SHEMONAH PERAKIM:
A TREATISE ON THE SOUL

Translation and Commentary by
LEONARD S. KRAVITZ and KERRY M. OLITZKY

UAHC PRESS
NEW YORK, NEW YORK

Library of Congress Cataloging-in-Publication Data

Maimonides, Moses, 1135-1204
    [Thamàniyat fuṣūl. English and Hebrew]
    Shemonah perakim : a treatise on the soul/translation and
commentary by Leonard S. Kravitz and Kerry M. Olitzky.
    p.   cm.
    Text in Hebrew and English; commentary in English.
    "A Companion Volume to Maimonides' Study of Pirke Avot."
    Includes bibliographical references and index.
    ISBN 0-8074-0704-6 (paperback : acid-free paper)
    1. Ethics, Jewish–Early works to 1800. 2. Maimonides, Moses,
1135-1204. Thàmaniyat fuṣūl. I. Kravitz, Leonard S. II. Olitzky,
Kerry M. III. Title.
BJ1287.M63T4713
296.3'6–dc21
                                         99-10918
                                          CIP

DESIGNER:
Typesetting: El Ot Ltd.
This book is printed on acid-free paper.
Copyright © 1999 by the UAHC Press
Manufactured in the United States of America
10 9 8 7 6 5 4 3 2 1

Acknowledgments

This book grew out of the long-time association of two colleagues whose lives span two generations and whose paths have crossed with mutual admiration and an ever-deepening friendship. So says the tradition, "When two come to study Torah, the Shekhinah dwells in their midst." Together we want to thank the following people, without whose help and assistance the development of this book would not have been possible. We are both privileged to teach and work at Hebrew Union College-Jewish Institute of Religion, where future generations of Jewish leaders are raised up, an honor and responsibility we do not take lightly. We extend particular appreciation to rabbinic students Rachel Smookler and Andy Vogel, who helped research various aspects of this volume. We are also indebted to administrative assistants Harriet Lewis and Nina Winer, who constantly find the wisdom to help make order out of chaos. Thanks also to Phil Miller, who was able to supply the Hebrew text. In addition, we thank our old and new friends at UAHC Press-particularly Seymour Rossel, Bennet Lovett-Graff and Ken Gesser, Hara Person, Stuart Benick, Debra Hirsh Corman, and especially Liane Broido for her fine attention to detail. They continue to support our efforts to bring sacred texts-unmitigated by selections or anthologies-directly to the people who desperately want to imbibe of their life-giving waters. To all that would come to drink, let their thirst be sated.

Rabbi Kerry M. Olitzky
Rabbi Leonard S. Kravitz
Pesach 5757

Contents

Introduction

As an introduction to his commentary on *Pirke Avot*, Moses Maimonides prepared a psycho-spiritual document called *Shemonah Perakim* (literally "Eight Chapters"). These writings are both part of his full commentary on the *Mishnah*, the compilation of Jewish law set down about 200 C.E. *Shemonah Perakim* is often published separately and sometimes subtitled *A Treatise on the Soul*. It reflects much of Maimonides' sentiments and advice regarding the pursuit of virtue and the avoidance of vice. It is also a statement of Jewish ethics-in the philosophical sense-and thereby introduces the reader to Maimonidean thinking in general.

Pirke Avot, a tractate of the *Mishnah* often called "Ethics of the Fathers," differs from all other tractates of the Mishnah because it is not associated with any specific *mitzvot*, or commandments, of the Torah. *Pirke Avot* gets its name from the fact that it deals with ethical statements of various teachers of the *Mishnah*. This emphasis on ethics suggests a literature reflective of the earlier wisdom literature of the Bible, rather than the legal literature of the *Mishnah*. It is the connection to wisdom in its broadest sense that links Maimonides' commentary to *Pirke Avot* and *Shemonah Perakim*, his introduction to that commentary. *Shemonah Perakim* deals with the nature and development of the human soul. It is the human soul that is shaped by ethics and will be influenced by the kinds of ethical statements found in *Pirke Avot*.

For Maimonides, the task of ethics is the healing of the soul. However, just as one who heals the body must first know the structure of the body, so one who heals the soul must first know the structure of the soul. Therefore, Maimonides begins his *Shemonah Perakim* with a description of the human soul. He stresses that the soul is a single entity although it may operate on a number of levels. Thus, the soul has different functions. Maimonides counts five different functions of the human soul: nutrititive, sentient, imaginative, desirous, and rational.

At first glance, modern readers may find the text and the terms Maimonides employs somewhat strange, unrelated to much that they know. Yet both *Pirke Avot* and *Shemonah Perakim* raise perennial questions regarding the relationship between personalities and ethical systems, how we think about the good and how the good relates to what is true. Much of the way we think has been shaped by what we learned of science as *wertfrei*, that is, objective and unrelated to value. In the social sciences, we offer descriptions of human behaviors before we make judgments regarding the values inherent in those behaviors. Living as we do in a world with many and different kinds of behavior, we have found a variety of definitions for what might be deemed moral or ethical. The optimism inherent in the ancient (and medieval) philosophers' notions that the ethical could be deduced from some kind of analysis of the human soul seems distant for us. Yet, as human beings who attempt to live decently, and as Jews who are part of a tradition devoted to the good, we are forced to be interested in the determination of what is good, as well as how we are to reach that good. If some of Maimonides' reasoning seems to be strange to us at first, further reflection will lead us to examine the Maimonidean positions as possible springboards to develop our own ethical positions.

Maimonides began with an analysis of the human soul, an analysis that seeks to establish the ways that the human soul (and hence being human) differs from the soul of other animals. The modern reader who is accustomed to psychological discourse dealing with instincts and drives may recognize that Maimonides' task is not so strange. As a rationalist and philosopher, he believes that the ability to think is specific to being human. Anything that impedes that ability is to be avoided or removed. The ethical life is a necessary requirement for the rational life. *Shemonah Perakim* is the means by which the ethical life will be purified so that the individual can then be enabled to get on with the more important business of thought.

According to Maimonides, when a soul is out of balance, individuals get themselves into trouble. While he describes this sense of being off-balance in terms of animal attributes of the soul (which might be easily recast in Freudian-like terms), it is clear that there are certain drives that pull on the individual that require exploration and explanation-through study. To make the work accessible to the people, Samuel ibn Tibbon translated *Shemonah Perakim* (from Arabic to Hebrew) during Maimonides' lifetime so that he might help the translator with difficulties in the text. Our English translation is based on Ibn Tibbon's Hebrew text. It is unknown why Ibn Tibbon chose to translate the text into Hebrew, but it is apparent that he communicated regularly with Maimondes. *Shemonah Perakim* was originally written in Arabic (as was Maimonides' entire commentary to the *Mishnah*), because that was the language the majority of Jews spoke at that time and he wanted to make it available to large numbers of people. In the introduction to Ibn Tibbon's translation, Maimonides admits that while the material is of universal importance, it may not be accessible to everyone. Moreover, he writes, "some of its elements will require further explication for a fuller elucidation so that all readers may be brought to full perfection and true success." He concludes his explanation by suggesting that only prophecy is higher than piety (*chasiduta*) and that piety is its prerequisite. He helps his readers to try to reach at least the level of piety and develop an appreciation for prophecy.

The method of relating particularity to universality is implicit in Maimonides' *Shemonah Perakim*. He begins with a discussion of reason's understanding of the psyche. After explaining how the health of the psyche is achieved through balance and moderation of the different psychic forces in the human, he explains (in chapter 4) that *halachah* provides a life-system that reflects reason's understanding of the psyche. According to David Hartman,[1] Maimonides understands *halachah* as a way of life that is the actualization of what philosophic reason understands to be essential for human perfection and the maintenance of society. What the psyche understands about moderation is known by reason rather than through studying the Talmud.

The all-pervasive longing for God is implicit throughout *Shemonah Perakim*. The writer also acknowledges the desire of the reader to use *halachah* as a means to experience something with profound religious significance. In *Shemonah Perakim*, Maimonides makes the distinction between laws in the *halachah* that are manifestly useful and laws whose usefulness can be discovered only after analysis and study. And so he invites the reader–as we do–to come and study.

---

1 David Hartman, *Maimonides Torah and Philosophic Quest*. Philadelphia: The Jewish Publication Society of America, 1976, p. 266, n. 65.

A Note to the Reader about This Volume

While the original (either in Arabic or in Hebrew) is simply divided into eight chapters (without any subsections), we have divided each chapter and numbered each paragraph (or section of a paragraph, depending on length) in order to make the volume more accessible to the reader. Commentaries introduce each section. These commentaries are often followed by explanations of particular concepts or ideas. Each chapter is followed by insights from parallel literature, which we have called "Gleanings."

In addition, many of the texts included in this volume date from an era yet insensitive to gender inclusivity in language. With apology, they are included in the original.

CHAPTER ONE

Maimonides' Introduction to the Soul

Maimonides begins his work at a place familiar to theologians and philosophers: the search for the soul and its purpose. He agrees with most of his contemporaries that possession of a soul distinguishes what is alive from what is not alive. For Aristotle, who serves as a source for Maimonides, the soul was the body in operation. However, since the body operates on a number of levels, there were those thinkers who thought that the body must have a number of souls. Maimonides initiates his discussion by arguing against those who believe that individuals have more than one soul. Instead, Maimonides suggests that each soul may be divided into three sections that will be loosely based on the major functions of each division, which he names vegetative, animal, and rational.

א:א דַּע, שֶׁנֶּפֶשׁ הָאָדָם אַחַת; וְיֵשׁ לָהּ פְּעֻלּוֹת רַבּוֹת חֲלוּקוֹת, יִקָּרְאוּן קְצָת הַפְּעֻלּוֹת
הָהֵן: נְפָשׁוֹת. וְיֵחָשֵׁב בַּעֲבוּר זֶה שֶׁיֵּשׁ לָאָדָם נְפָשׁוֹת רַבּוֹת, כְּמוֹ שֶׁחָשְׁבוּ
הָרוֹפְאִים, עַד שֶׁשָּׂם רֹאשׁ הָרוֹפְאִים בִּפְתִיחַת סִפְרוֹ, שֶׁהַנְּפָשׁוֹת שָׁלֹשׁ: טִבְעִית,
חִיּוּנִית, וְנַפְשִׁית. וּפְעָמִים שֶׁיִּקָּרְאוּ: כֹּחוֹת וַחֲלָקִים, עַד שֶׁיֵּאָמֵר: חֶלְקֵי הַנֶּפֶשׁ
— וְזֶה הַשֵּׁם יַעֲשׂוּהוּ הַפִּילוֹסוֹפִים הַרְבֵּה פְעָמִים. וְאֵינָם רוֹצִים בְּאָמְרָם:
"חֶלְקֵי", שֶׁהִיא מִתְחַלֶּקֶת כְּהֵחָלֵק הַגּוּפוֹת, אֲבָל הֵם מוֹנִים פְּעֻלּוֹתֶיהָ הַחֲלוּקוֹת
שֶׁהֵן לִכְלַל הַנֶּפֶשׁ, כַּחֲלָקִים לַ„כֹּל" הַמְחֻבָּר מֵהַחֲלָקִים הָהֵם.

1:1a You should know that each human being has only one soul, even though that soul has varied functions. Some have called these functions "souls" and therefore maintain that each human being has many souls. Some physicians hold this view, following the greatest of all [physicians, that is, Galen] who at the beginning of his book wrote that each human being has three souls: vegetative, animal, and rational. At times, these three are called capacities or divisions, so that one may speak of the divisions of a soul. Philosophers often speak in this manner without intending thereby to suggest that the soul may be divided as bodies are divided. They simply count the different functions of the soul as it operates in connection [with the body].

It is important to make a distinction between the human soul and the soul of an animal. While philosophers may use the same terms to describe a variety of functions in both the animal and human soul, they function differently among the species.

Three Aspects of the Soul

The Greek philosopher Plato (427-347 B.C.E.) taught that the human soul has three parts: reason or mind, spirit, and desire. He believed that only the mind could transcend the death of the body; since spirit and desire were linked to the body, they could not do so. On the other hand, Aristotle (384-322 B.C.E.) held that the three parts of the human soul related to different functions of the body. The nutritive aspect is related to the absorption of food and to reproduction. The sensitive part is related to the senses and to the commingling of the senses in a common sense that provided some material for the rational aspect of the soul. However, Aristotle seemed to think that the rational aspect of the soul was passive until it was activated on the outside by Divine active reason. Galen (129-199 C.E.), physician and philosopher, carried on Plato's threefold division of the soul. Thinkers in the Middle Ages understood him to maintain that there were actually three souls or one soul that operated on three levels. The vegetative soul level sustained the life of the body. The animal soul level enabled the body to move and react. The rational soul level gave humans the ability to think. While humans share the vegetative and animal aspects of the soul with animals, possession of this rational soul is what makes human beings unique.

Saadyah Gaon (882-942 C.E.) argued that the soul operates on three levels–when it is joined to the body–as if it had three separate faculties: reason, desire, and anger. For Saadyah, this explains the three names applied to the soul: *neshamah*, *nefesh*, and *ruach*. He explains two other names–*chayah* and *yechidah*–by making reference to the soul's possibility of endurance and its uniqueness.

וְאַתָּה יוֹדֵעַ, שֶׁתִּקּוּן הַמִּדּוֹת הִיא: רְפוּאַת הַנֶּפֶשׁ וְכֹחוֹתֶיהָ. וּכְמוֹ שֶׁהָרוֹפֵא אֲשֶׁר יְרַפֵּא הַגּוּפוֹת צָרִיךְ שֶׁיֵּדַע תְּחִלָּה הַגּוּף אֲשֶׁר יְרַפְּאֵהוּ: כֻּלּוֹ וַחֲלָקָיו מָה הֵם, רְצוֹנִי לוֹמַר: גּוּף הָאָדָם; וְצָרִיךְ שֶׁיֵּדַע אֵיזֶה דְּבָרִים יַחֲלוּהוּ וְיִשָּׁמֵר מֵהֶם; וְאֵיזֶה דְּבָרִים יַבְרִיאוּהוּ וִיכַוֵּן אֲלֵיהֶם — כֵּן רוֹפֵא הַנֶּפֶשׁ הָרוֹצֶה לְתַקֵּן מִדּוֹת הָאָדָם, צָרִיךְ שֶׁיֵּדַע הַנֶּפֶשׁ וְכֹחוֹתֶיהָ בִּכְלָלָה וַחֲלָקֶיהָ, וּמַה יַחֲלֶה אוֹתָה וּמַה-יַּבְרִיאָה. וּמִפְּנֵי זֶה אָמַר, שֶׁחֶלְקֵי הַנֶּפֶשׁ הֵם חֲמִשָּׁה: הַזָּן — וְהוּא נִקְרָא: צוֹמֵחַ; וְהַמַּרְגִּישׁ, וְהַמְדַמֶּה, וְהַמִּתְעוֹרֵר, וְהַשִּׂכְלִי.

1:1b You already know that the improvement of the ethical qualities is the healing of the soul and its functions. Just as the physician who would heal the human body must first know everything about the body in order to heal it and everything that causes diseases in order to be guarded from them and everything that brings healing in order to be

2

directed to them, so the one who would heal the soul by bringing improvement to its ethical qualities must know the soul and its functions and what, so to speak, makes it sick and what makes it healthy. For this reason, I will say that the soul, so to speak, has five different functions. The first is the nutritive, called the vegetable soul by some. The second is the sentient. Third is the imaginative. The fourth is the desirous. And the fifth is the intellectual.

Maimonides continues his discussion of the soul by suggesting that healing is possible through the ethical improvement of the individual. Using his practice of medicine as an analogy, he suggests that in order to know how to heal the soul, one must first know its anatomy. Having stated that most philosophers contend that the soul has three divisions, Maimonides now argues that there are actually five functions of the soul. These he names nutritive (alternatively, vegetative), sentient, imaginative, desirous, and intellectual.

If all that lives has a soul and that soul operates in a number of ways, one may wonder whether the functions of the soul of a human being are the same as the functions of an animal. Maimonides responds that while philosophers may use the same terms to describe the variety of functions of the human and animal soul, those functions differ among the species.

וּכְבָר הִקְדַּמְנוּ בְּזֶה הַפֶּרֶק, שֶׁדְּבָרֵינוּ אֵינָם רַק בְּנֶפֶשׁ הָאָדָם. כִּי כֹּחַ הַמָּזוֹן שֶׁיִּזּוֹן בּוֹ הָאָדָם, אֵינוֹ כְּכֹחַ הַמָּזוֹן שֶׁיִּזּוֹן בּוֹ הַסּוּס וְהַחֲמוֹר — כִּי הָאָדָם נִזּוֹן בַּחֵלֶק הַזָּן מִן־הַנֶּפֶשׁ הָאֱנוֹשִׁית; וְהַחֲמוֹר נִזּוֹן בַּחֵלֶק הַזָּן מִן־הַנֶּפֶשׁ הַחֲמוֹרִית; וְהַנֶּשֶׁר נִזּוֹן בַּחֵלֶק הַזָּן מִן־הַנֶּפֶשׁ אֲשֶׁר לָהּ. וְאָמְנָם יֵאָמֵר עַל־הַכֹּל: „נִזּוֹן" בְּשִׁתּוּף־הַשֵּׁם לְבַד, לֹא שֶׁהָעִנְיָן בְּכֻלָּם אֶחָד בְּעַצְמוֹ. וְכֵן יֵאָמֵר עַל־הָאָדָם וּשְׁאָר בַּעֲלֵי חַיִּים: „מַרְגִּישׁ" בְּשִׁתּוּף־הַשֵּׁם בִּלְבָד, לֹא שֶׁהַהֶרְגֵּשׁ אֲשֶׁר בָּאָדָם הוּא הַהֶרְגֵּשׁ אֲשֶׁר בִּשְׁאָר בַּעֲלֵי הַחַיִּים.

1:1c We have already suggested that this division of functions is not limited to the human soul, for the nutritive function by which the human being is sustained is not the same as the nutritive function by which a horse or a donkey is sustained. A human being is sustained by the nutritive function of the human soul as the donkey is sustained by the nutritive function of the donkey soul and as the eagle is sustained by the nutritive function of the eagle soul. The term "nutritive" is used in a composite manner, for its application is different in different species. The same is true with the sentient function of the soul; it differs in humans from other living beings.

Reflecting the sentiment that he expresses throughout his writings (that philosophy is difficult and may not be understood by all), Maimonides uses the analogy of light (and then sensation) to explain how similar functions in the souls of individual species appear as if they function in the same way but they do not. Noting that the issue is difficult for philosophers, Maimonides suggests (albeit in an unspoken manner) how much the more so is it difficult for nonphilosophers!

א:ב וְלֹא הַהֶרְגֵּשׁ אֲשֶׁר בְּזֶה הַמִּין, הוּא הַהֶרְגֵּשׁ בְּעַצְמוֹ אֲשֶׁר בְּמִין אַחֵר — אֲבָל כָּל־מִין וָמִין מֵאֲשֶׁר לוֹ נֶפֶשׁ, יֵשׁ לוֹ נֶפֶשׁ אַחַת בִּלְתִּי נֶפֶשׁ הָאַחֵר. וְיִתְחַיֵּב מִנֶּפֶשׁ זֶה פְּעֻלּוֹת אֵלֶּה, וּמִנֶּפֶשׁ זֶה פְּעֻלּוֹת אֲחֵרוֹת. וְאֶפְשָׁר שֶׁתִּדְמֶה פְּעֻלָּה לִפְעֻלָּה, וְיֵחָשֵׁב בִּשְׁתֵּי הַפְּעֻלּוֹת שֶׁהֵן דָּבָר אֶחָד בְּעַצְמוֹ — וְאֵין הַדָּבָר כֵּן. וְהַמָּשָׁל בָּזֶה: שְׁלֹשָׁה מְקוֹמוֹת חֲשׁוּכִים. הָאֶחָד מֵהֶם — זָרְחָה עָלָיו הַשֶּׁמֶשׁ וְהֵאִיר; וְהַשֵּׁנִי — הֵאִיר עָלָיו הַיָּרֵחַ וְהֵאִיר; וְהַשְּׁלִישִׁי — הֻדְלַק בּוֹ הַנֵּר וְהֵאִיר. הִנֵּה כָל־אֶחָד מֵהֶם נִמְצָא בּוֹ הָאוֹר; אֲבָל סִבַּת זֶה הָאוֹר וּפוֹעֲלוֹ — הַשֶּׁמֶשׁ, וּפוֹעֵל הָאַחֵר — הַיָּרֵחַ, וּפוֹעֵל הָאַחֵר — הָאֵשׁ. כֵּן פּוֹעֵל הַרְגָּשַׁת הָאָדָם — הוּא: נֶפֶשׁ הָאָדָם, וּפוֹעֵל הַרְגָּשַׁת הַחֲמוֹר — הוּא: נֶפֶשׁ הַחֲמוֹר, וּפוֹעֵל הַרְגָּשַׁת הַנֶּשֶׁר — הוּא: נֶפֶשׁ הַנֶּשֶׁר; וְאֵין לָהֶם עִנְיָן שֶׁיְּקַבְּצֵם אֶלָּא בְּשִׁתּוּף־הַשֵּׁם בִּלְבָד. וְהָבֵן זֶה הָעִנְיָן, שֶׁהוּא נִפְלָא מְאֹד; יִכָּשְׁלוּ בּוֹ הַרְבֵּה מֵהַפִּילוֹסוֹפִים, וְיִתְחַיְּבוּ בָּזֶה הָרְחָקוֹת וְדֵעוֹת בִּלְתִּי אֲמִתּוֹת.

1:2 The word "sentient" is used in the same composite manner. Each species has a specific soul. That soul has its own particular functions. Those functions may resemble the functions of another soul; one may think that they are the same, but they are not. Think, for example, of three dark places. The sun shines on one, and it is bright. The moon glimmers on another, and there is light. One lights a candle, and the last is lit up. You could say that all three places have been illuminated. However, the source of light of the first was the sun. The source of light of the second was the moon. And the source of light of the third was the candle. So it is with sensation in the human being; its source is the human soul, just as the source of sensation in the donkey is the donkey's soul and the source of sensation in the eagle is the eagle's soul. Only a term used in a composite manner can comprise all the separate meanings. Please understand that this is difficult; many philosophers have not understood it and have come up with notions that are false.

Maimonides now begins his explanation of the five individual functions of the soul. The first is the nutritive function, which is merely an extension of bodily function (digestion, growth, procreation).

א:ג וְאָשׁוּב אֶל כַּוָּנָתִי בְּחֶלְקֵי הַנֶּפֶשׁ, וְאֹמַר: הַחֵלֶק הַזָּן — מִמֶּנּוּ: הַכֹּחַ הַמּוֹשֵׁךְ, וְהַמַּחֲזִיק, וְהַמְעַכֵּל, וְהַדּוֹחֶה לַמּוֹתָרוֹת, וְהַמְגַדֵּל, וְהַמּוֹלִיד בְּדוֹמֶה, וְהַמַּבְדִּיל הַלֵּחוֹת עַד שֶׁיַּפְרִישׁ מַה־שֶּׁצָּרִיךְ לָהוּן בּוֹ, וּמַה־שֶּׁצָּרִיךְ לִדְחוֹתוֹ. וְהַדְּבָרִים עַל־אֵלּוּ שִׁבְעָה כֹחוֹת, וּמַה־יַּעֲשׂוּ, וְאֵיךְ יַעֲשׂוּ, וּבְאֵיזֶה אֵבָרִים פְּעֻלָּתָם יוֹתֵר נִרְאֵית וְיוֹתֵר נִגְלֵית, וּמַה־מֵּהֶם נִמְצָא תָּמִיד, וּמַה־יִּכְלֶה מֵהֶם לִזְמָן קָצוּב — זֶה כֻּלּוֹ רָאוּי בִּמְלֶאכֶת הָרְפוּאָה וְאֵין צֹרֶךְ לוֹ בָּזֶה הַמָּקוֹם.

1:3 And I return to what I intended to speak about regarding the functions of the soul. I would say that the nutritive function is that capacity to attract, retain, and digest food and to excrete the residue. Growth, procreation, and the ability to differentiate necessary from unnecessary are also included in that function. Matters dealing with these seven aspects of the nutritive function and how and why they operate and with what bodily organs they operate, whether internal or external, and which continually operate and which only operate occasionally are discussed in the science of medicine. There is no need to deal with them here.

Continuing his explanation from the previous paragraph, Maimonides indicates that the five senses–part of normal bodily function–find their origin in specific organs designated for specific functional purpose. Only touch is not seated in one organ alone. This explanation of the body will be important to recall as he explains the way the soul functions.

א:ד וְהַחֵלֶק הַמַּרְגִּישׁ — מִמֶּנּוּ הַכֹּחוֹת הַחֲמִשָּׁה הַמְפֻרְסָמִים אֵצֶל הֶהָמוֹן: הָרְאוּת, וְהַשֵּׁמַע, וְהַטַּעַם, וְהָרֵיחַ, וְהַמִּשּׁוּשׁ — וְהוּא נִמְצָא בְּכָל־שֶׁטַח הַגּוּף וְאֵין לוֹ אֵבָר מְיֻחָד, כְּמוֹ שֶׁיֵּשׁ לְאַרְבָּעָה הַכֹּחוֹת.

1:4 Every one knows the five senses, which are sight, hearing, taste, smell, and touch. Unlike the other senses, touch has no specific organ and is distributed throughout the body.

Standing in opposition to the *Mutakallimun* (school of Arabic philosophers explained below), Maimonides argues that one can conjure up things that are not real, that is, things that are impossible. This is a function of the soul. However, just because we can imagine it does not mean that it is real or that the image can be brought into reality.

The *Mutakallimun* taught the *Kalam*, ("word"), the first attempt at synthesizing religion and philosophy, who attempted to interpret the *words* of the Koran by the ideas of philosophy. This is a theological response to the philosophy as understood by Plato and Aristotle. This represented the leading school of thought in Maimonides' time. These Arabic philosophers opposed Aristotle because they attempted to defend religion against the philosophers. Maimonides agrees with the process but not with their result.

א:ה וְהַחֵלֶק הַמְדַמֶּה — הוּא הַכֹּחַ, אֲשֶׁר יִזְכֹּר רְשׁוּמֵי הַמּוּחָשִׁים, אַחַר הֵעָלְמָם מִקִּרְבַת הַחוּשִׁים אֲשֶׁר הִשִּׂיגוּם, וְיַרְכִּיב קְצָתָם אֶל קְצָתָם, וְיַפְרִיד קְצָתָם מִקְּצָתָם; וְלָזֶה יַרְכִּיב זֶה הַכֹּחַ מִן־עִנְיָנִים אֲשֶׁר הִשִּׂיגָם, עִנְיָנִים אֲשֶׁר לֹא הִשִּׂיגָם כְּלָל וְאִי אֶפְשָׁר לְהַשִּׂיגָם — כְּמוֹ שֶׁיְדַמֶּה הָאָדָם — סְפִינַת בַּרְזֶל רָצָה בָאֲוִיר; וְאָדָם שֶׁרֹאשׁוֹ בַּשָּׁמַיִם וְרַגְלָיו בָּאָרֶץ; וּבְהֵמָה בְּאֶלֶף עֵינַיִם, עַל־דֶּרֶךְ מָשָׁל, וְהַרְבֵּה מֵאֵלּוּ הַנִּמְנָעוֹת יַרְכִּיבֵם הַכֹּחַ הַמְדַמֶּה וְיַמְצִיאֵם הַדִּמְיוֹן. וּבְכָאן טָעוּ הַמְדַבְּרִים הַטָּעוּת הַמְגֻנָּה הַגְּדוֹלָה אֲשֶׁר בָּנוּ עָלֶיהָ פִּנַּת הַטְעָאָתָם בַּחֲלֻקַּת הַמְחֻיָּב, וְהָאֶפְשָׁר, וְהַנִּמְנָע. שֶׁהֵם חָשְׁבוּ, אוֹ הֵבִיאוּ בְּנֵי אָדָם לַחֲשֹׁב: כִּי כָּל־מְדֻמֶּה — אֶפְשָׁר; וְלֹא יָדְעוּ שֶׁזֶּה הַכֹּחַ יַרְכִּיב עִנְיָנִים שֶׁמְּצִיאוּתָם „נִמְנָע", כְּמוֹ שֶׁזָּכַרְנוּ.

1:5 The imaginative function operates by retaining sense impressions and combining them in such a way that some impressions are added and others are removed to create images different from what was perceived and indeed different from what could be perceived. As an example, one could imagine an iron ship flying through the air or a person whose head was in the heavens and whose feet were on earth or an animal with a thousand eyes. All these impossible things might be combined by the imagination and seem to have a reality in the imagination. Here the Mutakallimun erred greatly in using the imagination to determine what is necessary, what is possible, and what is impossible. They thought and convinced others to think that whatever could be imagined was possible. They did not realize that the imagination could make up things that were impossible.

The desirous function translates emotions into actions. For example, if one is angry with another individual, that person will probably want to move away from that individual. Maimonides sees this as a function of the soul. This function enables the body to take appropriate action.

וְהַחֵלֶק הַמִּתְעוֹרֵר — הוּא הַכֹּחַ, אֲשֶׁר בּוֹ יִשְׁתּוֹקֵק וְיִכְסֹף הָאָדָם לְדָבָר אֶחָד, א:ו
אוֹ יִמְאָסֵהוּ. וּמִזֶּה הַכֹּחַ יָבֹא אֶל פְּעָלוֹת: בַּקָּשַׁת דָּבָר, וְהַבְּרִיחָה מִמֶּנּוּ; וּבְחִירַת
דָּבָר אֶחָד, אוֹ הִתְרַחֵק מִמֶּנּוּ; וְהַכַּעַס וְהָרָצוֹן, וְהַפַּחַד וְהַגְּבוּרָה, וְהָאַכְזָרִיּוּת
וְהָרַחֲמָנוּת, וְהָאַהֲבָה וְהַשִּׂנְאָה, וְהַרְבֵּה מֵאֵלּוּ הַמִּקְרִים הַנַּפְשִׁיִּים. וּכְלֵי זֶה הַכֹּחַ
— כָּל־אֶבְרֵי הַגּוּף: כְּכֹחַ הַיָּד — עַל־לְקִיחַת דָּבָר וּנְגִיעָתוֹ; וְכֹחַ הָרֶגֶל — עַל
הַהֲלִיכָה; וְכֹחַ הָעַיִן — עַל הָרְאוּת; וְכֹחַ הַלֵּב — לְהִתְגַּבֵּר, אוֹ לִירֹא בְּעֵת
הַפַּחַד. וְכֵן שְׁאָר אֶבְרֵי הַגּוּף הַנִּרְאִים וְהַנִּסְתָּרִים הֵם וְכֹחוֹתֵיהֶם — כֻּלָּם כֵּלִים
לְזֶה הַכֹּחַ הַמִּתְעוֹרֵר.

1:6 The appetative (desirous) function is that aspect of the soul that moves one to or from a particular matter, or causes one to act or to refrain from acting in some specific way, or does not choose something. Anger, desire, fear, courage, compassion, cruelty, and other psychological dispositions are related to it. The outer and inner parts of the body, the hand's ability to grasp, the foot's ability to move, the eye's ability to see, the heart's ability to be brave or to fear, carry out this function.

The rational function–which Maimonides will consistently argue is the most important– reflects what we might call the rational mind. Abstract and theoretical learning/reasoning finds its origin in this function of the soul. This function even allows the person to determine whether or not something is possible.

וְהַחֵלֶק הַשִּׂכְלִי — הוּא הַכֹּחַ הַנִּמְצָא לָאָדָם, אֲשֶׁר בּוֹ יַשְׂכִּיל וּבוֹ תִּהְיֶה א:ז
הַהִשְׂתַּכְּלוּת, וּבוֹ יִקְנֶה הַחָכְמוֹת, וּבוֹ יַבְדִּיל בֵּין הַמְגֻנֶּה וְהַנָּאֶה מִן־הַפְּעֻלּוֹת.
וְאֵלּוּ הַפְּעֻלּוֹת: מֵהֶן — מַעֲשִׂי, וּמֵהֶן — עִיּוּנִי. וְהַמַּעֲשִׂי: מִמֶּנּוּ — מְלֶאכֶת־
מַחֲשֶׁבֶת, וּמִמֶּנּוּ — מַחֲשָׁבִי. וְהָעִיּוּנִי — אֲשֶׁר בּוֹ יֵדַע הָאָדָם הַנִּמְצָאוֹת שֶׁאֵינָן
מִשְׁתַּנּוֹת, כְּפִי מַה־שֶּׁהֵן עָלָיו, וְהֵן אֲשֶׁר יִקָּרְאוּ: "חָכְמוֹת" סְתָם. וּמְלֶאכֶת
מַחֲשֶׁבֶת — הוּא הַכֹּחַ אֲשֶׁר בּוֹ יִלְמַד הַמְּלָאכוֹת: כְּנַגָּרוּת, וַעֲבוֹדַת הָאֲדָמָה,
וְהָרְפוּאוֹת וְהַמַּלָּחוּת. וְהַמַּחֲשָׁבִי — הוּא הַכֹּחַ אֲשֶׁר בּוֹ יִסְתַּכֵּל הָאָדָם בַּדָּבָר
אֲשֶׁר יִרְצֶה לַעֲשׂוֹתוֹ: אִם אֶפְשָׁר לַעֲשׂוֹתוֹ, אִם לָאו; וְאִם אֶפְשָׁר לַעֲשׂוֹתוֹ, אֵיךְ
צָרִיךְ שֶׁיַּעֲשֶׂה? — זֶה שִׁעוּר מַה־שֶּׁצָּרִיךְ שֶׁנִּקַּח מֵעִנְיַן הַנֶּפֶשׁ הֵנָּה.

1:7 The rational function is the human ability to think, to reflect, to acquire the knowledge of the science, and to distinguish between acceptable and reprehensible acts. The rational function may operate in a practical or a theoretical manner. The practical may be involved with either crafts or computation. The theoretical is that by which one learns the unchanging realities to the extent that it is possible. This is known as science [*chochmah*]. The crafts [*malachot machashavot*] refer to the study of such things as carpentry, agriculture, medicine, and navigation. The computing skill is that by which one reflects on a thing one wishes to do to determine whether it is possible or not, and if possible, how to do it.

Although Maimonides has discussed the various functions of the soul, he wishes to stress its basic unity. Ultimately he views the soul as one spiritual structure. Even so, he directs us to consider the essential attribute of the human soul: its rationality. Thus, we should consider the intellect apart from the rest of the soul, as we would separate form from matter. However, if the soul does not fulfill its form (its potential), then it exists in vain.

Rational Skills

Aristotle said, "By their nature, all humans desire to know" (*Metaphysics, Book A*). Following Aristotle, Maimonides argues that while this might be theoretically true, in practice, men and women were constrained from knowing by a variety of factors from within and without. To know required a certain kind of training available to few and usable by still fewer. To truly *know* and therefore achieve human perfection required training in logic, mathematics, physics, and metaphysics (*Guide for the Perplexed* I:34).

Thus, the kind of knowing about which Maimonides speaks would belong to a particular elite group within the Jewish community, a group whose position and wealth could make that knowing possible. Rational skills, therefore, would be the province of that group. It should be noted that this elite group of individuals could and did study Greek philosophy and other literature developed outside of the context of Jewish tradition.

א:ח וְדַע, שֶׁזֹּאת הַנֶּפֶשׁ הָאַחַת אֲשֶׁר קָדַם סִפּוּר כֹּחוֹתֶיהָ וַחֲלָקֶיהָ — הִיא כַּחוֹמֶר, וְהַשֵּׂכֶל — לָהּ צוּרָה. וּכְשֶׁלֹּא הִגִּיעָה לָהּ צוּרָה — יִהְיֶה, כְּאִלּוּ מְצִיאוּת הַהֲכָנָה שֶׁבָּהּ לְקַבֵּל הַצוּרָה הַהִיא לְבַטָּלָה, וּכְאִלּוּ הִיא מְצִיאוּת הָבֶל. וְהוּא אָמְרוֹ: גַּם בְּלֹא־דַעַת נֶפֶשׁ לֹא־טוֹב (משלי יט, ב). רָצָה לוֹמַר: שֶׁמְּצִיאוּת־הַנֶּפֶשׁ שֶׁלֹּא הִגִּיעָה אֵלֶיהָ הַצוּרָה, אֲבָל תִּהְיֶה נֶפֶשׁ בְּלֹא דַעַת — לֹא טוֹב. אֲבָל הַדְּבָרִים עַל־הַצוּרָה, וְהַחֹמֶר, וְהַשִּׂכְלִי, וְהַדֵּעוֹת כַּמָּה הֵן, וְאֵיךְ יַגִּיעוּ אֲלֵיהֶן — אֵין זֶה מְקוֹמָם, וְלֹא יִצְטָרֵךְ בְּמַה שֶׁנִּרְצָה לְדַבֵּר עַל־הַמִדּוֹת; וְהוּא יוֹתֵר רָאוּי „בְּסֵפֶר הַנְּבוּאָה" אֲשֶׁר זָכַרְנוּ. וּבְכָאן אַפְסִיק בְּזֶה הַפֶּרֶק וְאַתְחִיל בְּאַחֵר.

1:8 This is all that we need to mention about the soul at this point. You should keep in mind that although we have enumerated the different functions and aspects of the soul, it remains a single entity. The soul can be compared to matter, and the intellect can be compared to form. Should the soul not fulfill its form, then the disposition [*hachanah*] to receive would be in vain and its existence would be purposeless. Scripture supports this view, as it says, "Also, the soul without knowledge is not good" [Prov. 19:2]. The verse teaches that it would not be proper for a soul to remain without knowledge and thus not to fulfill its form. However, this is neither the time nor the place for a full discussion of matter, form, intellect, and ideas, nor is it necessary for what we want to talk about when dealing with ethics. It would be more useful to discuss this in the Book of Prophecy, as we have already indicated. I will end this chapter and begin another.

GLEANINGS

REASONING FROM WITHOUT AND FROM WITHIN

Ever since men began to reflect, ever since they began to search for reasons and relationships in what they experienced and observed, and philosophy and religion began to develop, they came to understand that human life moves in two spheres. At times this insight was obscured; at times it was clear. Life disclosed itself to them from without, through the senses, and was quantified by measuring, weighing, and counting. Life also opened itself to them from within, through feelings and desires which became doubts, certainties, and decisions. At times men turned outwards; at times they harked within. Intellectual developments were carried by both spheres through the centuries. In both realms, certain proprieties, relationships, and anticipations have become knowledge: from without, certainty comes through rationality, through measuring, weighing, and building; from within, something different, the unmeasurable, the unweighable, the irrational, shows the way.

(Leo Baeck, *This People Israel: The Meaning of Jewish Existence*, trans. Albert H. Friedlander. New York: Holt, Rinehart and Winston, 1955)

LEO BAECK (1873-1956). *German-born rabbi who was a leader of Progressive Judaism in Europe. Rather than leaving Europe during the Nazi period, he dedicated himself to defending Jewish rights. Following his internment at Theresienstadt, he came to the United States, where he taught intermittently at Hebrew Union College-Jewish Institute of Religion in Cincinnati as a historian and "witness of his faith."*

THE CONSCIOUSNESS OF MORAL POWER

Reason being a ray from Divine Reason, ennobles man, awakens within him the desire more and more to rise toward the Supreme Reason. But the most essential element in him is the consciousness of his moral power, which is innate in man and is the foundation of his real nobility; and which, even because it awakens his aspiration to perfect purity, makes him feel his limitations along that line, and the bars to moral life so much the more. He feels that sensuality accompanies him from his infancy, that it is a part of his nature, so that a conflict is started between his sensuality and his spiritual ideas: "the desire of man's heart is evil from his youth." That sentence expresses the imperfection which is also manifested in the moral life, an appetite the allurements of which we have the power to resist. In ancient time the question was raised, why the bible begins with an account of the beginning of time instead of the first commands, and why all that introduction. The answer runs: "He hath showed to His people the power of His works," and though commandments do not occupy the first space, yet the pages contain considerations replete with religious element. The question was prompted by a narrow, literal view. But when *we* read that beginning of the bible, we discover a deep significance in the naive and simple presentation which even at this day not only fascinates us, but furnishes material for reflection. Not only that creation is presented in its well-constructed order, the conflict within man is brought in too. We behold man first in his innocence, then soon in struggle with craving that is, of course, part of his nature; he must control it if he does not want to become a prey to sin. Physical desire did not allure the first man only, it is part of the nature of all men and in that way the mother of sin which is not an involuntary inheritance from father to son but is committed by every one individually. Sin proceeds also from selfishness, from the narrow-minded separation of man from his fellow-man; it is the product of envy and manifests itself as discord; Cain is filled with ill-will against his brother. There we meet the great word: "Sin lurketh at the door, unto thee is its desire, *but thou canst rule over it.*"

(Abraham Geiger, *Judaism and Its History in Two Parts*, trans. Charles Newburgh. New York: The Bloch Publishing Co., 1911)

ABRAHAM GEIGER (1810-1874). *A leader of the Reform movement in Germany and an outstanding scholar of* Wissenschaft des Judenthums, *the scientific study of Judaism. He was a militant reformer who was active in several important Reform institutions in their incipient stages.*

THE ETHICS OF JUDAISM

The ethics of Judaism clings therefore to both prophet and priest; holds both the love of Israel and that of mankind; believes both in the world to come and in the imperatives to labor in this world; remembers both the power of human freedom and recalls its frustrating limitations; is both God-centered and aware of the centrality of the self. These conjunctions are not taken by the tradition as paralyzing paradoxes throwing man into despair. They are complementary values, expressions of a healthy tradition, rooted in the twin principles of reality and ideality, in what is and what ought to be. They manifest the dialectic of love and wisdom which reflects the complexity and maturity of life. Mature living and mature religion is not either/or. Polarities need not turn into polarizations, nor dualities into dualisms, nor ideologies into segregating sects. Judaism, to borrow a rabbinic metaphor, is like a mirror into which a thousand faces look. The mirror is one but it reflects the images of many. Each image is to be respected for its uniqueness. Together, they shape the form of Judaism.

(Harold M. Schulweis, The Single Mirror of Jewish Images: The Pluralistic Character of Jewish Ethics.
Los Angeles: University of Judaism, 1982)

HAROLD M. SCHULWEIS (1925-). *Rabbi, Valley Beth Shalom, Encino, California; adjunct professor of Jewish Contemporary Civilization at the University of Judaism, Los Angeles; and lecturer in Jewish Theology at Hebrew Union College-Jewish Institute of Religion, Los Angeles. A prolific writer, he is contributing editor to* The Reconstructionist, Sh'ma, *and* Moment *magazines and author of* For Those Who Can't Believe *(1994).*

LIFE IS FULL OF MORAL PURPOSE

Jewish Ethics is based essentially upon the fundamental principle that life is full of moral purpose. The world is not the work of mere chance, but has a Designer, a moral Ruler, and man, imbued with His spirit, has an object, a task to fulfil in this great plan of cosmos. Morality is conscious of purpose; it implies responsibility. Yet to whom are we responsible— responsible, not only for our actions, but also for our motives of action, for those intentions and purposes that make us moral beings? Not to society, which cannot read our thoughts, nor judge our motives, nor make us feel our responsibilities and duties, but to God alone, the living Power that permeates the world as the Source of Morality working for the highest ends and purposes. And here lies the fallacy of all agnostic reasoning, which says: "God cannot make morality; He cannot make badness divine; it is morality which lends God this authoritative power; hence morality is the supreme power to which even God must submit. Therefore have morality, and you need no God." The fact is, God is the very Power of Morality. He is not merely an Ideal of Justice and Purity, conceived of by the Jewish seers, lacking reality, not a mere "simile," a product of human fancy, existing only in the realm of imagination. He is the Power that speaks through conscience and reason to man as the great "I am"; the Mind that rules our mind, the Will that dictates our will, the Judge and Surveyor of our conduct, high above nature, which is unconscious, and above society, which exists only as an aggregate of individuals, yet enthroned as King and Father in every human soul. For man is not, as Aristotle and his modern followers say, a moral being because he is the product of society, born with a certain altruistic feeling that makes him a little less selfish than the brute is, and extends the love the stork or the hen has for her young over a larger household, and over a longer time than one generation. Man is not the result of certain biological, psychological, and social forces; he has a will of his own, he thinks and chooses of his own volition, he is free and able to determine his mode of conduct at every moment; he is the child of God. And this is the soul and essence of all morality, upon which Jewish Ethics lays all possible stress. The idea of God constitutes man's liberty of action and motive, his self-determination, upon which alone responsibility rests. It is neither reason and knowledge nor the emotions that make man free and strong. The will is the power that stands at the helm to direct action and to determine character. Yet this will of man must receive its dictates from a higher Will, from the supreme authority of an absolutely free Being, from God, the only

Redeemer of man. Only as the free son of God can he turn joy and sorrow, pleasure and pain, life and death, into means of moral perfection. The ultimate source of all Ethics, then is God–this is the truth conveyed by the first verse of the Decalogue.

(Kaufmann Kohler, *Studies, Addresses and Personal Papers*. New York: Hebrew Union College, 1931)

KAUFMANN KOHLER (1843-1926). *Rabbi, theologian, and scholar. President of Hebrew Union College and head of the philosophy and theology department of the* Jewish Encyclopedia. *He was also an editor for the Jewish Publication Society translation of the Bible (1931).*

HOLINESS–THE HIGHEST SPIRITUALITY

But the highest and loftiest of all principles of ethics, in fact its very essence, is holiness. There is no grander testimony to the religious genius of the Jew than is the attribute of holiness applied to God, in a spirit altogether contrasting with all other religions. All the gods of heathendom were steeped in sensuality and impurity, yet were called holy. The Jewish prophet called God holy as being too lofty, too sublime for sensuality or impurity. "His eyes are too pure to look with delight upon wrong." Holiness became the word for the highest spirituality, for the loftiest idealism. "Be holy, for the Lord your God is holy!" became the highest maxim and standard of Jewish morality; the whole of life, with its thinking and feeling, was henceforth to be lifted to that ideal of perfection. And this became at the same time the chief characteristic of Jewish Ethics. The thought of a holy God should pervade the whole life of man, and hallow it. Accordingly, the Fourth Commandment, the Sabbath Law, enjoins not merely the observance of a day of rest, but the hallowing of labor and industry as well as of pleasure and recreation, of the body as well as of the soul's life, of domestic as well as of religious affairs. And so the Fifth and Seventh Commandments proclaim the sanctity of the home and the holiness of marriage. Marriage for the Jew is not a concession to the flesh, but man's highest obligation to the race. Only a married man could serve as Israel's high priest, to perform the holy functions of the great Atonement Day. There is nothing so low in the life of man but that it should be permeated by the spirit of holiness; the table and the kitchen, the commonest needs of the flesh, should all be regulated by a law which testifies that a holy God rules in the affairs of men, and leaves nothing unhallowed. The Christian view regards him as a saint who renounces life, abstaining from the enjoyments of this world, which is of the Evil One, in order to live only for the other world. In contradistinction hereto Judaism wants this life, with all that it offers, to be elevated to the standard of holiness; and every enjoyment to be consecrated to God and man, and ennobled by purity of thought and purpose.

(Kaufmann Kohler, *Studies, Addresses and Personal Papers*. New York: Hebrew Union College, 1931)

MAKING AN ETHICAL COMMITMENT

A commentary: *Tikun olam* is a meaning that carried us throughout much of Jewish history. The shattering of the old ways, of the traditional culture with its implicit understandings and connections, requires that in our time it be formulated anew, explicitly. As we have seen, many American Jews have come to view ethics as the very essence of Judaism. It is the thread in Judaism's tapestry that weaves most neatly into America's own moral claims, and it can more readily be explained to our neighbors and to our children than Judaism's sometimes esoteric ritual. But a general ethical sensibility is not yet an active ethical commitment. American Jewry is distinguished not only by its understanding of pluralism, by the fact that it lives where particularism and universalism meet, but also by the opportunity it is offered, as an empowered community, to move from ethics to justice, to define itself as a partnership in *tikun olam*. In America, in our time, such as partnership can serve as our preeminent motive, the path through which our past is vindicated, our present warranted, and our future affirmed.

(Leonard Fein, Where Are We? New York: Harper and Row, 1988)

LEONARD FEIN (1934-). *Social critic, founding editor of* Moment *magazine and director of the Commission on Social Action of Reform Judaism, Union of American Hebrew Congregations.*

LIVING B'TZELEM ELOHIM, IN THE IMAGE OF GOD

It is the *tzelem Elohim* that enables Adam, the prototype of all humanity, to be on the same wavelength with God and thus be addressed by God. Adam is told to tend the garden. He is told from which trees he may eat and which are off-limits, what is permitted and what is forbidden. And Adam, with his *tzelem Elohim*, is capable of responding to the God who addresses him. Adam can obey the directive, ignore it, or even defy it. He can stand before God or he can hide. This ability, distinctively human, to be addressed and to respond or not to respond is what accords us our moral freedom, what allows us to make moral decisions. We can choose "what is right and good in the sight of *Adonai*" (Deut.6:18), we can choose something else, or we can make no choice at all–which is also a choice. What makes any behavior ethical or unethical in any given situation is determined by my response to what is ethically commanded in that situation. The question thus becomes: What is the *mitzvah*, the "commandment," that applies to such a situation?...

For the liberal Jew, however, these *mitzvot* and rulings constitute not the literal words of God but the inspired words of the Jewish people at a given moment in history to articulate what they believed the God of the covenant wanted them to do, ritually and ethically. Since we live during another time in history, we are entitled to be selective in our compliance with the traditional *mitzvot*: to accept ("do not wrong the stranger"), to reject ("an eye for an eye"), or to create anew (gender equality). The indispensable requirement, however, is that we make such selections out of knowledge and commitment, not out of ignorance and inconvenience.

But even with the accepting, rejecting, and creating anew, the liberal Jew embraces, no less than the Orthodox does, the *idea* of *mitzvah*, of being commanded. Our question is: In this situation, what response on my part, what course of action is "right and good in the eyes of *Adonai*"? Our response to that question, with all of its imperative urgency, with all that our ancestors have taught us, and with all that we have learned since, bears testimony to our ethical responsibility.

(Aron Hirt-Manheimer, ed., The Jewish Condition: Essays on Contemporary Judaism Honoring
Rabbi Alexander M. Schindler. New York: UAHC Press, 1995)

ARON HIRT-MANHEIMER (1948-). *Author, editor of* Reform Judaism, *the quarterly magazine of the Union of American Hebrew Congregations.*

SOUL OF FLESH AND SPIRIT

The notion of a dual soul–the soul of the flesh and the soul of the spirit–is also integral to our understanding of life, death, and life after death. Since we are both spirit and body, neither is extraneous to our being in this life or the next. Since the definition of our humanity must include our physical and spiritual natures, then the meeting of God and our humanity must include our body and our spirit.

This is the paradox of our nature and it is at the heart of the dual nature of our soul. Together, *neshama* and *nefesh* constitute a paradoxical duality, and a paradoxical duality itself constitutes a unity. *Neshama* and *nefesh* are aspects of the wholeness of ourselves. The two of them equal one soul and the soul unifies our complex being.

(Ira F. Stone, *Theological Meditations on God and the Nature of People, Love, Life And Death.* Woodstock, Vermont: Jewish Lights Publishing, 1992)

IRA F. STONE (1949-). *Rabbi of Temple Beth Zion-Israel in Philadelphia, teacher of theology at the Jewish Theological Seminary, and a member of the faculty of the New York Kollel, a center of adult Jewish study.*

THE SOUL RETURNING TO THE SOURCE

Consciousness flows through all being and wants to realize itself through the human substance. The idea of Messiah is greater than the last human being or the ultimate human being. It is the ultimate evolutionary form of consciousness. Through the person of the Messiah we are returned again to our source. We are reunited once again with all creation into one great common body of Adam. This is an Adam who did not die: the ultimate body of consciousness. Look: some day it will happen in an unequivocal way. Something will happen to one person. It will be a great transformation. The most hardened skeptic will have to confess that surely now everyone will change. The great yearning will be realized. Once again we will see our bodies mirrored in the heavens. For we will see ourselves mirrored in the anointed one. *Adam Kadmon*, the first one will have become *Adam Aharon*, the last one. We too will be no less than he/she is: in the image of God. And our transformation will change the ecosystem over which we have undisputed charge. Then the spirit shall break forth from everywhere.

(Lawrence Kushner, *The River of Light.* Woodstock, Vermont: Jewish Lights Publishing, 1981)

LAWRENCE KUSHNER (1943-). *Rabbi of Congregation Beth El of Sudbury, Massachusetts, adjunct member of the faculty at Hebrew Union College-Jewish Institute of Religion, New York, and author of numerous books on Jewish spiritual renewal.*

HEALING OF SOUL

This capacity for mutuality in human relations is the foundation for the moral life that also finds expression in human community. Human responsibility for the well-being of the world never can be fulfilled simply through personal action. Human beings come to accountability in the midst of communities that interpret and set out where obligations lie, and community is the context for fulfilling our obligations. Moreover, in coming together with others in mutual commitment to ideas or causes, we ever and again form new communities through which to renew and carry on our purposes. It is as we join with others, in a way that only human beings can, in shared engagement to a common vision, that we find ourselves in the presence of another presence that is the final source of our hopes and intentions, and that undergirds and sustains them. Whether the substance of our cause be our lives as women, the fate of the earth, the pursuit of justice in human community, or some more narrowly religious purpose, it is through the struggle with others to act responsibly in history that we come to know our own actions as encompassed and empowered by a wider universe of action and thus come to know God in a profound and significant way.

(Judith Plaskow, *Standing Again at Sinai: Judaism from a Feminist Perspective*. New York: HarperCollins, 1990)

JUDITH PLASKOW. *Contemporary feminist theologian and associate professor of Religious Studies at Manhattan College. She has presented a feminist reconstruction of Judaism.*

HEALING OF BODY AND SPIRIT

Jewish tradition has long recognized that there are two components of health: the body and the spirit. The *Mi Sheberach* prayer, traditionally recited for someone who is ill, asks God for *refuah shleima*, a complete healing, and then specifies two aspects: *refuat hanefesh*, healing of the soul/spirit/whole person, and *refuat haguf*, cure of the body. To cure the body means to wipe out the tumor, clear up the infection, or regain mobility. The heal the spirit involves creating a pathway to sensing wholeness, depth, mystery, purpose, and peace. Cure may occur without healing, and healing without cure. Pastoral caregivers and family members of seriously ill people know that sometimes lives and relationships are healed even when there is no possibility of physical cure; in fact, serious illness often motivates people to seek healing of the spirit.

(Nancy Flam, "Healing of Body and Spirit," *Reform Judaism*, summer 1994)

NANCY FLAM (1960-). *Rabbi. She pioneered the West Coast efforts of the National Jewish Center for Jewish Healing and is co-director of its national training program for Jewish professionals.*

THE ORIGINS OF ANGER

Anger results from our inability to admit the disparity between what we want and what is. It is a consequence of the impossibility of perfection in the created world in which the *idea* of perfection nevertheless exists. It is, therefore, grounded in the distance between the mortal and the immortal.

Anger generates great energy in both humans and God. God's anger results from the disparity between what He wants for us and what we are.

The energy generated by anger can be either constructive or destructive. When it reduces the moments-of-death in life, it is positive. When it causes us to be further removed from the presence of God, it is negative. In such stories as the destruction of Sodom and Gemorrah, the bringing of the flood, or the scattering of the builders of the Tower of Babel, God's anger and the energy it generates are models for acting on our anger and its energy. Typically, God's anger is ignited by injustice, by deceit, by cruelty and by unfaithfulness. He directs the energy generated by this anger at combating the causes of these conditions. God's anger can reestablish the equilibrium of the world. It aims to eliminate moments-of-death in life. It is life-giving.

(Ira F. Stone, *Seeking the Path to Life: Theological Meditations on God and the Nature of People, Love, Life And Death*. Woodstock, Vermont: Jewish Lights Publishing, 1992)

CHAPTER TWO

Concerning the Capacities of the Soul Where Good and Evil Qualities Are to Be Found

Having described the various functions of the soul, Maimonides proceeds to identify which functions are related to ethical behavior. *Mitzvah* and *averah*, commandment and transgression, are linked to the sentient and desirous functions of the soul. What we sense and what we desire are linked to what we do. Subsequently, what we do may be either in line with the will of God or opposed to it.

ב:א דַּע, שֶׁהָעֲבֵרוֹת וְהַמִּצְווֹת הַתּוֹרִיּוֹת, אָמְנָם, יִמָּצְאוּ בִּשְׁנֵי חֲלָקִים מֵחֶלְקֵי הַנֶּפֶשׁ, וְהֵם: הַחֵלֶק הַמַּרְגִּישׁ וְהַחֵלֶק הַמִּתְעוֹרֵר לְבָד; וּבִשְׁנֵי אֵלּוּ הַחֲלָקִים יִהְיוּ כָּל־הָעֲבֵרוֹת וְהַמִּצְווֹת. אָמְנָם, הַחֵלֶק הַזָּן וְהַחֵלֶק הַמְדַמֶּה — אֵין מִצְוָה בּוֹ וְלֹא עֲבֵרָה, שֶׁאֵין לַדַּעַת וְלַבְּחִירָה בְּאֶחָד מִשְּׁנֵיהֶם מַעֲשֶׂה כְּלָל; וְלֹא יוּכַל הָאָדָם בְּדַעְתּוֹ לְבַטֵּל מַעֲשֵׂיהֶם, אוֹ לְמַעֲטָם מִפְּעֻלָּה אַחַת. הֲלֹא תִרְאֶה שֶׁשְּׁנֵי הַחֲלָקִים הָאֵלֶּה, רְצוֹנִי לוֹמַר: הַזָּן וְהַמְדַמֶּה יַעֲשׂוּ בְּעֵת הַשֵּׁנָה הַפְּעֻלָּה הַמְיֻחֶדֶת לָהֶם. מַה־שֶׁאֵין־כֵּן בִּשְׁאָר כֹּחוֹת הַנֶּפֶשׁ.

2:1 You should know that the commission of transgressions and the performance of the *mitzvot* of the Torah are both related to two functions of the soul: the sentient and the desirous. Every transgression of and every performance of *mitzvot* are done with these two functions of the soul. Neither the nutritive nor the imaginative functions of the soul are involved with observance or sin, because those functions are not involved with thought or with choice. They operate unconsciously and cannot be diminished or stopped. The nutritive and the imaginative functions operate even when one is asleep; [this is] something no other function can do.

Truth for Maimonides (and for other philosophers) is not related to the sentient and desirous functions; rather, truth is related only to the rational function of the soul.

17

ב:ב   אַךְ הַחֵלֶק הַשִּׂכְלִי, יֵשׁ בּוֹ מְבוּכָה. אֲבָל אֲנִי אוֹמֵר שֶׁיֵּשׁ בְּזֶה הַכֹּחַ גַּם־כֵּן מִצְוָה
וַעֲבֵרָה: לְפִי אֱמוּנַת דֵּעַת בְּטֵלָה, אוֹ אֱמוּנַת דֵּעַת אֲמִתִּית; אֲבָל אֵין בּוֹ מַעֲשֶׂה
שֶׁיֵּאָמֵר עָלָיו שֵׁם מִצְוָה אוֹ שֵׁם עֲבֵרָה סְתָם. וְלָזֶה אָמַרְתִּי לְמַעְלָה, שֶׁבִּשְׁנֵי
הַחֲלָקִים הָהֵם יִמָּצְאוּ הָעֲבֵרוֹת וְהַמִּצְווֹת.

2:2   There is some confusion about the actions of the rational function. I might say that commandment and transgression apply to a true belief and a false belief; however, there is no act involved that one could label *mitzvah* or *averah*. Hence, as I have said, *mitzvah* and *averah* apply only to the two aforementioned [sentient and desirous] functions [of the soul].

Maimonides begins this section by pairing virtues and vices (as polar opposites), placing these virtues–and their corresponding vices–in particular functions of the soul. As might be expected, he places the intellectual virtue (with its various aspects of wisdom) in the rational function of the soul, the function he holds in highest esteem. Perhaps it is surprising then that Maimonides houses the virtue of ethics (and its opposing vice) in the desirous function. He explains this in further detail in the next paragraph.

ב:ג   אָמְנָם הַמַּעֲלוֹת — הֵן שְׁנֵי מִינִים: מַעֲלוֹת הַמִּדּוֹת וּמַעֲלוֹת הַשִּׂכְלִיּוֹת. וּכְנֶגְדָּן
שְׁנֵי מִינֵי פְּחִיתוּת. אָמְנָם, מַעֲלוֹת הַשִּׂכְלִיּוֹת הֵן יִמָּצְאוּ לַחֵלֶק הַשִּׂכְלִי. מֵהֶן —
הַחָכְמָה, וְהִיא: יְדִיעַת הַסִּבּוֹת הָרְחוֹקוֹת וְהַקְּרוֹבוֹת, אַחַר יְדִיעַת מְצִיאוּת הַדָּבָר
אֲשֶׁר יֵחָקְרוּ סְבוֹתָיו, וּמֵהֶן — הַשֵּׂכֶל, אֲשֶׁר מִמֶּנּוּ הַשֵּׂכֶל הָעִיּוּנִי, וְהוּא הַנִּמְצָא
לָנוּ בַּטֶּבַע, רְצוֹנִי לוֹמַר: הַמֻּשְׂכָּלוֹת הָרִאשׁוֹנוֹת; וּמִמֶּנּוּ — שֵׂכֶל נִקְנֶה, וְאֵין זֶה
מְקוֹמוֹ. וּמֵהֶן — זַכּוּת הַתְּבוּנָה, וְטוֹב הַהֲבָנָה, וְהוּא: לַעֲמֹד עַל־הַדָּבָר וְלַהֲבִינוֹ
מְהֵרָה בְּלֹא זְמָן, אוֹ בִּזְמָן קָרוֹב. וּפְחִיתוּת זֶה הַכֹּחַ — הֵפֶךְ אֵלּוּ, אוֹ שֶׁכְּנֶגְדָּם.

2:3   There are two kinds of virtues, ethical and intellectual, and correspondingly two different vices. The intellectual virtues relate to the rational function; the ethical virtues relate to the desirous function. Among the intellectual virtues are science [*chochmah*], which is the knowledge of ultimate and proximate causes, which one must investigate if one is to know anything; the innate intellect given to us by nature, which are the innate ideas; the acquired intellect, which we will not discuss here; and discernment and acumen, which are the ability to accurately and quickly grasp an idea. The intellectual vices are the reverse and the opposite of all the virtues.

By linking the ethical virtues to the desirous function of the soul, Maimonides makes the controlling of desire a virtue. To the modern reader, that claim may seem obvious. What is not so obvious is the method of controlling desire that Maimonides suggests. He contends that the individual must find some balance, a middle position between contrasting extremes. To the ancient and medieval philosopher, it was precisely this balance that constituted the ethical life. When this balance cannot be found, the result is what Maimonides describes as a vice.

ב:ד   אֲבָל מַעֲלוֹת הַמִּדּוֹת יִמָּצְאוּ לַחֵלֶק הַמִּתְעוֹרֵר לְבַדּוֹ; וְחֵלֶק הַמַּרְגִּישׁ בְּזֶה הָעִנְיָן אֵינוֹ רַק שַׁמָּשׁ לַחֵלֶק הַמִּתְעוֹרֵר. וּמַעֲלוֹת זֶה הַחֵלֶק רַבּוֹת מְאֹד: כַּזְּהִירוּת, כְּלוֹמַר: יִרְאַת חֵטְא, וְהַנְּדִיבוּת וְהַיֹּשֶׁר, וְהָעֲנָוָה, וְהַשְׁפְלוּת, וְהַהִסְתַּפְּקוּת, וְהוּא שֶׁקְּרָאוּהוּ חֲכָמִים: עֲשִׁירוּת, בְּאָמְרָם: אֵיזֶהוּ עָשִׁיר? — הַשָּׂמֵחַ בְּחֶלְקוֹ. וְהַגְּבוּרָה וְהָאֱמוּנָה וְזוּלָתָם. וּפְחִיתוּת זֶה הַחֵלֶק — הִיא: לַחְסֹר מֵאֵלּוּ, אוֹ לְהוֹסִיף בָּהֶן.

2:4 The ethical virtues are found only in the desirous function. The sentient function simply serves the desirous function. There are many ethical virtues such as caution, in the form of the fear of sin; generosity; humility; self-denial; contentment, what the sages called wealth, in their famous statement, "Who is rich? The one who rejoices in one's portion" [*Pirke Avot* 4:1]; courage; faithfulness; and similar things. The ethical vices are increases or decreases of those virtues.

For Maimonides, one might say that the nutritive and the imaginative functions of the soul are ethically neutral, since he considers the terms "virtues" and "vices" to be irrelevant to them. They simply function properly or they do not.

ב:ה   אֲבָל הַחֵלֶק הַזָּן וְהַמְדַמֶּה — לֹא יֵאָמֵר בּוֹ לֹא מַעֲלָה וְלֹא פְחִיתוּת; אַךְ יֵאָמֵר: שֶׁהוּא זָן עַל-יָשָׁר, אוֹ עַל-בִּלְתִּי יָשָׁר, כְּמוֹ שֶׁיֵּאָמֵר: אִישׁ פְּלוֹנִי עִכּוּלוֹ טוֹב, אוֹ בָטֵל עִכּוּלוֹ; אוֹ נִפְסַד דִּמְיוֹנוֹ אוֹ הוּא מְדַמֶּה עַל-יָשָׁר — אֵין בָּזֶה לֹא מַעֲלָה וְלֹא פְחִיתוּת וְזֶה מַה-שֶׁרָצִינוּ לְזָכְרוֹ בְּזֶה הַפֶּרֶק.

2:5 One does not apply the terms "virtues" and "vices" to the nutritive or the imaginative functions [of the soul]. One may say that these functions either work or they don't work as one might say that one person has proper digestion and that another does not have proper digestion and one person's imagination operates properly and another's does not do so. Neither "virtue" nor "vice" applies. This is what I wanted to mention in this chapter.

19

Mitzvah *and* Averah *(Commandment and Transgression)*

The terms *mitzvah* and *averah* reflect the commandment (*mitzvah*) system of the Torah as understood by Jewish tradition. The fulfillment of the 248 positive commandments and the avoidance of the 365 negative commandments constitute the *mitzvah* system. While Reform Judaism understands the *mitzvah* system differently (releasing individuals from its binding authority while asserting their personal autonomy), simply put, not doing what the Jew is commanded to do or doing what a Jew is commanded not to do would constitute an *averah*, a transgression against Divine Law. Thus, the life of Jew is to be lived between the *mitzvah* and the *averah*, following one and avoiding the other.

Acquired Intellect

Aristotle (382-322 B.C.E.) described the human intellect as both passive and active. Each human being was born with the passive intellect. It was that part that defined the human. This passive intellect required activation so that it might acquire information and become an acquired intellect. Thus, the active intellect activated the passive intellect. It was the origin of the active intellect that drew two of Aristotle's commentators–Alexander Aphrodisias (ca. 200 C.E.) and Themistius (ca. 400 C.E.)–into conflict. Aphrodisias maintained that the passive intellect was merely the capacity to receive forms; it was as mortal as the body. Aphrodisias identified God as the source of the active intellect. On the other hand, Themistius held that the passive intellect was an eternal, spiritual entity within the soul. The active intellect, therefore, was that aspect within the soul that activated the passive soul. Both commentators agreed that the contents of the activated soul were those universal forms that corresponded to elements of reality. The totality of these forms was the acquired intellect.

Fear of Sin

The notion of the fear of sin is necessarily related to the fear of Heaven; the latter drives the former. One fears sin because sin is an affront to God. Thus, one's commitment to God is measured by one's avoidance of sin. The fear of sin is a powerful motivation for the avoidance of sin. One rabbi said, "The fear of sin brings the individual to righteousness." Another said, "The fear of sin brings one to holiness" (Talmud, *Avodah Zarah* 20a-b). Yet the fear of sin never weighed heavily on the Jew. As one sage put it, "I fear in the midst of my joy, and I rejoice in the midst of my fear" (*Tanna de be Rabbi Eliyahu* 3). Sin can be avoided, because Judaism affirms that human beings have free will. The rabbis put it clearly, "All things are in the hands of Heaven except for the fear of Heaven." No person is predestined to be righteous or sinful. By their actions, individuals determine what they will be.

Generosity

In his *Nicomachean Ethics*, Aristotle presents a list of virtues that he determines are states of character. Maimonides follows Aristotle's notion of generosity. These virtues are balance points between excesses. For Aristotle, they represent the human ideal: to pursue the Golden Mean. Generosity or liberality, as it is often called, is the mean between the excesses of prodigality and meanness. Generous persons know how to use their wealth. As Aristotle puts it, the liberal person will give for the sake of the noble and rightly; that person will give to the right people, the right amounts, and at the right time, all the qualifications that accompany appropriate (or "right") giving. Such a person will give with pleasure and not with pain. Such giving, argue the philosophers, is an act of virtue. As such, virtue should provide pleasure and not pain.

Humility

In the balancing of behaviors to establish moral virtue, Aristotle argues that the mean between honor and dishonor is "proper pride," while excess in one direction is "empty vanity" and excess in the other direction is "undue humility." Although he generally follows Aristotle, Maimonides is constrained by Jewish tradition to skew the mean in favor of humility. For Maimonides, humility is too precious to be overly concerned with the balance of a mean. Undoubtedly, Maimonides remembered the other Moses who was described as "very humble" (Num. 12:3). For Maimonides, in attempting to establish a mean between Aristotle and rabbinic tradition, the mean favors moving toward humility.

Self-Denial

The idea of self-denial presents a significant challenge for Judaism. Although Jewish tradition had developed (or acknowledged) 365 negative commandments (behaviors that were forbidden to the Jew), the avoidance of such behaviors was not viewed as "self-denial." Instead, this avoidance was considered in accord with the individual's fulfillment of the Divine will. Adding on to such prohibited behaviors, as did the biblical Nazirites, was not acceptable to rabbinic Judaism. Indeed, in a clever midrashic move, the rabbis interpreted the requirement that the Nazirite bring an offering because he had come in contact inadvertently with the dead *maasher chatah al hanefesh* (Num. 6:11) to mean that the Nazirite had sinned against his own soul *al hanefesh* by refraining from permitted pleasures (*Sifre* 30). Although asceticism and self-denial have infrequently found their way into Judaism, usually after periods of persecution, Judaism has generally not found any value in prohibiting more than the Torah prohibits.

Contentment

The rabbis taught, "Who is rich? The one who rejoices in one's portion" (*Pirke Avot* 4:1), while Aristotle suggested that "happiness is activity in accordance with virtue" (*Nicomachean Ethics*, bk. X, chap. 7). Maimonides, who was obviously well-versed in both the teachings of the rabbis and the writings of Aristotle, suggests that contentment is to be found in knowledge: a treat for the mind, the main reason we were created as human beings.

Concerning the body, Maimonides felt differently. He argued that if one restricts oneself to what is necessary, then "this is the easiest of things and can be obtained with little effort." Thus, what makes for discontent is constant desire for those things that are unnecessary. If one wants silver, one then desires gold, and if one has gold, one desires crystal and then rubies and emeralds. Such desire causes unhappiness and even the loss of faith in God, for lacking luxury, one begins to complain about God's decrees and one imputes to the Creator a deficiency of power (*Guide for the Perplexed* III:12).

Courage

In the *Nicomachean Ethics* (bk. III, chaps. 6-8), Aristotle defines courage in relationship to fear. It is the mean or philosophical midpoint between those things that inspire confidence or provoke fear. For Aristotle, however, death–as an escape from poverty, love, or pain–is not the mark of courage; instead, it reflects cowardice. According to Aristotle, courage is the awareness of danger and the facing of it.

Like Aristotle, Maimonides argues that placing oneself needlessly in danger is not a mark of courage. Rather, it is a foolish act. For Maimonides and his family, a discussion of courage was not a matter of abstract philosophy. They waited out the onslaught of the Almohades, a group of Muslim fundamentalists who insisted that all within their realm become Muslims. Thus, many pretended to have converted. It took more courage to maintain Judaism in secret than it did to openly martyr oneself.

Truth and Faithfulness

Faithfulness (Hebrew, *emunah*) in Judaism may be applied to God or to human beings. In Deuteronomy 32:4, God is described as *El emunah*, "God of faithfulness." In Proverbs 20:6, a person is described as *ish emunim*, "a person of faithfulness." By ascribing the term both to the Deity and to human beings, Jewish tradition suggests that mortals can attain a particular Divine quality. Thus, by manifesting that quality of faithfulness, human beings can imitate the Deity. It is precisely because God is presented by Jewish tradition as the One in whom mortals can trust that belief in God can provide hope for fallible human beings. One can measure the depth of one's relationship with another human being by determining the extent of that relationship with God. Faithfulness in Jewish tradition is linked to truth, hence the phrase found in most prayer books: *emet v'emunah* (true and faithful).

Noting that the Hebrew word for truth (*emet*) is spelled with the first letter of the Hebrew alphabet (*alef*), the middle letter (*mem*), and the last letter (*tav*), the rabbis argued that *emet* (truth) was God's seal. One could depend on God, because God was truth. Likewise, one can depend on those who would serve God when they speak and maintain the truth. Thus, for both humans and God, faithfulness arises out of truth.

GLEANINGS

VIRTUE AND VICE

The rabbis believed people might rule over their capacity for evil but not because they esteemed human self-control. They knew us well enough not to trust in humankind alone. Despite our inertia, stupidity, malice, and aggressiveness they knew we remained God's covenant partners. They trusted God to help us even as we sought to do God's work. The rise of a new spirituality among liberal Jews, I am convinced, stems largely from our recognition that we share the rabbis' faith that trust in people cannot ultimately be dissociated from trust in God.

We also know much more about the effective motives for human behavior than they did. The rabbis believed that intellect, discipline, and will, reinforced by belief, rite, and community, would largely subdue our urge-to-evil. The high sanctity of many Jewish lives and of many Jewish communities over the centuries attests to the truth in their vision. But the way of rule and repression exacts a heavy toll. We modern Jews must take a somewhat different way. We propose to integrate our bodies and our emotions into our lives in ways the rabbis would have judged unthinkable. We need to alter our social relationships, particularly those which have been strongly hierarchical, to allow for greater self-expression.

(Eugene B. Borowitz, *Liberal Judaism*. New York: Union of American Hebrew Congregations, 1984)

EUGENE B. BOROWITZ (1924-   ). *Scholar and rabbi, regarded as one of the leading liberal Jewish theologians in the United States. Formerly the director of education at the Union of American Hebrew Congregations, he has been a member of the Hebrew Union College-Jewish Institute of Religion faculty in New York for over thirty years.*

SOCIAL RESPONSIBILITY FOR THE UNDERPRIVILEGED AND POWERLESS

Like the other principles, the idea of social responsibility for those who are in need–widows, orphans, aged, the poor–is closely related to a theological premise. When a farmer reaps his crops, they do not fully belong to him, even if he owns the field and has bought the seed and labors to make them grow. Still, he is only a partner in the enterprise, for without the help of God, in the form of rain, wind, proper temperatures, and so forth, all of the farmer's efforts will be in vain. God is, therefore, considered to be a part owner, and has the right to command the farmer to leave part of the crop for the poor. The farmer does not show any special kindness by doing this; he is expected to do so, and if he does not, then he sins.

The same principle applies to all wealth. Because in the final analysis, man is not considered to be the full owner of the possessions which he has accumulated, but only a partner, or a custodian who must render account to the Creator for his use of these possessions, he is therefore obligated to share them with others who have less than he. This sharing is not charity but *tz'dakah*, doing what is just. The powerless and the disenfranchised have a right to expect that society will fulfill its obligations toward them, and failure to fulfill these obligations is a severe condemnation of the society in the eyes of God.

(David Saperstein and Marc Saperstein, *Ethics in the Coming Decades*.
New York: Union of American Hebrew Congregations.)

DAVID SAPERSTEIN (1947-) *and* MARC SAPERSTEIN (1944-) *are both rabbis. David directs the Religious Action Center of Reform Judaism in Washington, D.C. while Marc is professor of Philosophy at Washington University in St. Louis.*

TORAH LISHMAH *AND* TORAT CHAYIM

It is no accident that it is precisely the greatest and most creative scholars who have been able to hold fast both to *Torah Lishmah* and *Torat Chayim*. On the one hand, *Torat Chayim*, the concern for learning for the sake of life, has given to *Torah Lishmah*, learning for its own sake, a vitality and a relevance that has enhanced its value and significance immeasurably. On the other hand, the standards of unswerving loyalty to the truth and freedom from ulterior considerations that are demanded by Torah for its own sake have prevented Torah for the sake of life from degenerating into the vulgar popularizations and the bigoted distortions that pass for Jewish learning in many quarters today.

To keep *Torah Lishmah* and *Torat Chayim* in creative tension and, thus, help make Jewish learning a significant instrument for Jewish living in our time is the great imperative for Jewish scholarship in our age. If Jewish studies are to be meaningful in the world and retain the respect of intelligent and sensitive men and women, and, what is more important, attract the attention and activity of creative men and women in the future, they must have an impact on life. We must strive, on the one hand, to hold fast to these two antinomies of objective and disinterested scholarship–not uninterested or uninteresting–and learning that is responsive to life, on the other.

(Robert Gordis, "On Judaism and Jewish Learning" in *Through the Sound of Many Voices: Writings Contributed on the Occasion of the 70th Birthday of W. Gunther Plaut*, ed. Jonathan V. Plaut. Toronto: Lester & Orpen Dennys Publishers, 1982)

ROBERT GORDIS (1908-1992). *Rabbi, Biblical Scholar, author. Taught at the Jewish Theological Seminary.*

THE OWNERSHIP OF POSSESSIONS

Jewish ethics is predicated upon a fundamental belief about the ownership of possessions. "The earth is the Lord's and all that is in it." Bless the earth, work its soil, but remember that your possessions are derived from God, and consequently all energy, power and good must be used in a Godly fashion–to heal, not to hurt; to profit, not to steal; to raise up, not to grind down the faces of the poor.

Let there be no misunderstanding. Greed, avarice, mendacity, are not temptations affecting Jews alone. Lying, cheating, white-collar crime, and corporate fraud are universal phenomena, transdenominational tragedies in our society. We read repeatedly of scores of indictments and arrests of non-Jewish violators. But that "everyone does it," that our society has gone berserk in its obsessive pursuit of wealth and power, does not alleviate our particularistic hurts and fears or justify our silence. It is a universal problem, but we are addressing our people, a talented, choosing people who chose to "love justice, love mercy, and walk modestly with God."

(Harold M. Schulweis, *In God's Mirror*. Hoboken, New Jersey, KTAV Publishing House, 1990)

24

WISDOM AS THE UNITY OF TEACHING AND LIFE

Among all the peoples in the world, Israel is probably the only one in which wisdom that does not lead directly to the unity of knowledge and deed is meaningless. This becomes most evident when we compare the biblical concept of *hokhmah* with the Greek concept of *sophia*. The latter specifies a closed realm of thought, knowledge for its own sake. It is totally alien to *hokhmah*, which regards such a delimitation of an independent spiritual sphere, governed by its own laws, as the misconstruction of meaning, the violation of continuity, the severance of thought from reality.

The supreme command of *hokhmah* is the unity of teaching and life, for only through this unity can we recognize and avow the all-embracing unity of God. In the light of our doctrine, He who gives life and gives that life meaning is wronged by a teaching which is satisfied with and delights in itself, which rears structures however monumental above life, and yet does not succeed in wresting even a shred of realization out of all the outer and inner obstacles we must struggle with in every precarious hour of our lives. For our God makes only one demand upon us. He does not expect a humanly unattainable completeness and perfection but only the willingness to do as much as we possibly can at every single instant.

(Martin Buber, *Israel and the World: Essays in a Time of Crisis*. New York: Schocken Books, 1948)

MARTIN BUBER (1878-1965). *Philosopher/theologian and religious existentialist best known for his dialogic conception of I–Thou as an approach to relationships with God and between people.*

CHAPTER THREE

The Sicknesses of the Soul

If good behavior is a function of balance, then it may be said that bad behavior is a function of being off-balance. Maimonides calls this "sickness of the soul."

ג:א אָמְרוּ הַקַּדְמוֹנִים: כִּי יֵשׁ לַנֶּפֶשׁ בְּרִיאוּת וָחֳלִי, כְּמוֹ שֶׁיֵּשׁ לַגּוּף בְּרִיאוּת וָחֳלִי. וּבְרִיאוּת הַנֶּפֶשׁ — הִיא: שֶׁתִּהְיֶה תְכוּנָתָהּ וּתְכוּנַת חֲלָקֶיהָ — תְּכוּנוֹת שֶׁתֵּעָשֶׂה בָהֶן תָּדִיר הַטּוֹבוֹת וְהַפְּעֻלּוֹת הַנָּאוֹתוֹת; וְחָלְיָהּ — הוּא: שֶׁתִּהְיֶה תְכוּנָתָהּ וּתְכוּנַת חֲלָקֶיהָ — תְּכוּנוֹת שֶׁתֵּעָשֶׂה בָהֶן תָּדִיר הָרָעוֹת וְהַפְּעֻלּוֹת הַמְגֻנּוֹת.

3:1 The ancients said that just as health and sickness applied to the body, so health and sickness applied to the soul. The soul is healthy when every aspect produces good and every action is fitting; the soul is sick when every aspect produces evil and every action is reprehensible.

Continuing the medical model as an analogy, Maimonides explains how physical illness impacts on the body.

ג:ב אָמְנָם, בְּרִיאוּת הַגּוּף וְחָלְיוֹ — מְלֶאכֶת הָרְפוּאוֹת תַּחְקֹר עָלָיו. וּכְמוֹ שֶׁחוֹלֵי הַגּוּף יְדַמּוּ, לְהֶפְסֵד הַרְגָּשׁוֹתֵיהֶם, בְּמַה־שֶׁהוּא מַר — שֶׁהוּא מָתוֹק, וּבְמַה־שֶׁהוּא מָתוֹק — שֶׁהוּא מַר; וְיָצִירוּ הַנָּאוּת — בְּצוּרַת בִּלְתִּי־נָאוּת; וְתֶחֱזַק תַּאֲוָתָם וְתִרְבֶּה הֲנָאָתָם בְּעִנְיָנִים שֶׁאֵין הֲנָאָה בָהֶם כְּלָל לַבְּרִיאִים; וְאֶפְשָׁר שֶׁיִּהְיֶה בָהֶם צַעַר: כַּאֲכִילַת עָפָר וּפֶחָמִים, וְהַדְּבָרִים הָעֲפוּצִים וְהַחֲמוּצִים מְאֹד, וְכַיּוֹצֵא בְאֵלּוּ מִן־הַמְּזוֹנוֹת אֲשֶׁר לֹא יִתְאַוּוּ לָהֶם הַבְּרִיאִים, אֲבָל יִמְאֲסוּ אוֹתָם — כֵּן חוֹלֵי הַנְּפָשׁוֹת, רְצוֹנִי לוֹמַר:

3:2 The practice of medicine deals with the health and illness of the body. Because of their illness, those who are physically sick may taste what is sweet as bitter and what is bitter as sweet. They may look at what is beautiful and see it as ugly. They may want things which no healthy person would want. And they may hurt themselves by eating dirt or charcoal or rotten or rancid food. No healthy person would want or find satisfaction in any of these things; a healthy person would reject them all.

A sickness of the soul (which Maimonides names as ''evils'') is caused by a kind of misconception similar to the misreading suffered by people who are physically ill. For example, they may confuse various tastes, as he explained in the previous paragraph. They may taste bitter as sweet or sweet as bitter. People who are ''soul sick'' incorrectly perceive good and evil, treating one as the other. Just as the treatment of those who are physically ill ultimately changes their perception of taste, so the treatment for those who are soul sick will ultimately change their perception of good and evil.

ג:ג הָרָעִים וּבַעֲלֵי מִדּוֹת הָרָעוֹת, יְדַמּוּ בְּמַה־שֶׁהוּא רַע, שֶׁהוּא — טוֹב, וּבְמַה־שֶׁהוּא טוֹב, שֶׁהוּא — רַע. וְהָאָדָם הָרַע יִתְאַוֶּה לְעוֹלָם הַפְלָגוֹת, אֲשֶׁר הֵן בֶּאֱמֶת רָעוֹת, וִידַמֶּה בַּעֲבוּר חֳלִי נַפְשׁוֹ שֶׁהֵן טוֹבוֹת.

3:3 The same is true with the sicknesses of the soul, in other words, with evils. Those who possess evil traits imagine that evil is good and good is evil. Constantly craving evil, they keep doing evil things, which–due to their sick souls–they imagine to be good.

The philosopher extends the disease model further with regard to the relationship between physician and patient. Individuals who are sick cannot determine what they must do to heal themselves. Illness impairs individuals' perception and therefore the judgment that is derived from that perception. So they seek advice from the physician.

ג:ד וּכְמוֹ שֶׁהַחוֹלִים הַגּוּפָנִיִּים, כְּשֶׁיֵּדְעוּ חֳלָיָם וְלֹא יֵדְעוּ מְלֶאכֶת הָרְפוּאוֹת, יִשְׁאֲלוּ הָרוֹפְאִים וְיוֹדִיעוּם מַה־שֶׁצָּרִיךְ לַעֲשׂוֹתוֹ, וְיַזְהִירוּם מִמַּה־שֶׁיְּדַמּוּהוּ עָרֵב, וְהוּא בְּהֶפֶךְ חָלְיָם; וְיַכְרִיחוּם לָקַחַת דְּבָרִים הַנִּמְאָסִים וְהַמָּרִים עַד שֶׁיַּבְרִיאוּ גוּפוֹתָם, וְיָשׁוּבוּ לִבְחֹר בַּטּוֹב וְלִמְאֹס בָּרָע.

3:4 Since they do not know medicine, when physically sick people become aware of their illness, they ask a physician, who will tell them what to do. The physician may tell them to avoid what seems pleasant and to take what seems unpleasant, even bitter, so that their bodies can be restored to health. A healthy body will be able to choose what is good for itself and reject what is bad.

Having been a physician to the body, Maimonides now operates as a physician to the soul by prescribing a kind of behavioral therapy for those who are soul sick. Such therapy moves the afflicted from one extreme to the other in order to arrive at the Golden Mean. This treatment is accomplished by a training regimen, administered by a scholar (a philosopher by the Maimonidean standard).

ג:ה כֵּן חוֹלֵי הַנְּפָשׁוֹת, צְרִיךְ לָהֶם שֶׁיִּשְׁאֲלוּ הַחֲכָמִים שֶׁהֵם רוֹפְאֵי הַנְּפָשׁוֹת וְיַזְהִירוּם מִן־הָרָעוֹת הָהֵן אֲשֶׁר יַחְשְׁבוּ בָהֶן שֶׁהֵן טוֹבוֹת, וִירַפְּאוּ אוֹתָם בַּמְּלָאכָה אֲשֶׁר יְרַפְּאוּ בָה מִדּוֹת הַנֶּפֶשׁ, אֲשֶׁר אֶזְכְּרָהּ בַּפֶּרֶק שֶׁאַחַר זֶה. אָמְנָם, חוֹלֵי הַנְּפָשׁוֹת אֲשֶׁר לֹא יַרְגִּישׁוּ בְּחָלְיָם וִידַמּוּ בוֹ שֶׁהוּא — בְּרִיאוּת; אוֹ יַרְגִּישׁוּ בּוֹ וְלֹא יִתְרַפְּאוּ.

3:5a The same is true for those suffering from sicknesses of the soul. They must seek out those scholars, those physicians of the soul, who will help them avoid the things that are evil that they think to be good and who will heal them. I will speak of the particular art used to repair the qualities of the soul in the next chapter. The problem with those who are soul sick is that they are not aware that they are ill; they imagine themselves to be well. Even if they are aware that they are ill, they will not heal themselves. Their prognosis is the same as for any other sick person.

It is clear that if the soul sick person does not seek help and follow the advice of the physician of the soul, then that person will surely die. The modern reader may find some elements of Maimonides' diagnosis and prescription congenial. Yet, some of the suggestions of the medieval philosopher will seem strange and primitive. Were we to place Maimonides' views within the context of modern psychology, we may find that those elements of his thought that seem strange provide more insight than first assumed. We are accustomed to the notion that our behavior is affected by past events, whether genetic or cultural. We know that our present life is shaped by the choices we made in the past. We have done things that we now wish that we had not done. But we cannot undo what has been done. However, we can strive to understand it. Maimonides provides us with another framework in which such understanding can take place.

אַחֲרִיתָם, מַה־שֶּׁתִּהְיֶה אַחֲרִית הַחוֹלֶה כְּשֶׁיִּמָּשֵׁךְ אַחַר הֲנָאוֹתָיו וְלֹא יִתְרַפֵּא, שֶׁהוּא יָמוּת בְּלִי סָפֵק. אֲבָל הַמַּרְגִּישִׁים, וְהֵם נִמְשָׁכִים אַחַר הֲנָאוֹתֵיהֶם — אָמְרָה בָהֶן הַתּוֹרָה הָאֲמִתִּית מְסַפֶּרֶת דִּבְרֵיהֶם: כִּי בִּשְׁרִרוּת לִבִּי אֵלֵךְ, לְמַעַן סְפוֹת הָרָוָה אֶת־הַצְּמֵאָה (דברים כט, יח). רְצוֹנִי לוֹמַר: שֶׁהוּא מְכַוֵּן לְרַווֹת צְמָאוֹ וְהוּא מוֹסִיף לְעַצְמוֹ צָמָא. אַךְ עַל־שֶׁאֵינָם מַרְגִּישִׁים בַּדָּבָר — אָמַר

שְׁלֹמֹה הַמֶּלֶךְ, עָלָיו הַשָּׁלוֹם, עֲלֵיהֶם: דֶּרֶךְ אֱוִיל יָשָׁר בְּעֵינָיו; וְשֹׁמֵעַ לְעֵצָה חָכָם (משלי יב, טו). רָצָה לוֹמַר: שׁוֹמֵעַ לַעֲצַת הֶחָכָם — חָכָם, מִפְּנֵי שֶׁיּוֹדִיעֶנּוּ הַדֶּרֶךְ שֶׁהוּא יָשָׁר בֶּאֱמֶת; לֹא אֲשֶׁר יַחְשְׁבֵהוּ הוּא ,,יָשָׁר". וְאָמַר: יֵשׁ דֶּרֶךְ יָשָׁר לִפְנֵי־ אִישׁ, וְאַחֲרִיתָהּ דַּרְכֵי מָוֶת (שם יד, יב).

3:5b If a sick person follows his/her own desires and does not seek treatment, s/he will surely die. Those who are aware that they are ill and still follow their own desires are described by the Torah [as saying], "I shall be safe, though I follow my own willful heart; this is as adding drunkenness to thirst" [Deut. 29:18]. The verse means that although one may intend to slake one's thirst, one only adds to it. Solomon described those who are not even aware of their illness with these words, "The way of a fool is straight in one's own eyes, but the one who is wise listens to advice" [Prov. 12:15]. Solomon meant that the wise person is the one who listens to a teacher, for that teacher can show him [or her] the proper path and thereby save them from error. Solomon also said, "There is a way that seems right to a human, but the end of it is the way of death" [Prov. 14:12].

We would probably find difficulty in the specific modalities of treatment that Maimonides prescribed. For example, we might not think that the way to stop being stingy is to be forced to spend or the way to stop being a spendthrift is to be forced to become stingy. Reflecting on some modern forms of behavioral therapy, such as aversion therapy, may make us wonder further whether the outcomes of modern therapy are any better than the outcomes of medieval therapy. One wonders which would indeed prove to be more effective if we were to set Maimonides' techniques against modern psycho-spiritual techniques and provided both with the same method of rigorous testing.

וְאָמַר עוֹד בְּחוֹלֵי הַנְּפָשׁוֹת הָאֵלֶּה, בִּהְיוֹתָם בִּלְתִּי יוֹדְעִים מַה־יַּזִּיקֵם וּמַה־יּוֹעִילֵם: דֶּרֶךְ רְשָׁעִים כָּאֲפֵלָה, לֹא יָדְעוּ בַּמֶּה יִכָּשֵׁלוּ (שם ד, יט). אַךְ מְלֶאכֶת רְפוּאַת הַנְּפָשׁוֹת הִיא, כְּמוֹ שֶׁאֲסַפֵּר בַּפֶּרֶק הָרְבִיעִי.

3:5c This applies to those who are soul sick and do not know what will help them and what will hurt them. This relates to what Solomon said in another passage, "The way of the wicked is like darkness; they do not know over what they stumble" [Prov. 4:19]. The work of the healing of souls will be discussed in the fourth chapter.

GLEANINGS

WICKEDNESS AND DEATH

Immortality is not a matter merely of duration of the spirit after death but also of the preservation of the values which give meaning to human life. We live in the works which we do, and which bind us to our fellowmen, in the visions we cherish and in the goals we further. Our lives are expressed not in the physical tracts of our bodies but within our ideal purposes, as creators of the values which sustain our civilization. Humble or great, our efforts are of moment to the entire social structure. What are our material achievements, our political attainments, and our cultural and spiritual refinements, but the distilled essence of human lives, of labor, love, thought, sacrifice? They are the fruitage of human souls. The world was made better or worse by their presence.

Only the person that strives to contribute, whether much or little, to the larger life of mankind may live on after his physical life draws to an end. Immortality thus considered appears not as an intrinsic attribute of the soul but an achievement. Through sacrificial service in the cause of human well-being, of right and of truth, a person may acquire the attributes that make for deathlessness, even as by selfishness, dissoluteness, and ignorance, he may dissipate the powers of his soul. The rabbis well expressed this thought in their saying: "The righteous live even in death; the wicked are dead even in life."

(Samuel S. Cohon, *Religious Affirmations*. Los Angeles: 1983)

SAMUEL S. COHON (1888-1959). *Rabbi, theologian, and professor of theology at Hebrew Union College, Cincinnati. He authored the Guiding Principles of Reform Judaism in 1937, which came to be known as the Columbus Platform, articulating a more positive approach to traditional Jewish observance than had his predecessors.*

CRUELTY AND COMPASSION

Because of his immense power, man is potentially the most wicked of beings. He often has a passion for cruel deeds that only fear of God can soothe, suffocating flushes of envy that only holiness can ventilate.

If man is not more than human, then he is less than human. Man is but a short, critical stage between animal and the spiritual. His state is one of constant wavering, of soaring or descending. Undeviating humanity is non-existent. The emancipated man is yet to emerge.

Man is more than what he is to himself. In his reason he may be limited, in his will he may be wicked, yet he stands in a relation to God which he may betray but not sever and which constitutes the essential meaning of his life. He is the knot in which heaven and earth are interlaced.

(Abraham Joshua Heschel, *To Grow in Wisdom*. Lanham, Maryland: Madison Books, 1990)

ABRAHAM JOSHUA HESCHEL (1907-1972). *Rabbi, scholar, and theologian. Perhaps the most influential Jewish thinker of the twentieth century. He taught at the Hochschule für das Wissenshaft des Judenthums and later replaced Martin Buber at the Juedisches Lehrhaus before coming to America to join the faculty at Hebrew Union College in 1940 and later at the Jewish Theological Seminary in 1945.*

WHERE INTROSPECTION LEADS

Many of our sins are due to an exaggerated egocentricity caused by the frustration of our social impulses. In such cases it must be obvious that introspection can result only in emphasizing the introvert bent of our minds. Herein lies one of the chief dangers of religious asceticism. Self-hate does not lead to love of our fellows, but to contempt and envy of them. "Be not wicked in thine own eyes" [*Pirke Avot* 2:13] is sound psychological as well as ethical advice. But to apply it means that we must sometimes cease worrying about our faults and try to interest ourselves in doing the things that are good, and forget about ourselves. Introspection may point out to us where we have made a mess of our lives; but a knowledge of the external factors which contribute to our failure and of the best methods by which these may be controlled so as to help restore our personality to its normal functioning is necessary to effect a genuine repentance, one that will truly make us *beriah hadashah*, a new creation, a regenerate personality.

(Mordecai M. Kaplan, *The Meaning of God in Modern Jewish Religion.* New York: The Jewish Reconstructionist Foundation, 1947)

MORDECAI M. KAPLAN (1881-1983). *Rabbi, scholar, and theologian. Founder of the Reconstructionist movement, he revolutionized the perspective on Judaism as a civilization in his magnum opus of the same name. He also initiated the Jewish community center as a concept and influenced generations of rabbis as a member of the faculty at the Jewish Theological Seminary.*

"HEALTH" AND ILLNESS

In a different context, if we awaken to religion, we keep its commandments. This keeping of the commandments expresses our awakening and sustains it but, more important, serves to transform the self so that what we once viewed as a commandment, we now see as the deepest expression of our own desire. When we first discover a friendship, we do things to help or please the other person because that's what friends do. In the process, we gradually come to do these things because we want to do them. The daily caring for our child at first expresses our gratitude and wonder. Later it sustains and strengthens this wonder. Finally the practice transforms us so that our caring becomes an expression of our being.

Purgation is not a one-time discipline but a way of life. It transforms our consciousness so that tasks once done out of duty are now done out of love, naturally and joyously springing from our transformed nature.

(Carol Ochs, *Women and Spirituality.* Totowa, New Jersey: Rowman & Allanheld, 1983)

CAROL OCHS (1939-). *Feminist theologian, instructor in pastoral theology at Hebrew Union College-Jewish Institute of Religion, New York, where she also directs its spirituality program. In addition, Dr. Ochs is an adjunct faculty member of the Union Institute Graduate School. From 1967 to 1992, she was professor of philosophy at Simmons College and is the author of* Song of the Self: Biblical Spirituality and Human Holiness; Women and Spirituality; *and* An Ascent to Joy: Transforming Deadness of Spirit.

THE RELIGIOUS PERSON

The religious man has a sense of wonderment for the mystery of the human soul, for the gift of life and for the pattern of the universe. This wonderment and awe add vision and depth to his life. He finds meaning and order in the world and appreciates deeply that he too is a thread in the fabric of the universe. Einstein, an agnostic by his own admission, still believed himself religious in the sense that he could experience a mystic awe as he reflected on the wisdom and radiant beauty of the universe. The sentiment of awe is, with the religious man, closely linked with a feeling of gratitude. He appreciates what has been given to him.

Nor does the religious man acknowledge his dependence on God with reluctance as though submitting against his will to a superior authority. He looks upon life itself as a blessing and freely acknowledges God as the author of his being. Can the religious man be said to be happy? He might not subscribe to happiness in the usual hedonistic sense but he would not be a stranger to joy.

(Robert L. Katz, "The Rabbi Asks," CCAR Journal, vol. 8, no. 2 [June 1960]: 50)

ROBERT L. KATZ (1917-). *Rabbi and founder of the Department of Human Relations at Hebrew Union College-Jewish Institute of Religion, Cincinnati. His book* Empathy: Its Nature and Uses *has become a classic in the field, and his* Pastoral Care and the Jewish Tradition *is used as the basic textbook in many Christian and Jewish seminaries.*

CHAPTER FOUR

Maimonides' Discussion of Virtue

In this chapter, Maimonides follows Aristotle's discussion of virtue as articulated in the *Nicomachean Ethics*, book II, book III, and book IV, beginning with the definition of virtue as "a state of character concerned with choice, lying in a mean, i.e., a mean relative to us, this being determined by a rational principle..." (bk. II, chap. 6). Aristotle then proceeds to a discussion of dispositions, "...two of them vices, involving excess and deficiency respectively, and one a virtue, viz., the mean, and all are in a sense opposed to all" (Bk II, Ch 8). He follows with a discussion of courage (bk. III, chap. 8), temperance (bk. III, chap. 10), liberality (bk. IV, chap. 1), magnificence (bk. IV, chap. 2), pride (bk. IV, chap. 3), honor (bk. IV, chap. 4), good temper (bk. IV, chap. 5), boastfulness (bk. IV, chap. 7), and shame (bk. IV, chap. 8).

ד:א הַמַּעֲשִׂים הַטּוֹבִים — הֵם הַמַּעֲשִׂים הַשָּׁוִים, הַמְמֻצָּעִים בֵּין שְׁתֵּי קָצָווֹת שֶׁשְּׁתֵּיהֶן רָע: הָאַחַת מֵהֶן — תּוֹסֶפֶת, וְהַשֵּׁנִית — חֶסְרוֹן. וְהַמַּעֲלוֹת — הֵן תְּכוּנוֹת נַפְשִׁיּוֹת וְקִנְיָנִים מְמֻצָּעִים בֵּין שְׁתֵּי תְכוּנוֹת רָעוֹת: הָאַחַת מֵהֶן — יְתֵרָה, וְהָאַחֶרֶת — חֲסֵרָה. מִן הַתְּכוּנוֹת הָאֵלֶּה יִתְחַיְּבוּ הַפְּעֻלּוֹת הָהֵן. וְהַמָּשָׁל בּוֹ: הַזְּהִירוּת, שֶׁהִיא מִדָּה מְמֻצַּעַת בֵּין רֹב הַתַּאֲוָה וּבֵין הֶעְדֵּר הֶרְגֵּשׁ־הַהֲנָאָה. הַזְּהִירוּת — הִיא מִפְּעֻלּוֹת הַטּוֹבוֹת; וּתְכוּנַת הַנֶּפֶשׁ, אֲשֶׁר תִּתְחַיֵּב מִמֶּנָּה הַזְּהִירוּת — הִיא מַעֲלַת הַמִּדּוֹת. אֲבָל רֹב הַתַּאֲוָה — הוּא הַקָּצֶה הָרִאשׁוֹן; וְהֶעְדֵּר הֶרְגֵּשׁ־הַהֲנָאָה לְגַמְרֵי — הוּא הַקָּצֶה הָאַחֲרוֹן, וּשְׁנֵיהֶם רַע גָּמוּר. וּשְׁתֵּי תְכוּנוֹת הַנֶּפֶשׁ, אֲשֶׁר מֵהֶן יִתְחַיֵּב רֹב הַתַּאֲוָה, וְהִיא: הַתְּכוּנָה הַיְתֵרָה; וְהֶעְדֵּר־הַהַרְגָּשָׁה, וְהִיא: הַתְּכוּנָה הַחֲסֵרָה — שְׁתֵּיהֶן יַחַד פְּחִיתֻיּוֹת מִפְּחִיתֻיּוֹת הַמִּדּוֹת.

4:1 Good acts are those midway between two extremes that are bad, namely, excess and absence. Virtues are those elements of character [lit., "psychic disposition and habits"] midway between two qualities that are bad: one excessive and the other absent. From virtues come good acts. Prudence, for example, is midway between excessive desire and its absence. Prudence is a good act; the quality of the soul that produces it is a virtue. Too much desire and no desire are the two bad extremes; the aspects of the soul that produced them are the quality of excess and the quality of absence, both of which are ethical defects.

In this section, Maimonides continues his exposition of dispositions that lead to specific actions. The mean between those extremes he describes are to be considered virtuous. If good psychic and moral health depends on being within the "Golden Mean," then Maimonides must inform the reader–those who are presently moved one way or the other away from that mean–to move toward that mean through a variety of mechanisms. It should be noted that the Golden Mean is not the same as the *mitzvah* system.

The Golden Mean

The notion of the Golden Mean is at the core of Maimonides' *Shemonah Perakim*. Maimonides learned this idea from Aristotle in his *Nicomachean Ethics*, books III and IV. The Golden Mean is the balance between two extremes that are vices. For example, courage is the mean between rashness and cowardice. Thus, the ethical life is a matter of discovering the balance between two extremes and then living that balance. However, since Maimonides' work reflects a history of Jewish tradition, he moves slightly away from an insistence upon an absolute middle position in *Shemonah Perakim*. Thus one may move toward humility even beyond the mean.

The notion of the Golden Mean is problematic when placed in the context of a legal system that is ascribed to God. This notion can also not be applied to most of what Maimonides calls "ritual commandments." It is also difficult to apply to many of the so-called "rational" commandments. One cannot determine how the Golden Mean will be applied to the Sabbath or to *mitzvot* like "Thou shalt not murder." While the Golden Mean may be used to develop a rational ethical system for a particular society, it seems unrelated to a Divine apodictic system.

ד:ב וְכֵן הַנְּדִיבוּת — מְמֻצַּעַת בֵּין הַכִּילוּת וְהַפִּזּוּר; וְהַגְּבוּרָה — מְמֻצַּעַת בֵּין הַמְּסִירָה לְסַכָּנוֹת וּבֵין רֹךְ הַלֵּבָב; וְהַסִּלְסוּל — מְמֻצָּע בֵּין הַהִתְנַשְּׂאוּת וּבֵין הַנַּבָלָה. וּפֵרוּשׁ סִלְסוּל — הוּא: מִי שֶׁמִּתְכַּבֵּד כָּרָאוּי וְאֵינוֹ מִתְנַבֵּל בְּדָבָר. וְהַהִתְנַשְּׂאוּת — הִיא שֶׁיִּתְכַּבֵּד הָאָדָם יוֹתֵר מִן־הָרָאוּי לוֹ. וְהַנְּבָלָה — יְדוּעָה, וְהִיא: שֶׁיַּעֲשֶׂה אָדָם מַעֲשִׂים בִּלְתִּי הֲגוּנִים שֶׁיֵּשׁ בָּהֶם פְּחִיתוּת הַרְבֵּה וְחֶרְפָּה. וְהַנַּחַת — מְמֻצַּעַת בֵּין הַקִּטְרוּג וְהַקַּנְטְרָנוּת, וּבֵין רַכּוּת הַטֶּבַע, מַה־שֶּׁקּוֹרִין בלע"ז: מוֹלד"ה וְהוּא: מִי שֶׁהוּא בְּלֹא דִבּוּר וּבְלֹא מַעֲשֶׂה לִכְבֵדוּת טִבְעוֹ וְקֹר מִזְגּוֹ, וְהוּא כְּנֶגֶד הַקִּטְרוּג שֶׁיָּבֹא מֵחִדּוּד טִבְעוֹ וְחֹם מִזְגּוֹ.

4:2a Generosity is midway between miserliness and extravagance. Courage is midway between recklessness and cowardice. Self-confidence is midway between arrogance and debasement. Dignity [*silsul*] is midway

34

between being overbearing and being obsequious. (One may define *silsul* as taking pride in oneself and not debasing oneself.) Arrogance is honoring oneself more than is fitting. Self-debasement is, as is well-known, the doing of shameful and reprehensible acts. Contentment is midway between contentiousness and apathy, called in Arabic *mavelad*. A person who is apathetic due to the sluggishness of one's nature can neither speak nor act. Apathy is the reverse of contentiousness, which arises from the irascibility of one's nature and the heat of one's mixture of humors.

Continuing the list, Maimonides goes so far as to identify those elements that have no parallel in the Hebrew language. While one might assume that they therefore are irrelevant to Judaism, Maimonides simply suggests that it is necessary to describe them.

וְהָעֲנָוָה — מְמֻצַּעַת בֵּין הַגַּאֲוָה וּבֵין שִׁפְלוּת הָרוּחַ. וְהַהִסְתַּפְּקוּת — מְמֻצַּעַת בֵּין אַהֲבַת הַמָּמוֹן וּבֵין הָעַצְלוּת. וְטוּב־לֵב — מְמֻצָּע בֵּין הַנִּבְזָלָה וְיִתְרוֹן טוּב הַלֵּבָב. (וּמִפְּנֵי שֶׁאֵין לַמִּדּוֹת הָאֵלֶּה שֵׁם יָדוּעַ בִּלְשׁוֹנֵנוּ — צָרִיךְ לְפָרֵשׁ עִנְיָנֵיהֶם, וּמַה־שֶׁרוֹצִים בּוֹ הַפִילוֹסוֹפִים: לֵב טוֹב — קוֹרְאִים: מִי שֶׁכָּל־כַּוָּנָתוֹ לְהֵיטִיב לִבְנֵי אָדָם בְּגוּפוֹ, וַעֲצָתוֹ, וּבְמָמוֹנוֹ בְּכָל יְכָלְתּוֹ, בִּלְתִּי שֶׁיַּשִּׂיגֵהוּ נֶזֶק אוֹ בִזָּיוֹן, וְהוּא: הָאֶמְצָעִי. וְהַנָּבָל — הוּא הֵפֶךְ זֶה, וְהוּא: מִי שֶׁאֵינוֹ רוֹצֶה לְהוֹעִיל לִבְנֵי אָדָם בְּדָבָר, אֲפִלּוּ בְּמַה־שֶׁאֵין לוֹ בּוֹ חֶסְרוֹן, וְלֹא טֹרַח, וְלֹא נֶזֶק — וְהוּא: הַקָּצֶה הָאַחֲרוֹן. וְיִתְרוֹן טוּב הַלֵּבָב — הוּא: שֶׁעוֹשֶׂה דְּבָרִים הַנִּזְכָּרִים בְּ„לֵב טוֹב", וַאֲפִלּוּ אִם יַשִּׂיגֵהוּ בָזֶה נֶזֶק גָּדוֹל, אוֹ בִזָּיוֹן, אוֹ טֹרַח רַב וְהֶפְסֵד מְרֻבֶּה — וְהוּא: הַקָּצֶה הָרִאשׁוֹן). וְהַסַּבְלָנוּת — מְמֻצָּע בֵּין הַכַּעַס וְהֶעְדֵּר הַרְגָּשַׁת חֶרְפָּה וָבוּז.

4:2b Humility is midway between pride and shame. Self-sufficiency is midway between the love of money and laziness. Being good-hearted is midway between being contemptible and being a "goody two-shoes." Because there is no name for these virtues in our [Hebrew] language, we must explain them clearly and indicate what the philosophers mean by these terms. For them, "good-hearted" means someone who wants to help other people physically or through advice or funds. Such a person acts with his/her total capacity, without incurring any harm or shame. The reverse of this is being a churl–such a person will not help someone else unless such help in no way causes him any injury or loss. That is one extreme. The other extreme is being good-hearted to a fault. Such a person does good without regard to the loss incurred, the disgrace faced, or the trouble suffered. Patience is midway between anger and the total loss of affect.

Maimonides wants to make sure that the reader fully understands his point. Thus, in addition to listing additional items for consideration, he goes to great length to explain certain items that at first may seem virtuous, even in the extreme. However, once the extreme position is probed, one can understand why it is indeed not a virtuous position to take.

וּבֹשֶׁת־פָּנִים — מְמֻצָּע בֵּין הָעַזּוּת וְהַבַּיְשָׁנוּת. (פֵּרוּשׁ נִרְאֶה לִי מִדִּבְרֵי רַבּוֹתֵינוּ, זִכְרוֹנָם לִבְרָכָה, שֶׁהַבַּיְשָׁן הוּא אֶצְלָם, מִי שֶׁיֶּשׁ־לוֹ רֹב בֹּשֶׁת; וּבֹשֶׁת פָּנִים, הִיא הַמְּמֻצָּע — מִמַּאֲמָרָם: לֹא הַבַּיְשָׁן לָמֵד (אבות פרק ב, משנה ה), וְלֹא אָמְרוּ: אֵין בֹּשֶׁת־פָּנִים לָמֵד; וְאָמְרוּ: בֹּשֶׁת־פָּנִים לְגַן־עֵדֶן (שם פרק ה, משנה כ), וְלֹא אָמְרוּ: הַ„בַּיְשָׁן" — וְלָזֶה סִדַּרְתִּים כָּךְ). וְכֵן שְׁאָר הַמִּדּוֹת יִצְטָרְכוּ עַל־כָּל־פָּנִים לִשְׁמוֹת מֻנָּחִים לָהֶם מֵהַסְכָּמָה, שֶׁיִּהְיוּ הָעִנְיָנִים מוּבָנִים. וְהַרְבֵּה פְּעָמִים יִטְעוּ בְּנֵי אָדָם בְּאֵלּוּ הַפְּעֻלּוֹת וְיַחְשְׁבוּ אֶחָד מֵהַקְּצָווֹת — טוֹב וּמַעֲלָה מִמַּעֲלוֹת הַנֶּפֶשׁ. פְּעָמִים יַחְשְׁבוּ הַקָּצֶה הָרִאשׁוֹן — טוֹב, כְּמוֹ שֶׁיַּחְשְׁבוּ הַמְּסִירָה לַסַּכָּנוֹת מַעֲלָה, וְיִקְרְאוּ הַמּוֹסְרִים עַצְמָם לַסַּכָּנוֹת: גִּבּוֹרִים; וּכְשֶׁיִּרְאוּ מִי שֶׁהוּא בְּתַכְלִית זֹאת הַמִּדָּה, רְצוֹנִי לוֹמַר: שֶׁמּוֹסֵר עַצְמוֹ לַסַּכָּנוֹת וּמוֹסֵר עַצְמוֹ לְמִיתָה בְּכַוָּנָה, וּפְעָמִים יִנָּצֵל בְּמִקְרֶה — יַחֲשִׁיבוּהוּ בָּזֶה וְיֹאמְרוּ עָלָיו שֶׁהוּא: גִּבּוֹר. וּפְעָמִים יַחְשְׁבוּ הַקָּצֶה הָאַחֲרוֹן שֶׁהוּא טוֹב, וְיֹאמְרוּ עַל־פְּחוּת הַנֶּפֶשׁ שֶׁהוּא: סַבְלָן; וְעַל־הֶעָצֵל — שֶׁהוּא: שָׂמֵחַ בְּחֶלְקוֹ; וְעַל־נֶעְדָּר הֶרְגֵּשׁ הַהֲנָאוֹת לְעֶבֶר־טִבְעוֹ — שֶׁהוּא: נִזְהָר, כְּלוֹמַר: יְרֵא־חֵטְא. וְעַל־זֶה הַמִּין מִן־הַטָּעוּת יַחְשְׁבוּ גַּם־כֵּן הַפִּזּוּר וְיִתְרוֹן־טוֹב־הַלֵּב מִן־הַפְּעֻלּוֹת הַטּוֹבוֹת — וְזֶה כֻּלּוֹ טָעוּת.

4:2c Being shamefaced is midway between being brazen and being ashamed. Being "shamefaced" seems to be an intermediate term for the rabbis, while "being ashamed" referred to the person who felt excessive shame. Thus they said, "The ashamed person will never learn," but they did not say, "The shamefaced person will never learn." The rabbis also said that "the shamefaced person will end in Paradise." They did not say that "the ashamed person will end in Paradise." [Following the rabbis] I have suggested this order. Thus, all the other terms must have a common agreement with regard to their meanings so that people do not err in their applications and think that one extreme is good and a virtue to be applied to the soul. At times, some may think that one extreme should be desired. For example, [one may mistakenly] think that placing oneself in danger [needlessly] is a virtue and that those who do so are brave. Seeing that the consequence of such a "virtue" is the intentional putting of oneself in mortal danger to be saved only by chance, some might think that such a person was brave. At other times, some might think that the other extreme is the one to be preferred. Thus, there are those who might think that a person who is mentally deficient is one who is patient. Others might call the person who is lazy the one who rejoices in one's portion. Still others might call one totally bereft of feeling, due to a nonresponsive nature, one who is careful or one who fears sin. Similarly, one might think that the spendthrift has a good heart. However, this would be an error.

The Torah does not tell us to be generous to the poor; instead, it tells us to leave the corners of the fields for them. The rabbis may raise questions as to the precise dimensions of the "corners of the field"; they do not raise the issue of whether or not the owner of the field is free to desist from the obligation of leaving those corners to the poor. The giving of *tzedakah* is a *mitzvah d'oraitah*, a commandment enjoined in the Torah, thus making it something that the individual Jew is not free to decide to do or not to do.

Vice, according to Maimonides, however, is the state of being unbalanced; consequently, virtue is being balanced. Thus, the return to virtue is the return to balance. Unlike the traditional notion of *teshuvah*, this return to virtue is not a product of either introspection or Divine forgiveness. This return is achieved through a change in behavior: by moving the affected person from the one extreme which he or she inclines toward the other. In the next section, Maimonides explains this position more specifically.

Gleanings, Corners of the Field, etc.

The Torah instructs us: "When you reap the harvest of your land, you shall not reap all the way to the edges of your field, or gather the gleanings of your harvest. You shall not pick your vineyard bare, or gather the fallen fruit of your vineyard; you shall leave them for the poor and the stranger: I *Adonai* am your God"(Lev. 19:9). This commandment is repeated in Leviticus 23:22 and Deuteronomy 24:19ff. A tractate of the *Mishnah, Peah* (Gleanings), expands the biblical requirements of the "edges of the field" and the "gleanings of the harvest." The *Mishnah* teaches that "whatever is used for food...and grows from the soil, is all reaped together, and is brought in for storage is liable to the law of *Peah*. Grain and pulse come within this rule" (*Peah* 1:4). It also teaches that "*Peah* should not be less that one-sixtieth part [of the harvest]" (*Peah* 1:2).

This concern for the poor, which is reflected in Torah and further interpreted by the rabbis, has remained a fundamental principle of Judaism throughout the history of the Jewish people. Such concern has been viewed as a *mitzvah*, a Divine commandment. It has been directed to all who are poor, whether Jewish or not. One easily sees in Reform Judaism's concern for social justice a modern application of the teaching about the edges of the fields and its gleanings.

וְאָמְנָם יְשֻׁבַּח בֶּאֱמֶת הַמְמֻצָּע, וְאֵלָיו צָרִיךְ לָאָדָם שֶׁיְּכַוֵּן וְיִשְׁקֹל פְּעֻלוֹתָיו כֻּלָּם תָּמִיד עַד שֶׁיִּתְמַצָּעוּ. וְדַע, שֶׁאֵלּוּ הַמַּעֲלוֹת וְהַפְּחִיתֻיּוֹת אֲשֶׁר לַמִּדּוֹת לֹא יַגִּיעוּ וְלֹא יִתְיַשְּׁבוּ בַּנֶּפֶשׁ, רַק בְּכֹפֶל הַפְּעֻלּוֹת הַבָּאוֹת מִן־הַמִּדָּה הַהִיא פְּעָמִים רַבּוֹת וּבִזְמָן אָרֹךְ וְהַרְגִּילֵנוּ בָּהֶן. וְאִם הָיוּ הַפְּעֻלּוֹת הָהֵן טוֹבוֹת, יִהְיֶה הַמַּגִּיעַ לָנוּ מֵהֶן — מַעֲלָה; וְאִם הָיוּ רָעוֹת, יִהְיֶה הַמַּגִּיעַ לָנוּ מֵהֶן — פְּחִיתוּת. וּמִפְּנֵי שֶׁאֵין אָדָם בְּטִבְעוֹ בִּתְחִלַּת עִנְיָנוֹ בַּעַל מַעֲלָה, וְלֹא בַעַל חִסָּרוֹן — כְּמוֹ שֶׁנְּבָאֵר בַּפֶּרֶק הַשְּׁמִינִי — וְהוּא יַרְגִּיל בְּלֹא סָפֵק פְּעֻלּוֹת מִקַּטְנוּתוֹ, כְּפִי מִנְהַג קְרוֹבָיו וְאַנְשֵׁי אַרְצוֹ. וְאֶפְשָׁר שֶׁיִּהְיוּ הַפְּעֻלּוֹת הָהֵן מְמֻצָּעוֹת, וְאֶפְשָׁר שֶׁיִּהְיוּ מוֹתָרוֹת, אוֹ מְחֻסָּרוֹת, כְּפִי שֶׁסִּפַּרְנוּ.

4:2d In truth, it is the middle way that should be praised. One should measure one's actions in order to achieve it. You should know that the ethical virtues or vices are not set into the soul unless and until they are repeated many times over a long period of time and one has been accustomed to them. As ethical actions–whether good or bad–they will affect us one way or the other, because no human being possesses virtue or vice by nature. This will be explained in the fifth chapter. Without a doubt, one gets used to doing certain things from one's youth due to the customs of one's relatives or the people of one's land. These actions may either be the middle way or they may be extremes in one direction or the other, just as we have reported.

Maimonides returns to the medical analogy in order to explain his position. Because the virtues imply an action, they must be considered the same way. As the loss of harmony in the body requires redress, so does the loss of harmony in the soul. Movement toward one extreme requires movement in the direction of the other. By changing behaviors, one can return to the Golden Mean position of being virtuous.

ד:ג וְתִהְיֶה נַפְשׁוֹ חוֹלָה — רָאוּי שֶׁיֵּלְכוּ בִּרְפוּאָתוֹ כְּדֶרֶךְ רְפוּאוֹת הַגּוּפוֹת בְּשָׁוֶה: כְּשֵׁם שֶׁהַגּוּף, כְּשֶׁיֵּצֵא מִשִּׁוּוּיוֹ נִרְאֶה אֶל אֵיזֶה צַד נָטָה וְיָצָא, וְנַעֲמֹד כְּנֶגְדּוֹ בְּהֶפְכּוֹ, עַד שֶׁיָּשׁוּב אֶל הַשִּׁוּוּי. וּכְשֶׁיִּשְׁתַּוֶּה, נָסַלֵּק יָדֵינוּ מִן הַהֶפֶךְ וְנָשׁוּב לַעֲשׂוֹת לוֹ מַה־שֶּׁיַּעֲמִידֵהוּ עַל שִׁוּוּיוֹ — כֵּן נַעֲשֶׂה בַּמִּדּוֹת בְּשָׁוֶה: כְּשֶׁנִּרְאֶה אָדָם שֶׁהָיְתָה לוֹ תְכוּנָה בְּנַפְשׁוֹ וְחָסֵר בָּהּ נַפְשׁוֹ מִכָּל־טוֹבָה לְרֹב הַכִּילוּת — וְזוֹ פְּחִיתוּת מִפְּחִיתֻיּוֹת הַנֶּפֶשׁ; וְהַפֹּעַל אֲשֶׁר יַעֲשֵׂהוּ — מִפְּעֻלּוֹת הָרַע, כְּמוֹ שֶׁבֵּאַרְנוּ בָּזֶה הַפֶּרֶק. וּכְשֶׁנִּרְצֶה לִרְפֹּאות זֶה הֶחֳלִי, לֹא נְצַוֵּהוּ לְהַרְגִּיל בִּנְדִיבוּת — שֶׁזֶּהוּ, כְּמוֹ שֶׁיְּרַפֵּא מִי שֶׁיִּגְבַּר עָלָיו הַחֹם בְּדָבָר הַמְמֻצָּע הַשָּׁוֶה, שֶׁלֹּא יַבְרִיאֵהוּ מֵחָלְיוֹ.

4:3a Should one's soul be ill, one should proceed in the same manner as one would proceed in the treatment of ills of the body. If the body loses its harmony and moves to one extreme or another, then one moves to reverse the process by moving to the other extreme until the body recovers its harmony. When that is accomplished, one ceases that movement. Then we do what is necessary to maintain that harmony. We do the same in dealing with the virtues. For example, we may find a person who in the past had a particular quality in his/her soul, like being charitable, for example, and all of a sudden has changed and become a miser. [This is] a most morally deficient quality, as we have explained in this chapter. Wishing to cure this disease, we would not tell that person to start being charitable. To do so would be like treating someone with a fever by covering that person with something that is lukewarm; that would hardly cure the patient.

Behavioral modification does not occur suddenly, quickly, nor with one slight change in behavior. To be cured, to be healed of one's soul sickness, a person must learn the new behavior (and be given the opportunity to practice this new behavior) many times. Once a person finally moves away from the extreme behavior, then that person must learn the behavior implied by the mean. One should not assume that both extremes represent the same challenge in behavioral modification. Maimonides cautions the reader that moving from one particular extreme to the mean can be more difficult than moving from the other extreme to the mean.

אֲבָל צָרִיךְ שֶׁנְּבִיאֵהוּ לְפַזֵּר, וְיִכְפֹּל מַעֲשֵׂה הַפִּזּוּר פַּעַם־אַחַר־פַּעַם פְּעָמִים רַבּוֹת, עַד שֶׁתָּסוּר מִנַּפְשׁוֹ הַתְּכוּנָה הַמְחַיֶּבֶת לַכִּילוּת, וְיִהְיֶה קָרוֹב לְהַגִּיעַ אֶל תְּכוּנַת הַפִּזּוּר — וְאָז נְסַלֵּק פְּעֻלּוֹת הַפִּזּוּר, וּנְצַוֵּהוּ לְהַתְמִיד עַל־פְּעֻלּוֹת הַנְּדִיבוּת וְיִשְׁקֹד עֲלֵיהֶן: לֹא יוֹתִיר וְלֹא יְחַסֵּר. וְכֵן כְּשֶׁנִּרְאֵהוּ מְפַזֵּר — נְצַוֵּהוּ לַעֲשׂוֹת פְּעֻלּוֹת הַכִּילוּת וְלִשְׁנוֹתָן; אֲבָל לֹא יִשְׁנֶה פֹּעַל הַכִּילוּת פְּעָמִים רַבּוֹת כִּשְׁנוֹתוֹ פֹּעַל הַפִּזּוּר. וְזֶה הַחִדּוּשׁ הַטּוֹב — הוּא סֵדֶר הָרְפוּאָה וְסוֹדָהּ, וְהוּא: שֶׁשּׁוּב הָאָדָם מִן־הַפִּזּוּר לַנְּדִיבוּת — יוֹתֵר קַל וְיוֹתֵר קָרוֹב, מִשּׁוּבוֹ מִן־הַכִּילוּת לַנְּדִיבוּת. וְכֵן שׁוּב נֶעְדַּר הַרְגָּשַׁת הַהֲנָאָה נִזְהָר וִירֵא־חֵטְא — יוֹתֵר קַל וְיוֹתֵר קָרוֹב לָשׁוּב, מִשּׁוּב בַּעַל הַתַּאֲווֹת נִזְהָר.

4:3b To be cured, the miser must be taught to be a spendthrift many times– not just once–until miserliness is removed from the soul and the former miser is on the verge of becoming a spendthrift. At that point, spendthrift training ceases and the person is directed to follow the middle path of being charitable, guided not to go beyond that in either direction. Similarly, should we see someone who is a spendthrift, we need to train that person to act in a miserly manner and to do so once or twice. Unlike our treatment of the miser, we need not do so more than that. What is remarkable about this method of treatment is that getting the spendthrift to become charitable is easier than getting the miser to become charitable. Likewise, it is easier to get someone who is devoid of feeling to become a person who is cautious. [And it is easier to get] one who fears sin than [it is to get] someone who is governed by his/her passions to become a person who is cautious.

Training implies drilling, the constant repetition of the desired behavior. The extent of repetition is determined by the specific extreme behavior that needs to be changed. Recognizing that his position differs slightly from the rabbis who preceded him–particularly in regard to avoiding passion or pleasure and instead remaining in control–Maimonides explains that maintaining control slightly more than is required is acceptable within the rubric of ''going beyond the strict measure of the law.''

וְלָזֶה נִכְפֹּל עַל־בַּעַל הַתַּאֲווֹת פְּעֻלַּת הֶעְדֵּר הַהֲנָאָה, יוֹתֵר מִשֶּׁנִּכְפֹּל עַל־נֶעְדַּר הָהַרְגָּשׁוֹת פְּעֻלַּת הַתַּאֲוָה; וּנְחַיֵּב עַל רַךְ־הַלֵּבָב מְסִירַת עַצְמוֹ לַסַּכָּנוֹת, יוֹתֵר מִשֶּׁנְּחַיֵּב הַמּוֹסֵר עַצְמוֹ לַסַּכָּנוֹת רַכּוּת הַלֵּבָב; וְנַרְגִּיל הַנָּבָל בִּיתְרוֹן טוֹב הַלֵּבָב, יוֹתֵר מִשֶּׁנַּרְגִּיל מִי שֶׁיֵּשׁ־לוֹ יִתְרוֹן לֵב טוֹב בִּנְבָלָה — זֶהוּ סֵדֶר רְפוּאוֹת הַמִּדּוֹת וְזָכְרֵהוּ. וְלָזֶה הָעִנְיָן לֹא הָיוּ הַחֲסִידִים מַנִּיחִים תְּכוּנַת נַפְשׁוֹתֵיהֶם תְּכוּנָה הַמְּמֻצַּעַת בְּשָׁוֶה — אַךְ הָיוּ נוֹטִים מְעַט לְצַד הַיֶּתֶר, אוֹ הַחֶסֶר, עַל־דֶּרֶךְ הַסְּיָג וְהַשְׁמִירָה. רְצוֹנִי לוֹמַר, עַל־דֶּרֶךְ מָשָׁל: שֶׁהָיוּ נוֹטִים מִן־הַזְּהִירוּת — לְצַד הֶעְדֵּר הֶרְגֵּשׁ־הַהֲנָאָה מְעַט; וּמִן הַגְּבוּרָה — לְצַד מְסִירוּת נֶפֶשׁ בַּסַּכָּנוֹת מְעַט; וּמִטּוֹב הַלֵּבָב — לְצַד יִתְרוֹן טוֹב הַלֵּבָב מְעַט; וּמִן־הָעֲנָוָה — לְצַד שִׁפְלוּת הָרוּחַ מְעַט, וְכֵן בִּשְׁאָר הָעִנְיָנִים. וְאֶל זֶה הָעִנְיָן רָמְזוּ בְּאָמְרָם: „לִפְנִים מִשּׁוּרַת הַדִּין".

4:3c For that reason, the passionate person must be drilled to control his/her feeling more than one without feeling must be drilled to have them. Similarly, we have to drill the person who is cowardly to place himself/herself into danger more than we have to drill the foolhardy to keep away from danger. Likewise, it is more difficult to get the cantankerous person to act properly than it is to get the overly refined person to act properly. The same is true with excessive humility. One should remember the method of healing ethical ills. The sages alluded to this method of healing when they suggested acting "beyond the strict measure of the law." For this reason [going beyond the strict measure of the law], the pietists of old did not leave the quality of their souls to remain at the midpoint, set equally between tendencies. Instead, they would lean toward that extreme that suggested more control. For example, they might lean away from caution toward the control of passion and away from pleasure. They might lean away from courage toward putting oneself in a bit of danger, from being good-hearted to being exceedingly good-hearted, from humility toward being abject, and so on in a similar manner to other things. That is what the sages referred to in their statement "going beyond the strict measure of the law."

Maimonides is dissatisfied with leaving this notion of going beyond the strict measures of the law and wants to probe more deeply. The proper use of the principle will depend on who applies it. Pietists in the past applied it to remedy the ills of individuals or society; fools in the present apply it merely to imitate those pietists or as an excuse to abuse their bodies to achieve religious ecstasy (to "get closer to God").

אֲבָל מַה שֶּׁעָשׂוּ אוֹתָם הַחֲסִידִים בְּקְצָת הַזְּמַנִּים, וּקְצָת הַמְּקוֹמוֹת, וּקְצָת אֲנָשִׁים מֵהֶם גַּם־כֵּן מִנְּטוֹת אַחַר הַקָּצֶה הָאֶחָד: בְּצוֹם, וְקוֹם בַּלֵּילוֹת, וְהַנָּחַת אֲכִילַת בָּשָׂר וּשְׁתִיַּת יַיִן, וְהַרְחָקַת הַנָּשִׁים, וְלָבֹשׁ הַצֶּמֶר וְהַשֵּׂעָר, וּשְׁכוּנַת הֶהָרִים, וְהִתְבּוֹדֵד בַּמִּדְבָּרוֹת — לֹא עָשׂוּ דָבָר מִזֶּה אֶלָּא עַל־דֶּרֶךְ רְפוּאוֹת, כְּמוֹ שֶׁזָּכַרְנוּ. וּלְהֶפְסֵד אַנְשֵׁי הַמְּדִינָה גַּם־כֵּן: כְּשֶׁיִּרְאוּ שֶׁהֵם נִפְסָדִים בְּחֶבְרָתָם וּרְאוֹת פְּעוּלוֹתֵיהֶם, עַד שֶׁיִּפְחֲדוּ מֵהֶפְסֵד מִדּוֹתֵיהֶם בַּעֲבוּרָם — וְעַל־כֵּן בָּרְחוּ לָהֶם לַמִּדְבָּרוֹת וּלְמָקוֹם שֶׁאֵין שָׁם אָדָם רָע. כְּמַאֲמַר יִרְמְיָה הַנָּבִיא, עָלָיו הַשָּׁלוֹם: מִי־יִתְּנֵנִי בַמִּדְבָּר מְלוֹן אֹרְחִים וְאֶעֶזְבָה אֶת־עַמִּי וְאֵלְכָה מֵאִתָּם, כִּי כֻלָּם מְנָאֲפִים עֲצֶרֶת בֹּגְדִים (ירמיה ט, א). וְכַאֲשֶׁר רָאוּ הַכְּסִילִים שֶׁהַחֲסִידִים עָשׂוּ אֵלֶּה הַפְּעוּלוֹת וְלֹא יָדְעוּ כַּוָּנָתָם, חָשְׁבוּ שֶׁהֵן טוֹבוֹת וְכִוְּנוּ אֲלֵיהֶן, בְּחָשְׁבָם שֶׁיִּהְיוּ כְמוֹתָם. וַיְעַנּוּ אֶת־גּוּפָתָם בְּכָל־מִינֵי עִנּוּי, וַיַּחְשְׁבוּ שֶׁהֵם קָנוּ לְעַצְמָם מַעֲלָה וּמִדָּה טוֹבָה וְשֶׁעָשׂוּ טוֹבָה, וְשֶׁבָּזֶה יִתְקָרֵב הָאָדָם לַשֵּׁם — כְּאִלּוּ הַשֵּׁם־יִתְבָּרֵךְ שׂוֹנֵא הַגּוּף וְרוֹצֶה לְאַבְּדוֹ. וְהֵם לֹא יָדְעוּ שֶׁאֵלּוּ הַפְּעֻלּוֹת רָע, וְשֶׁבָּהֶן תַּגִּיעַ פְּחִיתוּת מִפְּחִיתֻיּוֹת הַנֶּפֶשׁ. וְאֵין לְהַמְשִׁילָם אֶלָּא לְאִישׁ שֶׁאֵינוֹ יוֹדֵעַ בִּמְלֶאכֶת הָרְפוּאוֹת.

4:3d But what some of these pietists did in some places and at certain times in proceeding toward the extreme in fasting, in arising at night, not eating meat, not drinking wine, keeping far from women, wearing hair

41

shirts, climbing mountains, and wandering alone in deserts, was done only for reasons of health or because of the corruption of the society. They were afraid that association with the people of the society might affect their own ethical qualities. So they fled to the mountains or the desert places where no evil person might be found, even as the prophet Jeremiah said, "Would that I were in the wilderness, in a lodging-place of wayfaring people, that I might leave my people, and go from them! For they are all adulterers, an assembly of treacherous people" [Jer. 9:1]. When fools saw what the pietists had done, not knowing the purpose of pietists' actions, they still thought that their acts were worthy of emulation. Thus, they afflicted their bodies in every possible way thinking that they would acquire merit as a result and indeed [grow] closer to God. As if God hated the body and wanted its destruction. These fools did not know that these activities are dangerous and can lead to every kind of deficiency of the soul and can be applied only by someone who knows the science of medicine.

Maimonides will again bolster his position by using a medical analogy. People falsely reason that if a particular medicine or procedure helps heal an ill person, then it should move a healthy person to greater health. This is erroneous in the case of both the body and the soul. Such inappropriate actions would actually work in reverse and cause a healthy person to become ill.

ד:ד כְּשֶׁיִּרְאֶה בְּקִיאִים מֵהָרוֹפְאִים שֶׁהִשְׁקוּ חוֹלִים נוֹטִים לָמוּת סַמִּים הַנִּקְרָאִים בְּעַרְבִית: שַׁחַם, חַנְטָל וּמַחְמָדָה, ובלע״ז — קוֹלוֹקִינְטִידָא וְאַשְׁקְמוֹנִיָא; וְהַצַּבָּר, ובלע״ז — אֲלוֹאֵי וְכַיּוֹצֵא בָהֶם; וּפָסְקוּ מֵהֶם הַמָּזוֹן, וְנִרְפְּאוּ מֵחָלְיָם וְנִמְלְטוּ מִן־הַמָּוֶת הַצָּלָה גְמוּרָה — וְאָמַר הַסָּכָל הַהוּא: אַחַר שֶׁאֵלּוּ הַדְּבָרִים מְרַפְּאִים מִן־הַחֹלִי, כָּל־שֶׁכֵּן שֶׁיַּעֲמִידוּ הַבָּרִיא עַל־בְּרִיאוּתוֹ, אוֹ יוֹסִיפוּ כֹּחַ. וְהִתְחִיל לָקַחַת אוֹתָם תָּמִיד וּלְהִתְנַהֵג בְּהַנְהָגוֹת הַחוֹלִים, שֶׁהוּא יֶחֱלֶה בְּלֹא סָפֵק.

4:4a [Here is a parallel example:] When medical experts have prescribed certain potions for gravely ill patients to drink–called in Arabic *shacham chantal* and *machmuda*, and *kulkatraia* and *askamonia* in Latin–and also to be fed a plant called *aloes* in Latin and given no other food, and such patients have totally recovered, a fool might say that such drugs might heal any disease and how much the more so preserve the health of any healthy person. Were that person now to take such drugs continually and thus to operate as if he were ill, he would become ill without a doubt.

Maimonides concludes this section by stating that the Torah is a healing balm. It heals the individual soul by bringing it into balance. This pious statement may be seen as an attempt to balance the notion that virtue can be established by "...a rational principle," a notion that is far removed from Jewish tradition. Maimonides, following Aristotle, through his summary of the latter's discussion, adopts the search for that rational principle. As Aristotle saw it, that principle was one of equilibrium, of balancing between two extremes, as the "Golden Mean."

כֵּן הֵם חוֹלֵי הַנְּפָשׁוֹת אֵלּוּ בְּלֹא סָפֵק בְּלָקְחָם הָרְפוּאוֹת עַל-הַבְּרִיאוּת. וְזֹאת הַתּוֹרָה הַתְּמִימָה הַמַּשְׁלֶמֶת, כְּמוֹ שֶׁהֵעִיד עָלֶיהָ יוֹדְעָהּ: תּוֹרַת יְיָ תְּמִימָה מְשִׁיבַת נָפֶשׁ, עֵדוּת יְיָ נֶאֱמָנָה מַחְכִּימַת פֶּתִי (תהלים יט, ח) — לֹא זָכְרָה דָּבָר מִזֶּה. וְאָמְנָם כַּוָּנָה לִהְיוֹת הָאָדָם טִבְעִי הוֹלֵךְ בַּדֶּרֶךְ הָאֶמְצָעִי: יֹאכַל מַה-שֶּׁיֵּשׁ לוֹ לֶאֱכֹל — בְּשִׁוּוּי, וְיִשְׁתֶּה מַה-שֶּׁיֵּשׁ לוֹ לִשְׁתּוֹת — בְּשִׁוּוּי.

4:4b The same thing would occur were one to apply the methods of treatment for sick souls to healthy souls; those souls would become ill. The perfect Torah, which can perfect us all, as those who know it will attest and as the verse would have it, "The law of *Adonai* is perfect, restoring the soul. The testimony of *Adonai* is sure, making wise the simple" [Ps. 19:8] mentions nothing [of these extreme measures]. Its purpose is to have each person proceed naturally in the middle way. One should not eat too much or too little nor drink too much or too little.

Maimonides will continue to provide the reader with specific examples of behaviors that require modification and balance. It might be argued that the kind of vices that he discusses are dissimilar to those fitting into a halachic model. Indeed, one might argue that one could still commit these vices even if one also had fulfilled the *mitzvot*. As a result, this perspective has the potential to create the problem of vices that are unrelated to the Torah world. Thus, fulfilling the mandates of Torah would not give the individual personal religious direction in dealing with these kinds of virtue and vice.

Nazirite

According to the Torah (Numbers 6), Nazirites were persons who took an oath to devote themselves to God for a set period by refraining from eating grapes (or drinking wine) and by refraining from drinking any other intoxicant. In addition, during the designated period, Nazirites agreed not to cut their hair or have any contact with the dead (regardless of their relationship to the deceased). Should some contact be made–however inadvertently–the hair of the Nazirite was to be shaved. In addition, the Nazirite had to bring two doves or pigeons as an offering. On the completion of the period of the oath, the Nazirite brought two lambs (one as a burnt offering and one as a sin offering) and one ram as a peace offering.

According to the book of Judges (as exemplified in the story of Samson) and the Book of Samuel (as exemplified in the story of Samuel), parents could consecrate their children as lifetime Nazirites.

Rabbinic Judaism looked askance at the institution of the Nazirite. To the rabbis, the greatest sin of the Nazirites was not coming into contact with the dead or cutting their hair, but rather sinning against their own soul by not partaking in something that was permissible (that is, grapes and wine).

וְיִבְעַל מַה־שֶּׁמֻתָּר לוֹ לִבְעַל — בְּשִׁוּוּי, וְיִשְׁכֹּן בַּמְּדִינוֹת בְּיֹשֶׁר וּבֶאֱמוּנָה; לֹא שֶׁיִּשְׁכֹּן בְּמִדְבָּרִיּוֹת וּבֶהָרִים, וְלֹא שֶׁיִּלְבַּשׁ הַצֶּמֶר וְהַשֵּׂעָר, וְלֹא שֶׁיְעַנֶּה גוּפוֹ. וְהִזְהִירָה מִזֶּה, לְפִי מַה־שֶּׁבָּא בְקַבָּלָה. נֶאֱמַר בְּנָזִיר: וְכִפֶּר עָלָיו מֵאֲשֶׁר חָטָא עַל־הַנָּפֶשׁ (במדבר ו, יא). וְאָמְרוּ רַבּוֹתֵינוּ, זִכְרוֹנָם לִבְרָכָה: וְכִי עַל־אֵיזֶה נֶפֶשׁ חָטָא זֶה? — אֶלָּא עַל־שֶׁצִּעֵר עַצְמוֹ מִן־הַיַּיִן.

4:4c Similarly, one should have permitted sex in a fashion that is neither too much nor too little. One should dwell in cities and not out in the wilderness or on mountains. One should not wear hair shirts nor should one [otherwise] afflict one's body. We are warned against such practices by our tradition by what was taught about the Nazirite. The Torah stated, "And he shall atone for him because he sinned against the soul" [Num. 6:11]. The rabbis asked, "Which soul had he sinned against?" To which they answered, "[His own soul] in that he kept himself from wine" [B. Talmud, *Taanit* 11a; *Nedarim* 7a; *Nazir* 19a, 22a; *Baba Kamma* 91b; *Shevuot* 8a;].

While most of Maimonides' explanation seems like it is irrelevant to religion, here he introduces the reader to the notion of atonement. If the extremes represent vices and the practice of these vices represents sins, then even if individuals redirect themselves to a life of balance, they must atone for their sins. Through atonement, individuals can be brought back into balance. Using a prophetic text to prove his point, Maimonides then goes on to explain atonement through the principles of philosophy: truth is intellectual virtue, and peace is ethical virtue.

וַהֲלֹא דְבָרִים קַל־וָחֹמֶר. מַה־זֶּה שֶׁצִּעֵר עַצְמוֹ מִן־הַיַּיִן — צָרִיךְ כַּפָּרָה, הַמְצַעֵר עַצְמוֹ מִכָּל־דָּבָר וְדָבָר עַל־אַחַת כַּמָּה וְכַמָּה. וּבְדִבְרֵי נְבִיאֵינוּ וְחַכְמֵי תוֹרָתֵנוּ רָאִינוּ, שֶׁהָיוּ מְכֻוָּנִים עַל הַשִׁוּוּי וּשְׁמִירַת נַפְשָׁם וְגוּפָם, עַל מַה־שֶּׁחִיְּבֵם הַתּוֹרָה. וְעָנָה הַשֵׁם־יִתְבָּרֵךְ עַל־יַד נְבִיאוֹ לְמִי שֶׁשָּׁאַל לָצוּם יוֹם אֶחָד בָּעוֹלָם אִם יַתְמִיד אִם לָאו, וְהוּא אָמְרָם לִזְכַרְיָה הַנָּבִיא: הַאֶבְכֶּה בַּחֹדֶשׁ הַחֲמִשִׁי,

הַנֵּזֶר כַּאֲשֶׁר עָשִׂיתִי זֶה כַּמֶּה שָׁנִים? (זכריה ז, ג) וְעָנָה אוֹתָם: כִּי־צַמְתֶּם וְסָפוֹד בַּחֲמִישִׁי וּבַשְּׁבִיעִי וְזֶה שִׁבְעִים שָׁנָה, הֲצוֹם צַמְתֻּנִי אָנִי? וְכִי תֹאכְלוּ וְכִי תִשְׁתּוּ הֲלֹא אַתֶּם הָאֹכְלִים וְאַתֶּם הַשֹּׁתִים (שם, ה־ו). וְאַחַר־כָּךְ צִוָּה אוֹתָם בִּישֶׁר וּבְמַעֲלָה לְבָד, לֹא בְצוֹם, וְהוּא אָמְרוֹ לָהֶם: כֹּה אָמַר יְיָ צְבָאוֹת לֵאמֹר: מִשְׁפַּט אֱמֶת שְׁפֹטוּ, וְחֶסֶד וְרַחֲמִים עֲשׂוּ אִישׁ אֶת־אָחִיו; וְאַלְמָנָה וְיָתוֹם, גֵּר וְעָנִי אַל־תַּעֲשֹׁקוּ, וְרָעַת אִישׁ אָחִיו אַל־תַּחְשְׁבוּ בִּלְבַבְכֶם (שם, ט־י). וְאָמַר אַחַר־כָּךְ: כֹּה אָמַר יְיָ צְבָאוֹת: צוֹם הָרְבִיעִי וְצוֹם הַחֲמִישִׁי וְצוֹם הַשְּׁבִיעִי וְצוֹם הָעֲשִׂירִי יִהְיֶה לְבֵית־יְהוּדָה לְשָׂשׂוֹן וּלְשִׂמְחָה וּלְמֹעֲדִים טוֹבִים, וְהָאֱמֶת וְהַשָּׁלוֹם אֱהָבוּ (שם ח, יט). וְדַע, "שֶׁהָאֱמֶת" — הֵן הַמַּעֲלוֹת הַשִּׂכְלִיּוֹת, מִפְּנֵי שֶׁהֵן אֲמִתִּיּוֹת לֹא יִשְׁתַּנּוּ, כְּמוֹ שֶׁזְּכַרְנוּ בַּפֶּרֶק הַשֵּׁנִי; "וְהַשָּׁלוֹם" — הֵן מַעֲלוֹת הַמִּדּוֹת, אֲשֶׁר בָּהֶן יִהְיֶה הַשָּׁלוֹם בָּעוֹלָם.

4:4d Just as one who made oneself suffer by keeping oneself away from wine needs atonement, so anyone who has made oneself suffer by keeping oneself from any [permitted] pleasure requires atonement. We have noted both in the words of our prophets and the teaching of our sages of our Torah that they were intent upon harmony and the preservation of their souls and their bodies according to what the Torah required of them. Through the prophet, the Holy One answered the question asked by one who fasted one particular day and wanted to know whether he should persist in that fast, "Should I weep in the fifth month, separating myself, as I have done these so many years?" The prophet answered, "When you fasted and mourned in the fifth and seventh month, even these seventy years, did you fast at all to Me, even to Me? And when you eat, and when you drink, are you not they that eat, and they that drink?" [Zech. 7:3-5]. He then instructed them properly, speaking to them of ethics rather than fasting when he said, "Thus has *Adonai Tzevaot* spoken, saying: Execute true judgement and show mercy and compassion every person to one's neighbor; and do not oppress the widow, nor the parentless, the stranger, nor the poor; and let none of you devise evil against your neighbor in your heart" [Zech. 7:9-10]. At a later point, the prophet said, "Thus said *Adonai Tzevaot*: The fast of the fourth month, the fast of the fifth, the fast of the seventh, and the fast of the tenth, shall be to the house of Judah, joy and gladness, and cheerful seasons; therefore love you truth and peace" [Zech. 8:19]. You should know that "truth" refers to the intellectual virtues, which are immutable because they are true. "Peace" refers to the ethical virtues through which peace may obtain in the world.

Maimonides now wants to warn the reader about following the practices of non-Jews. It is not coincidental that he chooses sexual practice as an example. Not only are there specific sexual practices that are peculiar to Judaism that one may not find practiced among other peoples, but the Torah constantly uses the metaphor of sexuality when it relates God's displeasure with Israel's behavior. For Maimonides, the Torah's injunctions related to sex are mechanisms for movement toward balance. To offset the power of sexual desire, the *mitzvot* of the Torah are designed to move us a bit beyond the balance point toward the extreme of the lack of sexual feeling. Careful control of sexual desire keeps us far from the extremes that are unhealthy for the soul.

וְאָשׁוּב אֶל כַּוָּנָתִי. שֶׁאִם יֹאמְרוּ אֵלּוּ הַמִּתְדַּמִּים בָּאֻמּוֹת תּוֹרָתֵנוּ — שֶׁאֵינִי מְדַבֵּר אֶלָּא בָהֶם — שֶׁהֵם אֵינָם עוֹשִׂים מַה־שֶּׁעוֹשִׂים אוֹתוֹ: מֵהַטְרִיחוּת גּוּפוֹתָם, וּפְסוּק הֲנָאוֹתֵיהֶם, אֶלָּא עַל־דֶּרֶךְ הַלִּמּוּד לְכֹחוֹת הַנֶּפֶשׁ, כְּדֵי שֶׁיִּהְיוּ נוֹטִים אֶל הַצַּד הָאַחֵר מְעַט, כְּפִי מַה־שֶּׁבֵּאַרְנוּ בְּזֶה הַפֶּרֶק, שֶׁרָאוּי שֶׁיִּהְיֶה הָאָדָם כֵּן — זוֹהִי טָעוּת מֵהֶם, כַּאֲשֶׁר אֲבָאֵר. וְזֶהוּ: שֶׁהַתּוֹרָה לֹא אָסְרָה מַה־שֶּׁאָסְרָה, וְלֹא צִוְּתָה מַה־שֶּׁצִוְּתָה — אֶלָּא מִפְּנֵי זֹאת הַסִּבָּה, רְצוֹנִי לוֹמַר: כְּדֵי שֶׁנִּתְרַחֵק מִן־הַצַּד הָאֶחָד יוֹתֵר עַל־צַד הַהֶרְגֵּל. שֶׁאִסּוּר הַמַּאֲכָלוֹת הָאֲסוּרוֹת כֻּלָּן, וְאִסּוּר הַבְּעִילוֹת הָאֲסוּרוֹת, וְהָאַזְהָרָה עַל־הַקְּדֵשָׁה, וּמַה־שֶּׁהִצְרִיךְ בִּכְתֻבַּת אִשָּׁה וְקִדּוּשֶׁיהָ, וְעִם־כָּל־זֶה אֵינָהּ מֻתֶּרֶת תָּמִיד, אֲבָל תֵּאָסֵר בְּעֵת הַנִּדּוּת וְהַלֵּדָה; וְעִם־כָּל־זֶה גָזְרוּ רַבּוֹתֵינוּ, זִכְרוֹנָם לִבְרָכָה, לְמַעֵט הַמִּשְׁגָּל וּמִנָּעֻוֹהוּ בַיּוֹם, כְּמוֹ שֶׁבֵּאַרְנוּ בְּסַנְהֶדְרִין — זֶה כֻּלּוֹ, אָמְנָם, צִוָּנוּ הַשֵּׁם־יִתְבָּרֵךְ לְהִתְרַחֵק מִקְצֵה רֹב הַתַּאֲוָה רָחוֹק גָּדוֹל, וְלָצֵאת מִן־הַמְּצוּעַ אֶל הַצַּד הֶעְדֵּר הָרְגַּשְׁת־הַהֲנָאָה מְעַט, עַד שֶׁתִּתְחַזֵּב וְתִתְחַזֵּק בְּנַפְשׁוֹתֵינוּ תְּכוּנַת הַזְּהִירוּת.

4:4e I now return to my point: should you be asked by those Jews who imitate non-Jews–and I am speaking specifically of those who do what they do as a way of learning the capacities of their souls–so that they could incline a bit to one extreme as we have explained in this chapter, because they think that this is how people should be rather than because they want to afflict their bodies or control their pleasures. As I shall explain, this is a mistake. The Torah forbids what it does and permits what it does so that we can be kept from one extreme toward what is more common. This is the reason for all the prohibitions dealing with food and sex. This explains the warning about the cult prostitute, the wedding contract for a woman, and *kiddushin* for her. Even with the writing of a wedding contract and the performance of the rite of *kiddushin*, a married woman is not always permitted to her husband. She is forbidden at the time of menstruation and time of childbirth. Even when one's spouse is permitted, the sages advised a husband to limit sexual intercourse with his wife, not to engage in sex in the daytime. As we have explained in our commentary on *Mishnah Sanhedrin*, God has instructed us to go far from the extreme of excessive lust and to move somewhat toward the extreme of the lack of feeling so that the feeling of caution will become well established in our souls.

Using a few more examples primarily from the agricultural calendar, Maimonides makes his point once again. But if you examine all of the *mitzvot*, he suggests, you can draw the same conclusion: the *mitzvot* were designed to train the soul to achieve ethical virtue. They do so by moving us toward equilibrium and, in some cases, moving us a bit beyond so that we can be truly good hearted.

וְכֵן כֹּל מַה־שֶׁבַּתּוֹרָה: כִּנְתִינַת הַמַּעְשְׂרוֹת, וְהַלֶּקֶט, וְהַשִּׁכְחָה, וְהַפֵּאָה, וְהַפֶּרֶט, וְהָעוֹלֵלוֹת, וְדִין שְׁמִטָּה וְיוֹבֵל, וְהַצְּדָקָה „דֵי מַחְסוֹרוֹ" — זֶה כֻּלּוֹ קָרוֹב מִיִּתְרוֹן־לֵבָב, עַד שֶׁנִּתְרַחֵק מִקְצֵה הַנִּבְזָלָה רָחוֹק גָּדוֹל וְנִתְקָרֵב לִקְצֵה יִתְרוֹן־טוֹב־לֵבָב, עַד שֶׁיִּתְחַזֵּק לָנוּ „לֵב טוֹב". וּבְזֹאת הַבְּחִינָה בְּחַן רֹב הַמִּצְווֹת, תִּמְצָאֵן כֻּלָּן שֶׁהֵן מְלַמְּדוֹת וּמַרְגִּילוֹת כֹּחוֹת הַנֶּפֶשׁ.

4:4f This applies to all that is in the Torah from the aspect of tithes, what remains [in the harvested field], and what was forgotten [in the field], as well as the corner of the field, and what remains of the field, the law of the Sabbatical Year and the Jubilee, and the charity to fill a person's need. All of this is close to the excess of a good heart. We should keep far from the excess of boorish behavior so that we can establish the quality of being good-hearted. In this manner, you may examine most of the *mitzvot*; you will find them meant to teach and train the capacities of the soul.

More examples will be offered with specific texts from the Torah to bolster Maimonides' argument. (This is what is meant by using proof texts.) Fulfilling these *mitzvot* as derived from the Torah text will help the individual find the Golden Mean.

כְּמוֹ שֶׁאָסְרָה הַנְּקִימָה וְהַנְּטִירָה וּגְאָלַת־הַדָּם, בְּאָמְרוֹ: לֹא־תִקֹּם וְלֹא־תִטֹּר (ויקרא יט, יח); עָזֹב תַּעֲזֹב (שמות כג, ה); הָקֵם תָּקִים עִמּוֹ (דברים כב, ד) — עַד שֶׁיֵּחֱלַשׁ כֹּחַ הַכַּעַס וְהָרֹגֶז. וְכֵן הָשֵׁב תְּשִׁיבֵם (שם, א) — עַד שֶׁתָּסוּר תְּכוּנַת הַכִּילוּת. וְכֵן: מִפְּנֵי שֵׂיבָה תָּקוּם וְהָדַרְתָּ פְּנֵי זָקֵן (ויקרא יט, לב); כַּבֵּד אֶת־אָבִיךָ וְאֶת־אִמֶּךָ (שמות כ, יב); לֹא תָסוּר מִן־הַדָּבָר אֲשֶׁר־יַגִּידוּ לְךָ וְגוֹ' (דברים יז, יא)

עַד שֶׁתָּסוּר תְּכוּנַת הָעַזּוּת וְתַגִּיעַ תְּכוּנַת הַבֹּשֶׁת. וְאַחַר־כָּךְ הַרְחִיק
מִן־הַקָּצֶה הָאַחֲרוֹן, רְצוֹנִי לוֹמַר: רֹב הַבֹּשֶׁת, וְאָמַר: הוֹכֵחַ תּוֹכִיחַ אֶת־עֲמִיתֶךָ
(ויקרא יט, יז); לֹא תָגוּרוּ מִפְּנֵי־אִישׁ (דברים א, יז) — עַד שֶׁיָּסוּר רֹב הַבֹּשֶׁת
גַּם־כֵּן וְיִשָּׁאֵר בַּדֶּרֶךְ הָאֶמְצָעִי.

4:4g Similarly, the Torah has forbidden holding grudges, seeking revenge, and avenging blood, as the Torah teaches, "You shall not take vengeance, nor bear any grudge against the children of your people" [Lev. 19:18]; "You shall forbear to pass by him; you shall surely release it with him" [Exod. 23:5]; and "You shall surely help her to lift them up again" [Deut. 22:4] in order to weaken the capacity of anger and wrath. "You shall surely bring them back to your neighbor" [Deut. 22:1] is to be practiced until the quality of miserliness is removed. In the same way, "You shall rise up before the hoary head, and honor the face of the old person..." [Lev. 19:32]; "Honor your father and your mother" [Exod. 20:12]; and "You shall not turn aside from the sentence which they will declare to you" [Deut. 17:11] are to remove from you the quality of arrogance and move to the quality of shame and then leave that extreme of shame. Hence, the Torah teaches, "You shall surely rebuke your neighbor" [Lev. 19:17] and also "You shall not be afraid of the face of any person" [Deut. 1:17] so that the person will cease being overly shameful and return to the middle way.

For those who are anxious to bolster the Golden Mean, Maimonides reminds us of the commonly held rabbinic notion that you cannot add or delete from the system of *mitzvot*. If we added or subtracted from the *mitzvot*, which the rabbis warn us against, we would lose our balance.

ד:ה וּכְשֶׁיָּבֹא הָאִישׁ הַסָּכָל בְּלֹא סָפֵק וְיִשְׁתַּדֵּל לְהוֹסִיף עַל־אֵלּוּ הַדְּבָרִים, כְּמוֹ:
שֶׁיֶּאֱסֹר הַמַּאֲכָל וְהַמִּשְׁתֶּה, מוּסָף עַל־מַה־שֶּׁנֶּאֱסַר מִן־הַמַּאֲכָלִים; אוֹ יֶאֱסֹר
הַזִּוּוּג יוֹתֵר עַל־מַה־שֶּׁנֶּאֱסַר מִן־הַבְּעִילוֹת; וְיִתֵּן כָּל־מָמוֹנוֹ לַעֲנִיִּים אוֹ לַהֶקְדֵּשׁ,
מוּסָף עַל מַה־שֶּׁבַּתּוֹרָה עַל־הַהֶקְדֵּשׁוֹת וְעַל־הַצְּדָקוֹת, וְעַל־הָעֲרָכִים — יִהְיֶה
עוֹשֶׂה מַעֲשֶׂה הָרָעִים וְהוּא לֹא יֵדַע, וְיַגִּיעַ אֶל הַקָּצֶה הָאַחֵר וְיֵצֵא מִן־הַמְּצוּעַ
לְגַמְרֵי. וְלַחֲכָמִים בְּזֶה הָעִנְיָן דָּבָר, לֹא שָׁמַעְתִּי כְּלָל יוֹתֵר נִפְלָא מִמֶּנּוּ, וְהוּא
בַּגְּמָרָא דִּבְנֵי מַעֲרָבָא בַּפֶּרֶק הַתְּשִׁיעִי מִנְּדָרִים, דִּבֵּר בִּגְנוּת הַמְקַבְּלִים עַל־עַצְמָם
שְׁבוּעוֹת וּנְדָרִים עַד שֶׁיִּשָּׁאֲרוּ כְּעֵין אֲסוּרִים. אָמְרוּ שָׁם בְּזֶה הַלָּשׁוֹן: „אָמַר רַב
אִידִי בְּשֵׁם רַבִּי יִצְחָק: לֹא דַיֶּךָ בְּמַה־שֶּׁאָסְרָה תּוֹרָה, אֶלָּא שֶׁאַתָּה אוֹסֵר עָלֶיךָ

48

דְּבָרִים אֲחֵרִים"? וְזֶה הָעִנְיָן שֶׁזְּכַרְנוּ בְּשָׁוֶה בְּלֹא תּוֹסֶפֶת וּבְלֹא חִסָּרוֹן. הִנֵּה
הִתְבָּאֵר־לְךָ מִכָּל מַה־שֶּׁזְּכַרְנוּהוּ בְּזֶה הַפֶּרֶק.

4:5a If some fool were to come and attempt to add on to these things and, for example, add to the list of what may not be eaten or drunk or add on further restrictions to sexual intercourse or add on to what the Torah instructs concerning what is devoted to the sanctuary and charity given to the poor, and the evaluation gifts given to the sanctuary, so that one would give all of one's money to the poor or to the sanctuary, one would be doing something wrong and unknowingly go to the other extreme and totally miss the middle way. I have never heard anything more marvelous then what the sages taught in the *Gemara* of the people of the west [the Jerusalem Talmud], in the ninth chapter of *Nedarim*, concerning reprehensible matters that they had taken upon themselves. Thus, certain things have become prohibited by oaths and vows. The sages responded in this manner: "Rabbi Idi said in the name of Rabbi Isaac, 'Was it not enough for you that the Torah prohibited what it did that you had to add other prohibitions?'" We referred to this when we spoke of equilibrium–neither adding nor subtracting. Behold it has been explained to you concerning all that we have mentioned in this chapter, that we should direct our actions toward the middle way.

Maimonides the philosopher and physician will relate the soul sickness to bodily illness once again. In both, Maimonides tells the reader to attempt to arrest the illness before it reaches the extreme lest extreme measures be required to cure it.

שֶׁצָּרִיךְ לְכַוֵּן אֶל הַפְּעֻלּוֹת הַמְמֻצָּעוֹת, וְשֶׁלֹּא יֵצֵא מֵהֶן אֶל־קָצֶה מִן־הַקְּצָווֹת —
אֶלָּא עַל־צַד הָרְפוּאוֹת וְלַעֲמֹד כְּנֶגְדּוֹ בְּהֶפֶךְ. כְּמוֹ שֶׁהָאָדָם הַיּוֹדֵעַ בִּמְלֶאכֶת
הָרְפוּאוֹת, כְּשֶׁיִּרְאֶה מִזְגוֹ שֶׁנִּשְׁתַּנָּה מְעַט שִׁנּוּי, לֹא יִשְׁכַּח וְלֹא יַנִּיחַ הַחֳלִי
לְהִתְחַזֵּק עַד שֶׁיִּצְטָרֵךְ אֶל רְפוּאָה חֲזָקָה בְּתַכְלִית; וּכְשֶׁיֵּדַע שֶׁאֵבֶר מֵאֵבָרָיו
חָלוּשׁ, יִשְׁמְרוֹ תָּמִיד וְיִתְרַחֵק מִדְּבָרִים הַמַּזִּיקִים לוֹ וִיכַוֵּן לְמַה־שֶּׁיּוֹעִילֵהוּ, עַד
שֶׁיִּבְרִיא הָאֵבֶר הַהוּא, אוֹ עַד שֶׁלֹּא יוֹסִיף חֻלְשָׁה.

4:5b One should not go to either extreme except as a matter of medicine when one operates to the reverse of the particular malady until the afflicted person sees something of a change in one's physical nature. One should not forget and allow a sick person to get so sick that the person needs the strongest kind of medicine. Should someone know that one part of one's body is weak, one should constantly take care of it, keep harmful things from it, get helpful things to it, and try to improve it or at least not allow it to be further weakened.

Maimonides next focuses his attention on "normal" people. It is easy to speak of people whose behaviors represent the extremes, but what about the majority of people, who operate close to the middle? How can they monitor and modulate their behavior? Since it is highly improbable that any individual is born entirely virtuous (ethically and intellectually), we must all work toward reaching the mean. And even when we have successfully reached the mean, then we must pay careful attention to our own behavior in order not to move away from the mean toward either extreme.

כֵּן הָאָדָם הַשָּׁלֵם צָרִיךְ לוֹ שֶׁיִּזְכֹּר מִדּוֹתָיו תָּמִיד, וְיִשְׁקֹל פְּעֻלּוֹתָיו, וְיִבְחַן תְּכוּנוֹת נַפְשׁוֹ יוֹם יוֹם. וְכָל־מַה־שֶּׁיִּרְאֶה נַפְשׁוֹ נוֹטָה לְצַד קָצֶה מִן הַקְצָווֹת, יְמַהֵר בִּרְפוּאָה וְלֹא יַנִּיחַ הַתְּכוּנָה הָרָעָה לְהִתְחַזֵּק בִּשְׁנוֹתוֹ מַעֲשֶׂה רָע, כְּמוֹ שֶׁזָּכַרְנוּ. וְכֵן יָשִׂים לְנֶגֶד עֵינָיו הַמִּדּוֹת הַפְּחוּתוֹת אֲשֶׁר לוֹ וְיִשְׁתַּדֵּל לְרַפְּאתָם תָּמִיד, כְּמוֹ שֶׁזָּכַרְנוּ — שֶׁאִי־אֶפְשָׁר לְאָדָם מִבִּלְתִּי חֶסְרוֹן. שֶׁהַפִילוֹסוֹפִים כְּבָר אָמְרוּ: „כָּבֵד הוּא וְרָחוֹק שֶׁיִּמָּצֵא מִי שֶׁהוּא בְטֶבַע לְמַעֲלוֹת כֻּלָּן, ר"ל: לְמַעֲלוֹת הַמִּדּוֹת וּלְמַעֲלוֹת הַשִּׂכְלִיּוֹת, מְזֻמָּן וּמוּכָן". אֲבָל בְּסִפְרֵי הַנְּבִיאִים נִמְצָא זֶה בָּהֶם הַרְבֵּה. אָמַר: הֵן בַּעֲבָדָיו לֹא יַאֲמִין וּבְמַלְאָכָיו יָשִׂים תָּהֳלָה (איוב ד, יח); וּמַה־יִּצְדַּק אֱנוֹשׁ עִם־אֵל, וּמַה־יִּזְכֶּה יְלוּד אִשָּׁה (שם כה, ד). וּשְׁלֹמֹה הַמֶּלֶךְ, עָלָיו הַשָּׁלוֹם, אָמַר סְתָם: כִּי אָדָם אֵין צַדִּיק בָּאָרֶץ, אֲשֶׁר יַעֲשֶׂה־טּוֹב וְלֹא יֶחֱטָא (קהלת ז, כ).

4:5c A perfect person should always keep ethical qualities in mind and consider one's actions. One should examine the qualities of one's soul each day; should one note movement toward an extreme, one should speedily move to heal it and not allow it to become fixed in the soul and generate bad behavior. One should always keep one's bad qualities in mind and constantly strive to improve them. It is not possible that a person not have some bad quality. The philosophers said that it is improbable that any person have all the virtues by nature, that is, the ethical and the intellectual virtues. This has been stated many times in the books of the prophets, as the verse has it, "Behold, You put no trust in Your servants, and Your angels You charge with folly" [Job 4:18] and "And how can a human be just with God?" [Job 9:2]; "And one that is born of a woman, that one should be righteous?" [Job 15:14]. Solomon the king said it simply, "For there is not a righteous person on earth, that does good and does not sin" [Eccles. 7:20].

For the Jewish tradition, to exhibit anger is reprehensible. For Maimonides, anger negatively affects the soul. How then could *Moshe Rabbaynu* (Moses, our teacher)–the greatest prophet of all–pour out his anger against the Israelites? They strayed from the mean. Moses got angry, and Aaron was too patient. God punished both Moses and Aaron for sinning, for both profaning God's name by their extreme actions.

וְאַתָּה יוֹדֵעַ שֶׁאֲדוֹן הָרִאשׁוֹנִים וְהָאַחֲרוֹנִים: מֹשֶׁה רַבֵּנוּ, עָלָיו הַשָּׁלוֹם, כְּבָר אָמַר אֵלָיו הַשֵּׁם-יִתְבָּרֵךְ: יַעַן לֹא-הֶאֱמַנְתֶּם בִּי לְהַקְדִּישֵׁנִי לְעֵינֵי בְּנֵי יִשְׂרָאֵל (במדבר כ, יב); עַל אֲשֶׁר-מְרִיתֶם אֶת-פִּי לְמֵי מְרִיבָה (שם, כד); עַל אֲשֶׁר לֹא-קִדַּשְׁתֶּם אוֹתִי בְּתוֹךְ בְּנֵי יִשְׂרָאֵל (דברים לב, נא). וְחֶטְאוֹ, עָלָיו הַשָּׁלוֹם, הוּא: שֶׁנָּטָה לְצַד אֶחָד מִן-הַקְּצָווֹת מִמַּעֲלַת הַמִּדּוֹת, וְהִיא: הַסַּבְלָנוּת. כַּאֲשֶׁר נָטָה לְצַד הָרַגְזָנוּת בְּאָמְרוֹ: שִׁמְעוּ-נָא הַמֹּרִים (במדבר כ, י), דִּקְדֵּק עָלָיו הַשֵּׁם-יִתְבָּרֵךְ: שֶׁיִּהְיֶה אָדָם כָּמוֹהוּ כּוֹעֵס לִפְנֵי עֲדַת יִשְׂרָאֵל בְּמָקוֹם שֶׁאֵין רָאוּי בּוֹ הַכַּעַס?! וְכַיּוֹצֵא בָזֶה בְּדִין הָאִישׁ הַהוּא — חִלּוּל הַשֵּׁם הוּא.

4:5d   You also know that it was said even about Moses our teacher, the master of all who preceded him and all who followed him, "Because you did not believe in Me, to sanctify Me in the eyes of the Israelites . . . [Num. 20:12]. Because you trespassed against Me in the midst of the Israelites at the waters of *Merivat-kadesh* [Deut. 32:51] [the text has *meritem b'mei merivah*], because you did not sanctify Me in the midst of the Israelites" [Deut. 32:51, end]. Both Aaron and Moses had sinned; one moved too much to the extreme of patience, and the other moved too much to the extreme of anger. It was Moses who had said, "Hear now, you rebels; are we to bring you forth water out of this rock?" [Num. 20:10]. God dealt with Moses in a very exacting manner, for a man such as he should not have become angry in the presence of the Israelites. It was not fitting for him to become angry. As a result, Moses profaned the name of God.

Surely, both Moses and Aaron knew that ethical instruction is best conveyed by what we do and not by what we say. Moses' anger might have been taken as an acceptable model! So Maimonides will try to justify Moses' anger and indicate his punishment. The punishment will demonstrate the error of his anger. As a result of Moses and Aaron's behaviors, the Israelites learned what not to do. It was particularly problematic because the people saw Moses get angry, but they did not see God rebuke Moses for his anger. They only saw the positive results of his anger. And anger, perhaps more so than other behaviors, affects the qualities of the soul.

מִפְּנֵי שֶׁמִּתְנוּעוֹתָיו וּמִדְּבָרָיו כֻּלָּם לְמֵדִים, וְהָיוּ מְקַוִּים לְהַגִּיעַ בָּהֶם אֶל הַצְלָחַת הָעוֹלָם הַזֶּה וְהָעוֹלָם־הַבָּא — וְאֵיךְ יֵרָאֶה בּוֹ הַכַּעַס, וְהוּא מִפְּעֻלּוֹת הָרַע, כְּמוֹ שֶׁבֵּאַרְנוּ, וְלֹא יָבֹא כִּי אִם מִתְּכוּנוֹת רָעוֹת מִתְּכוּנוֹת הַנֶּפֶשׁ. אֲבָל אָמְרוּ בָּעִנְיָן: „מְרִיתֶם אֶת־פִּי" — הוּא כְּמוֹ שֶׁאֲבָאֵר, וְהוּא: שֶׁלֹּא הָיָה מְדַבֵּר עִם סְכָלִים, וְלֹא עִם מִי שֶׁאֵין לוֹ מַעֲלָה; אֲבָל עִם אֲנָשִׁים שֶׁהַקְּטַנָּה שֶׁבִּנְשֵׁיהֶם הָיְתָה כִּיחֶזְקֵאל בֶּן־בּוּזִי, כְּמוֹ שֶׁזָּכְרוּ הַחֲכָמִים, וְכָל־מַה־שֶּׁיֹּאמַר אוֹ יַעֲשֶׂה יִבְחָנוּהוּ. וְכַאֲשֶׁר רָאוּהוּ שֶׁכָּעַס, אָמְרוּ: שֶׁהוּא, עָלָיו הַשָּׁלוֹם, וַדַּאי אֵין לוֹ פְּחִיתוּת מִדָּה, וְלוּלֵא שֶׁהָיָה יוֹדֵעַ שֶׁהַשֵּׁם־יִתְבָּרֵךְ כָּעַס עָלֵינוּ בְּבַקָּשַׁת הַמַּיִם וְשֶׁאֲנַחְנוּ הִכְעַסְנוּהוּ, יִתְבָּרֵךְ, לֹא הָיָה כּוֹעֵס — וְאָנוּ לֹא מָצִינוּ שֶׁהַשֵּׁם־יִתְבָּרֵךְ כָּעַס בְּדַבְּרוֹ אֵלָיו בְּזֶה הָעִנְיָן, אֲבָל אָמַר: קַח אֶת־הַמַּטֶּה וְהַקְהֵל אֶת־הָעֵדָה וְגו׳ (במדבר כ, ח).

4:5e The Israelites learned the wrong things by his actions and his words. They had wished to achieve success in this world and in the next; how could he show them anger? (Anger is, as we have explained, a most base activity!) It also affects the qualities of the soul. The sages interpreted "You have rebelled against My word" that Moses was not speaking with fools or even with worthless people. He was speaking with people that the least of them [literally, the youngest of the women, a phrase whose meaning we have chosen to transcend] was the equivalent of Ezekiel ben Buzi. Whatever Moses would say or do, the people would examine [as a possible model of action]. When they saw Moses become angry, they said that perhaps anger is not a bad quality. Were it not that Moses knew that God became angry with us when we asked for water and that we provoked God, Moses would not have become angry. However, we did not see that God became angry with Moses in speaking with him in this matter. Rather, God said, "Take the rod; assemble the congregation, you and Aaron, your brother..." [Num. 20:8].

Concerned as he often is that he has strayed from his original direction in explaining about the soul, Maimonides wants to answer the question that others want to know as well: What was the real nature of the sin that Moses committed that resulted in God's refusing him permission to enter the Promised Land? The answer: Moses strayed from the Golden Mean, exhibiting behaviors that represented the extreme.

Salvation

While this word has a Christian ring to it (particularly in English), salvation has had different meanings in Jewish history. Salvation meant Divine deliverance from danger and evil in the Bible. The Song of the Sea trumpets the deliverance of the Israelites. The text sings, "*Adonai* is my strength and song; God has become my salvation" [Exod. 15:2]. Later, when the Israelites attempted to establish their presence in the Land of Israel and were opposed by the Philistines and the Aramites, they cried out to God to save them. God answered them by sending them a "savior" in the person of Othnael ben Kenaz (Judg. 3:9ff.). Samson carried out another act of salvation by battling the Philistines (Judg. 15:18ff.). When David delivered himself from danger, this was viewed as an act of salvation (I Sam. 25:26). It was God's activity that people believed directly brought salvation (Isa. 25:9).

The Psalmist understood salvation as deliverance from something other than immediate danger. Salvation may refer to a restoration of the sense of God's nearness to one who feels bereft of Divine favor and the demonstration of that favor to one's opponents (Ps. 22:8ff.). It may refer to a response to radical loneliness (Ps. 27:9-10), or it may refer to deliverance from the problems of poverty (Ps. 34:7).

It must be emphasized that the notion of salvation in Judaism is directed to this life, regardless of whether it is as deliverance from immediate danger or from other problems. Salvation in Judaism does not refer to what may occur in life after death or in the world to come. While Reform theologians generally disagree with this understanding of classical Jewish tradition, what will occur in the next life is a function of observance of the *mitzvah* system and of the hope expressed in the rabbinic view that every Jew had a portion in the world to come.

ד:ו וְהִנֵּה יָצָאנוּ מִכַּוָּנַת הַשַּׁעַר; אֲבָל הִתַּרְנוּ סָפֵק מִסְפְקֵי הַתּוֹרָה, שֶׁנֶּאֱמַר בּוֹ דְּבָרִים רַבִּים, וְנִשְׁאַל פְּעָמִים רַבּוֹת: „אֵיזֶה חֵטְא חָטָא"? וּרְאֵה מַה־שֶּׁנֶּאֱמַר בּוֹ וּמַה־שֶּׁאָמַרְנוּ בּוֹ אֲנַחְנוּ — וְהָאֱמֶת תַּעֲשֶׂה דַּרְכָּהּ. וְאָשׁוּב אֶל כַּוָּנָתִי: כִּי כְּשֶׁיִּהְיֶה הָאָדָם שׁוֹקֵל פְּעֻלּוֹתָיו תָּמִיד וּמְכַוֵּן אֶל אֶמְצָעוּתָם, יִהְיֶה בְּמַדְרֵגָה עֶלְיוֹנָה מִמַּדְרֵגַת בְּנֵי אָדָם, וּבָזֶה יִתְקָרֵב אֶל הַשֵּׁם־יִתְבָּרֵךְ וְיַשִּׂיג אֶל טוֹבוֹ — וְזֶה הַדֶּרֶךְ הַשָּׁלֵם שֶׁבְּדַרְכֵי הָעֲבוֹדָה. וּכְבָר זָכְרוּ הַחֲכָמִים, זִכְרוֹנָם לִבְרָכָה, זֶה הָעִנְיָן וְכָתְבוּ עָלָיו וְאָמְרוּ: כָּל־הַשָּׂם אָרְחוֹתָיו וּמַשְׁגִּיחַ בָּהֶם — זוֹכֶה וְרוֹאֶה בִּישׁוּעָתוֹ שֶׁל הַקָּדוֹשׁ־בָּרוּךְ־הוּא, שֶׁנֶּאֱמַר: וְשָׂם דֶּרֶךְ אַרְאֶנּוּ בְּיֵשַׁע אֱלֹהִים (תהלים נ, כג). אַל תִּקְרֵי: „וְשָׂם", אֶלָּא „וְשָׁם". וְהַ„שִּׂימָה" — הוּא הַשִּׁעוּר וְהַסְּבָרָא. זֶה הָעִנְיָן אֲשֶׁר פֵּרַשְׁנוּ בְּזֶה הַפֶּרֶק כֻּלּוֹ בְּשָׁוֶה, וְזֶהוּ שִׁעוּר מַה־שֶּׁרְאִינוּהוּ שֶׁצָּרִיךְ בְּזֶה הָעִנְיָן.

4:6 Behold we have gone far from the purpose of this section, but we have explained one of the doubtful passages of the Torah. We shall speak more about it and we will ask many times, "Precisely what sin did Moses commit?" Pay attention to what we have said and what we will say about the matter and particularly that pursuing the mean is the

53

highest goal of human activity. Let truth find its way. Through this one approaches God and one will receive God's reward. It is the most perfect manner of worship [of God]. The sages have already remarked about this and said [B. Talmud, *Moed Katan* 5b; *Sotah* 5b], "Whoever carefully considers one's ways and watches them will be meritorious and will see the salvation of the Holy Blessed One, as the verse says, 'There will I show the person the way of the salvation of God' [Ps. 50:23]. [We are translating the verse to fit the interpretation of the sages, who may have had a different biblical text.]" The sages said, "Do not read *v'sam* ('and place') but rather *v'sham* ('that orders'), which means 'placing and reasoning.'" This is the matter of balance of which we have spoken in this chapter. This is the evaluation that we have looked for in this matter.

GLEANINGS

HEROISM

The fundamental concepts with which women think about themselves and in terms of which they evaluate their lives have come to them from a one-sided view of experience. It is essential that women understand the role models offered to them so that they may choose in light of their self-awareness rather than in terms of a confused image of who they can become. The role models men have offered women, even in the case of Esther, conform to a male concept of heroism. Although her mode of success is "feminine" (in the traditional sense of the word) in that she succeeds in terms of beauty, Esther is regarded as heroic because she accomplishes what she sets out to do. Heroism is achieved, traditionally, by accomplishing a goal, by conquering adversity, or by sacrificing oneself for some "noble" cause. But women can choose to redefine heroism in terms that take into account more natural processes. They can opt for a heroism that is achieved by (a) becoming who they are meant to be by being open to those forces that transform them; (b) being able to endure and find nourishment even in the most arid times; or (c) being able to live and to pass on the gifts of life, trust, openness, and the capacity to love. With our new definition of heroism in mind, we can look for biblical countermodels to the Deborahs, Judiths, and Esthers.

It is time to look more closely at biblical women who appear to have failed by men's standards, but who nevertheless are able to remain true to themselves in the face of a harsh, unsupportive environment. Two such women are Hagar and Leah. Hagar, the handmaid of Abraham's wife Sarah, becomes pregnant by Abraham at Sarah's suggestion, is abused by Sarah as a result, bears a son Ishmael, and is finally cast out into the desert and left to die. Leah, grandniece of Abraham, is, through her father's trickery, given in marriage to Jacob, who has just worked for seven years to earn the right to marry her younger sister Rachel, his true love. Leah must endure, one week after her own wedding, the marriage of her husband and her sister. She bears six sons and a daughter, Dinah, who is raped, and serves as stepmother to the two sons of Rachel (who dies giving birth to the younger one). At first glance, Hagar and Leah hardly suggest themselves as role models. Nevertheless, by piecing together their stories from the meager information about them in Genesis, we see that they succeed admirably in transcending such highly unfavorable conditions. Through them we can witness resilience, joy, devotion, and strength.

(Carol Ochs, *Women and Spirituality*. Totowa, New Jersey: Rowman & Allanheld, 1983)

HUMILITY

Perhaps we can get a little nearer to him [the holy man] by expanding his humility. May we not say of him that he aspires? He wants to be better than he is. Do you answer: "Then he is like everybody else. For who does not want to be better than he is?" The point perhaps comes in as to the measure of the wanting. It is a question of degree. You may want a thing in the abstract, tepidly, as a matter of theory; or you may want a thing eagerly, warmly, as a matter of fact. This paradox is, I think, true: the holy man is holy because he is dissatisfied with himself, because he has a keen and constant sense of his own imperfection, of the contrast between his ideal and his performance. Without such a sense, how can there be aspiration? Though holiness is a divine attribute, and though we are bidden to be holy inasmuch as and because God is holy, yet between the holiness of God and the holiness of man there would seem to be the large difference that the one can subsist in the perfection of everlasting attainment, the other only in the process of becoming. Human holiness must be ever conscious of a beyond.

(Claude G. Montefiore, *Truth in Religion*. New York: Macmillan, 1906)

CLAUDE G. MONTEFIORE (1858-1938). *Theologian and leader of Liberal Judaism in England, founder of the* Jewish Quarterly Review, *and president of the World Union for Progressive Judaism.*

HONOR THE ELDERLY

The need for a sense of connectedness lies at the heart of the issue of how to adequately deal with the problems of the aged, and of those who must be responsible for the aged. Perhaps it is time we once again looked to the wisdom of our ancestors for a solution and guidelines. Perhaps the wisdom of Hillel in warning against separating oneself from the community can be seen as seminal to this issue. Each of us has a need to feel a sense of purpose to our existence, and a sense of belonging to the world in which we live.

Perhaps, ultimately it is to the family that we must turn for an answer. The Jewish people are sustained by the strength of the families, and by the values that are learned within them. Perhaps it is time we once again embraced the values of the family and of the central need for a sense of connectedness among people. Through such an avenue, we might be able to find our way back to the innocence of being that produced a sense of awe and wonder at the miracles of our everyday lives. There are no simple answers to the problems that plague the aged in our society. But, if our hearts and minds are once again tuned to the need for reaching out to those around us, for experiencing an innate sense of personal responsibility for the emotional and physical well-being of our families both immediate and extended, and to the need for each of us to experience that vital sense of connectedness to our past, our people, and our personal relationships, then we will at least have made a large step, on the road to personal and social well-being. I leave you with the wisdom of ben Sira, who summarized the essence of every individual's personal stake in the fate of the aged, when he said, "Don't shame the aged, for we shall all be numbered among them."

(Steven C. Reuben, "Honor the Elderly," *Journal of Aging and Judaism*, vol. 2, no. 2 [winter 1987]: 117-222)

STEVEN CARR REUBEN (1949-). *Rabbi, songwriter, and religious leader of Congregation Kehillath Israel, Pacific Palisades, California.*

ASCETICISM

Asceticism is in one sense the negation of selfishness; in another sense it may be regarded as a phase of self-development. For he who would labor for the good of others, for the welfare of family, community, or state, must first of all be master of himself. The familiar phrase, to be a slave of one's habits or passions or desires, contains a truth. Only he who is completely self-controlled and self-disciplined is really free, and spiritual freedom implies a measure of asceticism. Just as the old Rabbi argued that he who toils in the Torah, who, in other words, leads the consecrated life, must "live a life of trouble," so too he urged that no man is really free but "he who labors in the Torah." The finest life has often been described as conditional upon a kind of death. "Arise and fly," says the poet, "the reeling faun, the sensual feast; move upward, working out the beast, and let the ape and tiger die." The Talmud tells a story that Alexander of Macedon asked the "wise men of the South" what should a man do that he may live? And the answer was "Let him die." So, too, a false life is said to be equivalent to a living death. That the higher may live it may even be necessary for the lower to die. Still, therefore, true asceticism is something positive: the rejection of the lower for the sake of the higher, a conscious loss for the sake of gain. The true ascetic is not less a man because of his asceticism: he is more a man. This distinguishes the false from the true. The false or erroneous ascetic loses without gain; the right ascetic gains through his loss.

(Claude G. Montefiore, *Truth in Religion*. New York: Macmillan, 1906)

SABBATICAL AND JUBILEE

. . . Jeremiah also invoked the Jubilee vision as a vision of hope (Chapter 32), even though the Babylonians were on the verge of conquering the land and he was prophesying their victory. At this dire moment Jeremiah, using precisely the legal form delineated in Leviticus 25, paid seventeen shekels to redeem a plot of land in his tribal village. He placed the deed of its redemption in a pottery jar, to remain buried until someday when the redemption could actually take place. And he proclaimed that someday the whole land would be redeemed as well, so that houses, fields, and vineyards could be bought and sold again.

Thus he affirmed that the great liberation of the Jubilee applies both to each individual and to the whole people.

Does this vision from another age have any implications for our time?

In this vision, there is a coherent model of a "sustainable economy" in which the people are fed for many generations and millennia, and the land is not tortured into desolation. Today, ecologists and economists focus on how to create just such a sustainable economy. This is no abstraction: It is as personal as Jeremiah's pottery jar. When people who are struggling over how to protect ancient forests and to use lumber resources properly define their battle in terms of "spotted owls" versus "logger jobs," that is what they are fighting over.

This vision contains a coherent model of how to encourage both entrepreneurship and equality. Political theorists and activists struggle over which of these values is more important, and how to balance them. When people battle over "safety nets" and "tax incentives," over "welfare" and "empowering the poor," those are the issues they are fighting over.

This vision is not only about the grand design of a society, it is also about the details of everyday life. It presents us a coherent model of how families and individuals should borrow from and lend to each other, how they should buy from each other, and contains many other teachings about interpersonal ethics over money, issues that we encounter in our lives every day.

(Arthur Waskow, *Down-to-Earth Judaism: Food, Money, Sex, and the Rest of Life*. New York: William Morrow, 1995)

ARTHUR WASKOW (1933-). *Well-known for his work in the Jewish renewal movement and as leader of the Shalom Center, he is the editor of* The New Menorah Journal *and author of several books.*

VEGETARIANSIM

As a human being, I am not only part of but a custodian of nature. God has commanded me to multiply and be fruitful, to fill the earth and rule over the fish of the sea, the birds of the sky, and all living things. The Bible call me *nefesh*, which some biblical scholars translate as throat-through which food and drink and air pass and give me life. As part of nature I take in nutrients to live. God said: "I give you every seed bearing plant that is upon all the earth and every tree that has seed bearing fruit they shall be yours for food. And to every breath of the earth and to every fowl of the air and to everything that creepeth upon the earth wherein there is a living soul I have given every green herb for food" (Gen. 1:29).

Set before us is the ideal of creation, God's original intention: a world of herbivorous animals, a vegetarian universe. That ideal reappears in the vision of the Prophet Isaiah, who imagines the world at the end of history transformed from carnivorous to herbivorous living: "The wolf shall dwell with the lamb, the leopard lie down with the kid, the calf and the beast of prey together, and a little child shall herd them. The cow and the bear shall graze, their young shall lie down together, and the lion, like the ox, shall eat straw" (Isaiah 11:6). The optimal vision of creation is thus embodied in a vegetarian diet.

(Harold M. Schulweis, "Thou Shalt Eat Vegetable," *Reform Judaism*, vol. 23, no. 4 [1995]: 23-25)

FASTING

Incidentally, Judaism does not sanction overly long periods of self-abnegation. It would not look favorably on a week-long hunger strike. Our tradition prescribes a fast of one day as sufficient. Abstaining from food for more than one day is considered excessive and irresponsible.

Fasting also provides us with a way of exerting self-discipline. For a period of over twenty-four hours, we are obligated to say "No" to our cravings. In fact, one of the purposes of Yom Kippur is for us to regain control of our appetites and passions.

Yom Kippur should involve the reconstruction of our moral lives. Our ardor for sinful ends should now be re-directed for good. Our passion for amassing material goods should be rechanneled into helping others.

In other words, on Yom Kippur, we heal the split that has ever-widened over the past year between our animal desires and our human conscience. On Yom Kippur, desire and conscience become one. Hence, we have another understanding of the word "at-one-ment" or atonement. Passion and discipline are fused together.

In addition, fasting should help us to identify with those who are poor and hungry. Fasting should arouse our compassion. We experience pangs of hunger which we voluntarily impose upon ourselves. In this way, we can be more understanding of those millions in the world who are hungry, not from choice, but from a deprivation over which they have no control. One estimate is that two-thirds of the world's population is ravaged by starvation.

Yes, fasting is to be more than just the mere ritual of avoiding food and drink for twenty-four hours. It has many other functions. Fasting can cause us pain for the sins we have committed. Fasting can give us an opportunity to pause to thank God for the blessings we may enjoy in the year ahead. Fasting can help us to develop self-discipline by our refusing to give in to our appetites for over twenty-four hours. Fasting can heighten our sense of solidarity with the destitute and the hungry throughout the world. Fasting can transform and sensitize us to the woes and the hurts of others.

(Samuel M. Stahl, *Making The Timeless Timely: Thoughts and Reflections of a Contemporary Reform Rabbi*. Austin, Texas: Nortex Press, 1993)

SAMUEL M. STAHL (1939-). *Rabbi and spiritual leader of Temple Beth El in San Antonio, Texas; former editor of the* CCAR Journal: A Reform Jewish Quarterly.

CHAPTER FIVE

A Person's Use of the Powers of the Soul to Achieve a Particular Purpose

The purpose of the body is to maintain the soul. The purpose of the soul is to sustain the intellect. The purpose of the intellect is to know God. "Knowing God" resonates differently in the mind of the religious believer than it does in the mind of the philosopher. For the believer, "knowing God" is achieved by doing God's commandments. For the philosopher, as Maimonides indicates in *Guide for the Perplexed* (I:34), "knowing God is achieved by studying logic, mathematics, physics, and metaphysics." In *Shemonah Perakim*, Maimonides directs his attention to achieving both the intellectual and ethical virtues. Control of the passions figures in the attainment of both. That control is achieved by pursuing the Golden Mean.

ה:א צָרִיךְ לָאָדָם שֶׁיְּשַׁעְבֵּד כֹּחוֹת נַפְשׁוֹ כֻּלָּם לְפִי הַדַּעַת, כְּפִי מַה־שֶׁהִקְדַּמְנוּ בַּפֶּרֶק שֶׁלְּפָנֵי זֶה. וְיָשִׂים לְנֶגֶד עֵינָיו תָּמִיד תַּכְלִית אַחַת, וְהִיא: הַשָּׂגַת הַשֵּׁם־יִתְבָּרֵךְ, כְּפִי יְכֹלֶת הָאָדָם לָדַעַת אוֹתָהּ. וְיָשִׂים פְּעֻלּוֹתָיו כֻּלָּן: תְּנוּעוֹתָיו וּמְנוּחוֹתָיו וְכָל־דְּבָרָיו מְבִיאִים לְזוֹ הַתַּכְלִית, עַד שֶׁלֹּא יִהְיֶה בִּפְעֻלּוֹתָיו דָּבָר מִפֹּעַל הַהֶבֶל, רְצוֹנִי לוֹמַר: פֹּעַל שֶׁלֹּא יָבִיא אֶל זֹאת הַתַּכְלִית. וְהַמָּשָׁל בּוֹ: שֶׁיָּשִׂים הַכַּוָּנָה בַּאֲכִילָתוֹ וּבִשְׁתִיָּתוֹ, וּמִשְׁגָּלוֹ, וּשְׁנָתוֹ וִיקִיצָתוֹ, וּתְנוּעָתוֹ וּמְנוּחָתוֹ — בִּבְרִיאוּת גּוּפוֹ לְבַד. וְהַכַּוָּנָה בִּבְרִיאוּת גּוּפוֹ — שֶׁתִּמָּצֵא הַנֶּפֶשׁ כֵּלִים בְּרִיאִים וּשְׁלֵמִים לִקְנוֹת הַחָכְמוֹת וְקָנוֹת מַעֲלוֹת הַמִּדּוֹת וּמַעֲלוֹת הַשִּׂכְלִיּוֹת עַד שֶׁיַּגִּיעַ לַתַּכְלִית הַהִיא.

5:1 One should control all the powers of the soul in the manner in which we have spoken in the previous chapter. One should have the knowledge of God as an ultimate goal as far as one is humanly able to achieve it. Every action, every movement, every pause, every word should be directed to that goal—so that nothing is directed in any other direction. As an example, one's eating, drinking, sex life, sleeping, and waking should be directed to the end of bodily health. The purpose of bodily health is the formation and maintenance of perfect and healthy instruments through which the soul will be able to acquire the sciences, the ethical virtues, and the intellectual virtues.

If the knowledge of God is the ultimate purpose in life, then Maimonides will tell us how to set our priorities. What is beneficial is important. What is pleasurable is unimportant. What is beneficial to the body will ultimately be beneficial to the soul. What is beneficial to the soul will be beneficial to the intellect. Through the intellect, we come to know God.

ה:ב וְעַל־זֶה הַהֶקֵשׁ לֹא תִהְיֶה אָז כַּוָּנָתוֹ אֶל הַהֲנָאָה לְבָד עַד שֶׁיִּבְחַר מִן־הַמָּזוֹן וְהַמִּשְׁתֶּה הֶעָרֵב, וְכֵן בִּשְׁאָר הַהַנְהָגוֹת — אֲבָל יְכַוֵּן אֶל הַמּוֹעִיל. וּכְשֶׁיִּזְדַּמֵּן שֶׁיִּהְיֶה עָרֵב — יִהְיֶה; וּכְשֶׁיִּזְדַּמֵּן שֶׁיִּהְיֶה בִּלְתִּי עָרֵב — יִהְיֶה.

5:2 Since that [knowledge of God] is the purpose, bodily pleasure should not be a goal. One should not choose on the basis of pleasure what one should eat and drink. Rather, one's goal should be to eat and drink what is beneficial. The same is true with all other practices. What is beneficial–and not what is pleasant–should be the goal.

While it may seem that there are some specific (medicinal) cases in which people are behaving in response to the pleasure principle, Maimonides wants to make sure that the reader understands that the pleasure itself is irrelevant. The pleasure is simply the means through which the individual is brought to the goal of healing the body so that the soul might acquire the wisdom it seeks in the form of knowledge of God.

ה:ג אוֹ יְכַוֵּן אֶל הֶעָרֵב עַל־דֶּרֶךְ חָכְמַת הָרְפוּאָה: כְּמִי שֶׁחָלְשָׁה תַאֲוָתוֹ לַמַּאֲכָל — יְעִירֶהָ בִּמְזוֹנוֹת הַמְתֻבָּלִים הָעֲרֵבִים שֶׁנֶּפֶשׁ הָאָדָם מִתְאַוָּה לָהֶם. וְכֵן מִי שֶׁהִתְעוֹרְרָה עָלָיו מָרָה שְׁחוֹרָה — יְסִירָהּ בִּשְׁמִיעַת הַנִּגּוּנִים, וּבְמִינֵי זֶמֶר, וּבְטִיּוּל הַגַּנּוֹת, וּבְבִנְיָנִים הַנָּאִים, וְחֶבְרַת הַצּוּרוֹת הַיָּפוֹת וְכַיּוֹצֵא בָהֶם מִמַּה־ שֶׁיַּרְחִיב הַנֶּפֶשׁ, וְיָסִיר חֳלִי הַמָּרָה הַשְּׁחוֹרָה מִמֶּנּוּ. וְהַכַּוָּנָה בְּכָל־זֶה — שֶׁיַּבְרִיא גוּפוֹ. וְתַכְלִית הַכַּוָּנָה בִּבְרִיאוּת גוּפוֹ — לִקְנוֹת חָכְמָה.

5:3a What is pleasant may be employed for medical reasons, as in the case of a person whose appetite has been diminished. For such a person, well-seasoned food may be prescribed to increase the appetite. Similarly, a person affected by melancholy may be treated by listening to pleasant music and the sound of musical instruments, by walking through verdant gardens, by passing through magnificent buildings, by seeing beautiful objects. What will expand the desires of the soul will be efficacious in treating melancholy. The purpose of all this is to heal the body; the purpose of healing the body is the soul's acquisition of wisdom.

The human task is to know God as far as is humanly possible. Our intellects should direct all bodily activities. Thus, all of our actions (from eating to sex) should be motivated by the desire to take care of the body so that we might follow the necessary path and come to know God. To allow the body to direct itself would be to function on the animal level. Sometimes this path includes doing things that are not pleasant but are necessary. Finally, an analysis of our activities may yield insight into our essential virtue.

Wisdom

Wisdom has meant a variety of things during the history of Jewish thought. In the Bible, wisdom refers to a specific grouping of literature that suggests a pragmatic and prudential view of ethics. These books, Proverbs, Ecclesiastes, and Job, for example, reflect a view generally paralleled by other Near Eastern literature. During the rabbinic period, rabbis used the term "wisdom" to refer to Torah, particularly the Oral Torah, as the rabbinic method of understanding the Written Torah. They held that the Oral Torah was given at Sinai along with the Written Torah. Whether this Torah was written or passed down orally, it was only a taste of the sublime Divine wisdom (what they literally called "the unripened fig"). Divine wisdom was understood by medieval philosophers as the essence of the Deity. Some philosophers understood Divine wisdom as the sum total of all possible knowledge. They also believed that individual thinkers–through training and diligence–could activate their own intellect and apprehend some bits of that Divine knowledge and thereby come into contact with the Divine intellect.

Regardless of whether it was in the biblical, rabbinic, or medieval mind-set, wisdom was a goal. The writer of Proverbs put it this way: "The beginning of wisdom is: Get wisdom" (Prov. 4:7). Throughout their history the Jewish people have sought wisdom. They believed they could "get wisdom" by studying Torah; by studying Torah, they might understand the world and the Ultimate Value behind it. And that is the basic motivation behind seeking it.

וְכֵן כְּשֶׁיִּתְעַסֵּק לִקְנוֹת מָמוֹן — תִּהְיֶה תַכְלִית כַּוָּנָתוֹ בְקִבּוּצוֹ, שֶׁיּוֹצִיאוֹ בְּמַעֲלוֹת וְשֶׁיִּמְצָאֵהוּ לְחוּשֵׁי גוּפוֹ וּלְהַמְשִׁיךְ מְצִיאוּתוֹ, עַד שֶׁיַּשִּׂיג וְיֵדַע מֵהַשֵּׁם-יִתְבָּרֵךְ מַה-שֶּׁאֶפְשָׁר לְדַעְתּוֹ. וְעַל-זֶה הַהֶקֵּשׁ יֵשׁ לִמְלֶאכֶת הָרְפוּאוֹת מָבוֹא גָדוֹל מְאֹד בְּמַעֲלוֹת הַשְּׂכְלִיּוֹת וְהַמִּדּוֹת וּבִידִיעַת הַשֵּׁם-יִתְבָּרֵךְ, וּבְהַגִּיעַ אֶל הַהַצְלָחָה הָאֲמִתִּית. וְיִהְיֶה לִמּוּדָהּ וּבַקָּשָׁתָהּ עֲבוֹדָה מִן-הָעֲבוֹדוֹת הַגְּדוֹלוֹת, וְלֹא תִהְיֶה אָז כַּאֲרִיגָה וּכְנַגָּרוּת. כִּי בָהּ נְשַׁעֵר פְּעֻלּוֹתֵינוּ, וְיָשׁוּבוּ פְּעֻלּוֹת אֱנוֹשִׁיּוֹת מְבִיאוֹת אֶל הַמַּעֲלוֹת הָאֲמִתִּיּוֹת. כִּי הָאָדָם שֶׁיָּבֹא וְיֹאכַל מָזוֹן עָרֵב אֶל הַחֵךְ, טוֹב הָרֵיחַ

שֶׁנֶּפֶשׁ אָדָם מִתְאַוָּה לוֹ, וְהוּא מַזִּיק לוֹ; וְאֶפְשָׁר שֶׁיִּהְיֶה סִבָּה לַחֲלָי קָשֶׁה, אוֹ
לְמִיתַת פִּתְאֹם — זֶה וּבְהֵמוֹת אֶצְלִי שָׁוִין. וְאֵין זֶה פֹּעַל הָאָדָם, מֵאֲשֶׁר הוּא
אָדָם בַּעַל שֵׂכֶל; אָמְנָם הוּא פֹּעַל אָדָם מֵאֲשֶׁר הוּא חַי, נִמְשָׁל כַּבְּהֵמוֹת נִדְמוּ.
וְאָמְנָם יִהְיֶה פֹּעַל אֱנוֹשִׁי, כְּשֶׁיֹּאכַל הַמּוֹעִיל לְבָד. וּפְעָמִים יַנִּיחַ הָעָרֵב וְיֹאכַל
הַנִּמְאָס, כְּפִי בַּקָּשַׁת הַמּוֹעִיל — וְזֶה פֹּעַל לְפִי הַדַּעַת, וּבָזֶה נִבְדָּל הָאָדָם
בִּפְעֻלּוֹתָיו מִזּוּלָתוֹ. וְכֵן כְּשֶׁיִּבְעַל כְּשֶׁיִּתְאַוֶּה, מִבִּלְתִּי שֶׁיִּשְׁמֹר הַנֶּזֶק וְהַתּוֹעֶלֶת
— יֵשׁ לוֹ זֶה הַפֹּעַל מֵאֲשֶׁר הוּא בַּעַל חַי, לֹא מֵאֲשֶׁר הוּא אָדָם.

5:3b Similarly, were one to be occupied in making and amassing money, one's purpose should be in spending it wisely and taking care of the needs of the body, so that one's life might be preserved in order to know, as far as is possible, about God. There is an analogy between the acquisition of the intellectual and moral virtues leading to the apprehension of God and the attainment of true success in the study of medicine. Unlike weaving or carpentry, medicine requires great study and requires specific actions. Similarly, we must evaluate our activities in order to achieve true virtues. A person might eat delicious and aromatic food, the kind of food that most people would want; yet, that food might harm the individual and cause some grave illness or even sudden death. Such eating would be animal rather than human activity, due to the animal nature that we share with other animals, not due to our possession of an intellect. Indeed, the human may be compared to the animal, as it is written, "*ka'behaymot nidmu*, like beasts that perish" [Ps. 49:13, 21 is interpreted midrashically as "compared to the beasts"]. To be truly human, one should eat only what is beneficial. To eat what is beneficial might require a person to eat what is not appetizing instead of what is appetizing. Such eating would follow the intellect. It is by the intellect that the human person is distinguished from all other animals. The same is true with regard to sexual intercourse. One should engage in it without regard to any benefit or danger linked to it. Such activity relates to the individual by virtue of our being an animal rather than by virtue of being human.

Don't be deceived, cautions Maimonides. There is more to living a virtuous life than just preserving the body. If one's goal is simply to keep one's body healthy (rather than it serving as a means to the end–knowledge of God), then that person is no different than the one who eats or does anything else solely for the sake of pleasure.

ה:ד וְאֶפְשָׁר שֶׁתִּהְיֶה הַנְהָגָתוֹ כֻּלָּהּ לְפִי הַמּוֹעִיל, כְּמוֹ שֶׁזָּכַרְנוּ, אֶלָּא שֶׁיָּשִׂים הַתַּכְלִית: בְּרִיאוּת גּוּפוֹ וּשְׁלֵמוּתוֹ מֵהֶחֳלָיִים לְבַד — וְאֵין זֶה חָסִיד. כִּי כְמוֹ שֶׁבָּחַר זֶה הֲנָאַת הַבְּרִיאוּת, בָּחַר זֶה הָאַחֵר הֲנָאַת הַמַּאֲכָל, אוֹ הֲנָאַת הַמִּשְׁגָּל — וְכֻלָּם אֵין תַּכְלִית אֲמִתִּי לִפְעוּלּוֹתָם; אֲבָל הַנָּכוֹן: שֶׁיָּשִׂים תַּכְלִית כָּל מַה־שֶׁיִּתְעַסֵּק בּוֹ בִּבְרִיאוּת גּוּפוֹ וְהֶמְשֵׁךְ מְצִיאוּתוֹ עַל־הַשְּׁלֵמוּת, כְּדֵי שֶׁיִּשָּׁאֲרוּ כְּלֵי כֹחוֹת נַפְשׁוֹ — אֲשֶׁר הֵם אֶבְרֵי הַגּוּף — שְׁלֵמִים; וְתִתְעַסֵּק נַפְשׁוֹ מִבְּלִי מוֹנֵעַ בְּמַעֲלוֹת הַמִּדּוֹת וּבְמַעֲלוֹת הַשִּׂכְלִיּוֹת.

5:4 As we have mentioned, it is possible to consider all behaviors in their relation to what is beneficial. However, the one whose sole purpose is keeping the body healthy and free from ailments does not become thereby a pious person but is simply choosing the delights of health in the same way as another might choose the delights of food or the delights of sex–all of which have no ultimate purpose. Instead, the purpose of health and the perfection of the body should be that the body–through its various capacities–may serve as instruments for the soul. No part of the body should be an impediment to the acquisition of moral and intellectual virtues.

Every intellectual science may be used to prepare the intellect for its ultimate goal. Even the study of solid geometry and mechanics, which seem unrelated to philosophy, trains the mind in the ways of logical proof (of the existence of God).

ה:ה וְכֵן כָּל־מַה־שֶׁיִּלְמָדֵהוּ מִן־הַחָכְמוֹת וּמִן־הַדֵּעוֹת שֶׁיַּשִּׂיג. מַה־שֶׁהוּא מֵהֶן דֶּרֶךְ לַתַּכְלִית הַהִיא — אֵין בּוֹ דִין וּדְבָרִים; וּמַה־שֶׁאֵין בּוֹ תּוֹעֶלֶת בַּתַּכְלִית הַהִיא: כִּשְׁאֵלַת הַחֶשְׁבּוֹן, וְסֵפֶר הַחֲרוּטִים וְהַתַּחְבּוּלוֹת, וּלְהַרְבּוֹת מִשְׁאָלוֹת אֶל־הַהַנְדָּסָה, וּמְשִׁיכַת הַמִּשְׁקָלִים, וְהַרְבֵּה כַּיּוֹצֵא בָאֵלּוּ — תִּהְיֶה הַכַּוָּנָה בָּהֶם לְחַדֵּד הַשֵּׂכֶל וּלְהַרְגִּיל כֹּחַ הַשִּׂכְלִי בְּדַרְכֵי הַמּוֹפֵת, עַד שֶׁיַּגִּיעַ לָאָדָם קִנְיַן יְדִיעַת הֶקֵּשׁ הַמּוֹפְתִי מִזּוּלָתוֹ, וְיִהְיֶה לוֹ זֶה הַדֶּרֶךְ שֶׁיַּגִּיעַ בּוֹ לִידִיעַת אֲמִתַּת מְצִיאוּת הַשֵּׁם־יִתְבָּרַךְ. וְכֵן בְּדִבְרֵי הָאָדָם כֻּלָּם.

5:5 What is derived from the sciences and similar notions that lead to the desired end is never in question. However, those notions that [seem] to have no purpose in themselves and that [seem to] convey no benefit such as the study of mathematics, the Book on Conic Sections, mechanics, geometry, and the [study of the] suspension of weights, as well as similar studies, may have as their purpose the sharpening of the intellect and the [training in the] use of proofs so that a person will acquire the methods of logical proof. In this manner, one will come to the true knowledge of the existence of God. Similarly, in all that touches human beings, one should be concerned only with what will bring benefit to the soul.

Maimonides provides further instruction to the reader. Even if one pursues mathematics for the sake of sharpening the intellect, one should remember that the true purpose of all learning is to come to know God. However, if this pursuit somehow brings harm to the body or soul, it must be rejected. But the individual's responsibility does not stop there. If someone's activities potentially might harm someone–including the person's self–then the individual has the responsibility to condemn the other's actions. Likewise, one must offer praise to the other person who acts in ways that are beneficial to the body or soul. This behavior not only will help society but will draw the individual's own attention away from the path of evil, as well.

ה:ו אֵין צָרִיךְ שֶׁיְּדַבֵּר בָּהֶם אֶלָּא בְּמַה־שֶׁיָּבִיא בּוֹ תוֹעֶלֶת, אוֹ יַרְחִיק הֶזֵּק מִנַּפְשׁוֹ, אוֹ מִגּוּפוֹ; אוֹ בְּחָכְמָה, אוֹ בְּמַעֲלָה; בְּשֶׁבַח מַעֲלָה, אוֹ מְעֻלָּה; אוֹ לִגְנוֹת גְּנוּת, אוֹ מְגֻנֶּה. כִּי קִלְלַת בַּעֲלֵי הַחֶסְרוֹנוֹת וְזִכְרָם לִגְנוּת — אִם יִהְיֶה הַכַּוָּנָה בּוֹ לְחַסְּרָם אֵצֶל בְּנֵי אָדָם, עַד שֶׁיִּתְרַחֲקוּ מֵהֶם וְלֹא יַעֲשׂוּ כְּמַעֲשֵׂיהֶם — הוּא דָּבָר מְחֻיָּב, וְהִיא מַעֲלָה. הֲלֹא תִרְאֶה אָמְרוֹ יִתְבָּרֵךְ: כְּמַעֲשֵׂה אֶרֶץ־מִצְרַיִם אֲשֶׁר יְשַׁבְתֶּם־בָּהּ לֹא תַעֲשׂוּ (ויקרא יח, ג). וְסִפּוּר הַסְּדוֹמִים וְכָל־מַה־שֶׁבָּא בַּמִּקְרָא מִסִּפּוּר גְּנוּת בַּעֲלֵי הַחֶסְרוֹנוֹת וְזִכְרָם לִגְנַאי, וְשֶׁבַח הַטּוֹבִים וְהַגְדָּלָתָם — אֵין הַכַּוָּנָה בּוֹ רַק מַה־שֶׁזְּכַרְתִּי לָךְ: עַד שֶׁיִּמָּשְׁכוּ בְּנֵי אָדָם אַחֲרֵי הַדְּרָכִים הַטּוֹבִים הָאֵלֶּה, וְיִתְרַחֲקוּ מִדַּרְכֵי הָרָעִים הָהֵם. וּכְשֶׁיָּשִׂים הָאָדָם כַּוָּנָתוֹ אֶל זֶה הָעִנְיָן, — יְבַטֵּל מִפְּעֻלּוֹתָיו וִיחַסֵּר מִמַּאֲמָרָיו הַרְבֵּה מְאֹד. כִּי מִי שֶׁיְּכַוֵּן אֶל זֶה הָעִנְיָן — לֹא יִתְעוֹרֵר לְפַתֵּחַ הַכְּתָלִים בְּזָהָב, אוֹ לַעֲשׂוֹת רָקוּם זָהָב בִּבְגָדָיו הַנָּאִים. הָאֱלֹהִים! אִם לֹא יְכַוֵּן בָּזֶה לְהַרְחִיב נַפְשׁוֹ כְּדֵי שֶׁתַּבְרִיא וְיַרְחִיק מִמֶּנָּה חָלְיָה, עַד שֶׁתִּהְיֶה בְּהִירָה זַכָּה לְקַבֵּל הַחָכְמוֹת. וְהוּא אָמְרָם, זִכְרוֹנָם לִבְרָכָה: "שְׁלֹשָׁה מַרְחִיבִין דַּעְתּוֹ שֶׁל אָדָם: אֵלּוּ הֵן דִּירָה נָאָה, וְאִשָּׁה נָאָה, וְכֵלִים נָאִים". מַאי "וַתִּזְנַח מִשָּׁלוֹם נַפְשִׁי"? ר' אַבָּא אָמַר "זוֹ מִטָּה מֻצַּעַת וְאִשָּׁה מְקֻשֶּׁטֶת לְתַלְמִידֵי חֲכָמִים". כִּי הַנֶּפֶשׁ תִּלְאֶה וְתֵעָכֵר הַמַּחֲשָׁבָה בְּהַתְמָדַת עִיּוּן הַדְּבָרִים הָעֲכוּרִים, כְּמוֹ שֶׁיִּלְאֶה הַגּוּף בַּעֲשׂוֹתוֹ הַמְּלָאכוֹת הַכְּבֵדוֹת עַד שֶׁיָּנוּחַ וְיִנָּפֵשׁ, וְאָז יָשׁוּב לְמִזְגּוֹ הַשָּׁוֶה.

5:6 One should reject anything that brings harm to the soul or to the body, whether it relates to a matter of knowledge or a matter of status, whether it be to praise or to demean. However, one should demean those who have [spiritual] defects and contemn them—if one's intention is to keep the masses from associating with them or imitating their actions. That doing so is a virtue is indicated by the Torah verse, "After the doings of the land of Egypt, where you have dwelled, you shall not do..." [Lev. 18:3] and from the story of the people of Sodom [Gen. 18-19] and from other passages in the Bible that decry the actions of persons lacking virtue. Just as Scripture mentioned such people for condemnation, it mentioned good people for praise. The purpose for both praise and condemnation is that people should follow the ways of goodness and keep far from the ways of evil. When one directs one's attention to such matters, one will keep far from evil acts and will greatly limit one's speech. Such a person will not inlay one's walls with gold or embroider one's clothes with gold (unless the purpose was [as a method of treatment] to comfort the soul in order to heal it and make it able to absorb the sciences). The sages referred to such a notion when they said, "Three things expand a person's consciousness: a nice house, a beautiful spouse, and nice clothes" [B. Talmud, *Berakhot* 57b]. "What is the meaning of 'My life was bereft of peace;'... Rabbi Aba referred it to as a prepared bed and a bejeweled spouse for the disciples of the wise" [B. Talmud, *Shabbat* 25b]. In the same way that the body becomes fatigued when it continually does heavy work, the soul becomes fatigued and thought eludes it when its attention is continually directed to ugly things. The soul will return to equilibrium when it is rested and refreshed.

Maimonides interrupts his directive with a bit of home remedy, for this work of praise and condemnation may cause fatigue. Thus, he directs us to relax and be refreshed by a visit to his version of an art gallery or nature reserve. He teaches that we must remember that, in one way or another, they are all part of God's creation. Even here, we must be careful not to be seduced by the beauty of these objects, whether they are natural or crafted by human beings. They are all potential objects of lust and desire. This train of thought will eventually lead Maimonides to discuss whether persons who struggle to control their passions are on a higher or lower level than persons who by nature are not troubled by their passions. From a rabbinic perspective, "according to the suffering is the reward" (*Pirke Avot* 5:23)—which Maimonides will cite in the next chapter; thus, persons who struggle and succeed to control their passions should be on a higher level than those who do not have to struggle at all. From a philosophical perspective, it would seem that persons who are not troubled by their passions are on a higher level, since they need not expend effort that is better spent on philosophical study. Maimonides provides a kind of harmonization by suggesting that both positions are the same. The philosopher's ideal is the person who would not be interested in committing major crimes, while the rabbis were directing their statements to those persons who had no difficulty in observing the ritual *mitzvot*, since they had no interest in committing moral transgressions.

ה:ז כֵּן צְרִיכָה הַנֶּפֶשׁ גַּם־כֵּן לְהִתְעַסֵּק בִּמְנוּחַת הַחוּשִׁים בְּעִיּוּן לַפִּתּוּחִים וְלָעִנְיָנִים הַנָּאִים, עַד שֶׁתָּסוּר מִמֶּנָּה הַלֵּאוּת. כְּמוֹ שֶׁאָמְרוּ: „כִּי הֲווֹ חָלְשֵׁי רַבָּנָן מִגִּרְסַיְהוּ הֲווֹ אָמְרִי מִלְּתָא דִּבְדִיחוּתָא". וְיַחְשֹׁב שֶׁעַל־זֶה הַצַּד — לֹא יִהְיוּ אֵלֶּה רָעוֹת וְלֹא מַעֲשֵׂה הֶבֶל, רְצוֹנִי לוֹמַר: עֲשִׂיַּת הַפִּתּוּחִים וְהַצִּיּוּרִים בַּבִּנְיָנִים וּבַכֵּלִים וּבַבְּגָדִים. וְדַע, שֶׁזֹּאת הַמַּדְרֵגָה הִיא מַדְרֵגָה עֶלְיוֹנָה מְאֹד וַחֲמוּרָה, לֹא יַשִּׂיגוּהָ אֶלָּא מְעַט מִזְעָר וְאַחַר הֶרְגֵּל גָּדוֹל. וּכְשֶׁיִּזְדַּמֵּן מְצִיאוּת הָאָדָם שֶׁזֶּה עִנְיָנוֹ — אֵינִי אוֹמֵר שֶׁהוּא לְמַטָּה מִן־הַנְּבִיאִים. רְצוֹנִי לוֹמַר: שֶׁיְּשַׁמֵּשׁ כֹּחוֹת נַפְשׁוֹ כֻּלָּם וְיָשִׂים תַּכְלִיתָם — יְדִיעַת הַשֵּׁם־יִתְבָּרֵךְ לְבַד; וְלֹא יַעֲשֶׂה מַעֲשֶׂה קָטֹן אוֹ גָּדוֹל, וְלֹא יְדַבֵּר דָּבָר — אֶלָּא שֶׁהַפֹּעַל הַהוּא, אוֹ הַדָּבָר הַהוּא מֵבִיא לְמַעֲלָה, אוֹ לְמַה־שֶּׁמֵּבִיא אֶל מַעֲלָה. וְהוּא יַחְשֹׁב וְיִסְתַּכֵּל בְּכָל־פֹּעַל וּתְנוּעָה וְיִרְאֶה אִם יָבִיא אֶל הַתַּכְלִית הַהִיא, אוֹ לֹא יָבִיא — וְאָז יַעֲשֵׂהוּ. וְזֶהוּ אֲשֶׁר בִּקֵּשׁ מִמֶּנּוּ יִתְבָּרֵךְ שֶׁנְּכַוֵּן אֵלָיו, בְּאָמְרוֹ: וְאָהַבְתָּ אֵת יְיָ אֱלֹהֶיךָ בְּכָל־לְבָבְךָ וּבְכָל־נַפְשְׁךָ וּבְכָל־מְאֹדֶךָ. רָצָה לוֹמַר: בְּכָל־חֶלְקֵי נַפְשֶׁךָ.

5:7a The soul must be involved with resting the senses by concentration on beautiful engravings and beautiful objects. Even a joke may diminish fatigue as we read. "The rabbis were weary from their studies; therefore, they responded [to Rabba] with a joke." [B. Talmud, Shabbat 30b] Their act was neither evil nor folly. In a similar way, one might say that the making of beautiful engravings, beautiful pictures in buildings, beautiful painting on objects, and beautiful clothes is very important and much to be desired. Its importance can only be understood by a few and then only after much training. Should such a person exist, I would say that his/her level would be only less than the prophets. Such a person would use all the faculties of his/her soul and direct them only to the knowledge of God. No other act, great or small, would interest him/her. S/he would say nothing. S/he would only be concerned that a particular act or a particular matter would bring him/her to that particular virtue or to what was anticipatory of a virtue. S/he would reflect on every act and every movement to see if it would fulfill his/her purpose or not. If it would not, s/he would make it so it did. It is this which God asks of us in the verse, "And you shall love *Adonai* with all your heart, with all your soul, and with all your might" [Deut. 6:5], that is, with every aspect of your soul.

It should be noted that the control of the passions is a necessary but insufficient condition to achieve the knowledge of God. Only philosophical study (see 5:1) can achieve that knowledge. One may consider the discussion of the control of the passions as directed to readers who have just begun their philosophical studies. Consequently, further study will teach them that control of the passions is not enough to achieve human perfection; only the knowledge of what can be known provides us with the opportunity for human perfection. Ethical perfection is required, but it is not the equal of intellectual perfection. That perfection is achieved by knowing what can be known, particularly of God.

שֶׁתַּעֲשֶׂה תַכְלִית כָּל־חֵלֶק מִמֶּנָּה תַכְלִית אַחַת וְהִיא: לְאַהֲבַת הַשֵּׁם־
יִתְבָּרֵךְ. וּכְבָר הִזְהִיר הַנָּבִיא, עָלָיו הַשָּׁלוֹם, עַל־זֶה גַּם־כֵּן וְאָמַר: בְּכָל־דְּרָכֶיךָ
דָעֵהוּ (משלי ג, ו) וּפֵרְשׁוּ הַחֲכָמִים, זִכְרוֹנָם לִבְרָכָה, וְאָמְרוּ: „אֲפִלּוּ לִדְבַר
עֲבֵרָה". וּרְצוֹנָם לוֹמַר: שֶׁתָּשִׂים לַפֹּעַל הַהוּא תַּכְלִית, וְהִיא — הָאֱמֶת, אַף־עַל־
פִּי שֶׁיֵּשׁ בּוֹ עֲבֵרָה מִצַּד אֶחָד. וּכְבָר כָּלְלוּ הַחֲכָמִים, זִכְרוֹנָם לִבְרָכָה, זֶה הָעִנְיָן
כֻּלּוֹ בִּקְצָרָה בְּמִלּוֹת מוּעָטוֹת מוֹרוֹת עַל־זֶה הָעִנְיָן הוֹרָאָה שְׁלֵמָה מְאֹד, עַד
כְּשֶׁאַתָּה תִּבְחַן הַמִּלּוֹת אֵיךְ סִפְּרוּ זֶה הָעִנְיָן הַגָּדוֹל וְהֶעָצוּם כֻּלּוֹ, אֲשֶׁר חִבְּרוּ בוֹ
חִבּוּרִים וְלֹא הִשְׁלִימוּהוּ — תֵּדַע שֶׁנֶּאֱמַר בְּכֹחַ אֱלֹהִים בְּלֹא סָפֵק, וְהוּא אָמְרָם
בְּצַוָּאוֹתֵיהֶם: „וְכָל־מַעֲשֶׂיךָ יִהְיוּ לְשֵׁם שָׁמַיִם". וְזֶהוּ הָעִנְיָן אֲשֶׁר בֵּאַרְנוּהוּ בְּזֶה
הַפֶּרֶק; וְזֶהוּ שִׁעוּר מַה־שֶּׁרְאִינוּהוּ רָאוּי לְזָכְרוֹ הֵנָּה, לְפִי זֹאת הַהַקְדָּמָה.

5:7b Every aspect of your soul should have the love of God as its purpose. This too is what the prophet meant by the statement, "In all your ways acknowledge God, and God will direct your paths" [Prov. 3:6]. Commenting on the verse, the [rabbis in the] Talmud noted, "Rabba said, 'Even involving a transgression'" [B. Talmud, *Berakhot* 63a]. They meant that you should set truth as the purpose of your particular action even if a transgression should be involved with it when viewed one way. The sages summed this up in a few words, which are filled with meaning when you examine them. They recounted this important matter, which many have written about and never completed. With Divine assistance, you should know that we will speak of this without doubt. In their ethical wills, the sages said, "Let all of your acts be for the sake of Heaven." This is what we have spoken of in this chapter; and this is what we have seen fit to mention in this introduction.

GLEANINGS

THE MYSTIC UNION WITH GOD

While to some minds a view of the soul's destiny that is not connected with either the resurrection of the physical body or of final judgment may appear unsatisfying, other find it manna for their hungry hearts. In the mystic union with God the soul attains its highest reward, whether it retains consciousness of individuality or not. The drop has joined the ocean. The spark has merged into the radiant light. In the words of the *El Male Rahamim, it is* "sheltered under the wings of the Shechinah." Without pressing further into the realm that is enveloped in mystery, the lover of God rests satisfied. With the Jewish poet he says, "Thou livest, God, I live in thee." "The essence of the hereafter," says Rabbi Nahman of Bratzlav, "is the consciousness of His divinity." The highest aspiration is voiced in the prayer of Rabbi Shneor Zalman of Liadi, "Lord of all the world! I gladly forego my reward in the hereafter and my portion in Gan Eden. Only one thing do I ask for and seek: Thee, Thee!" In this spirit, too, Jehudah Halevi exclaimed, "When I am afar from Thee, my death is my life; when I cleave to Thee, my life is my death." With these sentiments of Jewish mystics and saints we may associate the thought of the American philosopher Josiah Royce: "Just because God is One, all our lives have various and unique places in the harmony of the divine life. And just because God attains and wins and finds this uniqueness, all our lives win in our union with Him, the individuality which is essential to their true meaning." (*Conception of Immortality*, p. 75.) God, in the words of Emily Brontë, is indeed "the steadfast rock of immortality."

(Samuel S. Cohon, *What We Jews Believe*. Cincinnati: Union of American Hebrew Congregations, 1931)

LOVING GOD

The event at the Red Sea is but one of many in Israel's history where God is said to have revealed Himself, where God has given man the ability to experience "that intercourse of mind and event which is the essence of revelation." Why does God give this ability to man? Why, at certain moments in the course of history, does He lift happenings and events from the level of the routine and the ordinary to that of Revelation? Again, we have to answer these questions in very much the same way in which we have tried to account for the Election of Israel: It is because of God's *Love*. "For God so loved the world . . . ," says the Christian (John 3:16). "With everlasting love hast Thou loved the House of Israel, Thy people," says the Jew at the daily evening service; "Torah and commandments, statutes and judgments, hast Thou taught us." Indeed, as Franz Rosenzweig would have it, the Divine Love is *the only* content of Revelation. Man, becoming conscious of this Love of God, hears the divine command: "Thou shalt love the Lord thy God with all thy heart, with all thy soul, and with all thy might." Ordinarily, of course, love cannot be *commanded*. Only a lover, in a moment of aroused love, might, and does, demand of his beloved that she return his love, that she reciprocate the love shown to her. But that is precisely what the moment of Revelation does imply. God shows His Love, and longs for man's love in return. All the rest is commentary and interpretation.

(Jakob J. Petuchowski, *Ever Since Sinai: A Modern View of Torah*. New York: Scribe Publications, 1968)

JAKOB J. PETUCHOWSKI (1925-1991). *Rabbi and theologian. At the time of his death, Dr. Petuchowski was the Sol and Arlene Bronstein Professor of Judeo-Christian Studies and Research Professor of Jewish Theology and Liturgy at Hebrew Union College-Jewish Institute of Religion, Cincinnati, where he had taught for many years. He had been the first director of Jewish Studies at HUC-JIR, Jerusalem. Dr. Petuchowski was a prolific writer, well-known for his sensitive approach to Jewish ritual and tradition. In* Ever Since Sinai, *he articulated a belief in the authority of revelation and halakhah.*

KNOWING GOD

Once one is convinced that the most reliable path to the knowing of God and to the discerning of his way with nature and humankind is to be found in these modes of revelation–intuitive insight, historical experience, and the spirit of critical inquiry and the scientific quest–then we have a revealing and concealing God, a God both knowable and unknowable, both near and far away, both mind and heart, both all-powerful and helpless, both redemptive and damning. In a word, we have a God who was both present and absent in Auschwitz; who made the Holocaust a possibility but did not bring it about; who suffered with its victims but could not lift a finger to alleviate the pain, the anguish, and the heartlessness of it all; who remained true to his covenant with Israel and humankind but could not alter its conditions. Never in all of human history had God revealed himself so fully, or hidden himself so effectively. This awesome paradox becomes intelligible once one looks for God and his ways with nature and humankind through the prisms of the three modes of revelation which the spirit of free critical inquiry has vouchsafed us.

Let us take a hard, dispassionate, even clinical look at the Holocaust in the same way as we would take a look at some frightening and mystifying disease such as cancer or AIDS; or some frightening and partly mystifying natural phenomenon such as earthquakes or tornadoes; or some frightening and in part mystifying human tragedy such as war, starvation, terrorism, and homelessness. Must we not, first of all, recognize that such frightening phenomena are real possibilities in our universe, actualities that will not simply dissolve themselves by justified rage, pious pleas for divine intervention, or bitter tears? Whether or not there be a God, the only realistic option that is open to us if we seriously wish to lessen the mystery and to end the pain, the suffering, and the tragedy, is to have recourse to those laws of nature to which we have access and which, when understood and co-opted, offer us redemption from the evil which had held us in thrall. Scientists draw on these dependable laws to invent vaccines; to detect the ravaging forces of nature untamed and reduce their devastating effects; to manipulate genes to increase the food supply; to understand the workings of the brain and the trials and tribulations of the psyche and the divided self. What we do, in effect, in order to alleviate our affliction is to turn to the mind of God and tap those mathematical formulae, dependable laws, and enduring principles which made both our affliction and our healing possible. God thus is both all-knowing and all-causing, on the one hand, and not-knowing and not-causing on the other. God "knows" the formulae, the laws, and the principles, but God does not "know" how to activate them to serve human ends prior to their having been discovered by men and women through the spirit of free critical inquiry and the scientific quest. God is indeed a redemptive God, but only when the means for gaining redemption become know through the free, restless, and prying minds of men and women.

(Ellis Rivkin, *The Life of Covenant: The Challenge of Contemporary Judaism, Essays in Honor of Herman E. Schaalman.* Chicago: Spertus College Press, 1986)

ELLIS RIVKIN (1918-). *Historian. Dr. Rivkin is the Adolph S. Ochs Professor Emeritus of Jewish History at the Hebrew Union College-Jewish Institute of Religion, Cincinnati. He is particularly well-known for his application of the Marxist theory of economic determinism to leadership in Jewish history, particularly evident in his book* A Hidden Revolution: The Pharisees' Search for the Kingdom Within. *Dr. Rivkin applied the "unity principle" of monotheism in his work in Jewish history and demonstrated a "transhistoric" methodology to his work.*

BEARING WITNESS

As we begin to set our agenda for the 21st century, I hope that those of us who care about the future of Reform Judaism will begin by acknowledging the centrality of God in our understanding of Jewish self-identity. Scholars have pointed out, and I think rightly so, that part of what distinguished modern Orthodoxy, Conservatism, and Reform from one another, at least in the late 19th and early 20th centuries, was their differing emphasis on the three major elements of Judaism: God, Torah, and Israel. Orthodoxy placed greatest emphasis on Torah; Conservatism on Israel, i.e., on Jewish peoplehood; and Reform on God. Indeed, one can argue, that for the Classical Reformers of the late 19th and early 20th centuries who viewed much of Torah as inessential and had little, if any, sense of Jewish peoplehood, belief in God and in God's moral teachings was seen as the core, the "essence" if you will, of Jewish self-identity. To lose sight of this God-centeredness is, I think, to lose sight of Classical Reform's greatest legacy. What made Classical Reform an authentic expression of Judaism and what continues to authenticate Reform today is, I believe, its emphasis on bearing witness.

(Ellen M. Umansky, "Addresses and Papers," *Central Conference of American Rabbis One-Hundred-First Convention,* vol. C, June 1990, pp. 63-69)

ELLEN M. UMANSKY (1950-). *Feminist theologian. Carl and Dorothy Bennett Professor of Judaic Studies Fairfield University in Connecticut. She is well-known as the biographer of Lily Montagu and Tehilla Lichtenstein and as the co-editor of* Four Centuries of Jewish Women's Spirituality: A Source Book.

THE HIGHER KNOWLEDGE OF GOD

How do we come to know the deeper, the higher knowledge and thought of God? God reveals Himself to man only in man. If you want to know how God speaks, if you want to know the wisdom of God, you cannot find it on the mountain top, not in cave or cavern; you can find it only in the human life. Then we must study human life. When we say "God speaks", it can only mean that He speaks literally through human organs, that He looks upon us through human eyes, that He draws us to Him in human love. For of Him, the Highest

Wisdom, the Infinite Love, the Perfect Beauty, we can know nothing except through the channels of our own inmost spiritual life, and that life opens its fountains to us in the depths of human experience. As in the fountain is reflected the image of the stars invisible in the glare of daylight, so in the depths of the soul is revealed the image of Him who is the Life and Love of all beings.

(Isaac S. Moses, "Sources of Spirituality–Conference Sermon," Central Conference of American Rabbis Twenty-eighth Annual Convention, Buffalo, 1917, pp. 220-334)

ISAAC S. MOSES (1847-1926). *Rabbi. Trained in Santamichel, Gleiwitz, and Breslau, he served numerous congregations before serving Central Synagogue in New York City. He wrote his own prayer book,* Tefillah Lemoshe, *which led him to prepare a manuscript on which the first draft of the* Union Prayer Book *(1892) was prepared. He edited the weekly* Zeitgeist *in Milwaukee with Adolph Moses and Emil G. Hirsch.*

GOD AS A MYSTERIOUS FORCE

Utilizing the concepts of our day, when we speak of God we think of the living and creative essence of the universe, the ultimate ground of all existence, the unique One who unifies the multiplicity of warring natural phenomena, the self-conscious intelligence whose workings are discernible in the net-work of law which holds the universe together. For us God is the mysterious source from which all things derive their being, the power eternal expressing Himself in solar systems and in the tiniest atom and electron, in organic matter and in human life. He is self-existent, limitless in power, infinite in resources, wondrous in manifestations. He reveals Himself in baffling phenomena and in ordinary processes of nature. The microscope no less than the telescope displays His wonders. The tiniest living cell or drop of water is charged with the mystery which overwhelms us when we gaze upon the stars.

(Samuel S. Cohon, What We Jews Believe. New York: Union of American Hebrew Congregations, 1931)

CHAPTER SIX

The Difference between the Tzadik and the One Who Controls Oneself

Is virtue a matter of nature or nurture? Are there naturally virtuous people? If a person were not naturally virtuous, yet had achieved virtue by great moral exertion, would that person be at a higher or lower ethical level than the person who was naturally virtuous? Maimonides will wrestle with these questions in this section. His difficulties will be compounded by the traditional Jewish notion of free will and by the rabbinic idea that reward should comport with exertion as he prepares to discuss the difference between the *tzadik* (the person virtuous by nature) and the "one who controls oneself" (the one who has achieved virtue).

ו:א אָמְרוּ הַפִּילוֹסוֹפִים: שֶׁהַמּוֹשֵׁל בְּנַפְשׁוֹ — אַף־עַל־פִּי שֶׁעוֹשֶׂה הַמַּעֲשִׂים הַטּוֹבִים וְהַחֲשׁוּבִים — הוּא עוֹשֶׂה אוֹתָם וְהוּא מִתְאַוֶּה אֶל הַפְּעֻלוֹת הָרָעוֹת וְנִכְסָף אֲלֵיהֶן וְיִכְבֹּשׁ אֶת־יִצְרוֹ; וְיַחֲלֹק עָלָיו בִּפְעֻלוֹתָיו, עַל מַה־שֶׁיְּעִירוּהוּ אֵלָיו כֹּחוֹתָיו וְתַאֲוָתוֹ וּתְכוּנַת נַפְשׁוֹ וְיַעֲשֶׂה הַטּוֹבוֹת — וְהוּא מִצְטַעֵר בַּעֲשִׂיָתָם וְנִזּוֹק.

6:1 The philosophers have said that the one who controls oneself is that person who can do good and important things while, at the same time, intensely desiring to do evil things. By exerting self-control, such a person can direct one's actions toward good in spite of the other aspects of one's personality pushing the individual to do evil. The exertion, however, is painful and injurious.

Maimonides' conclusions may seem counterintuitive to the modern reader. We might think that the one who wrestled with temptation and won would be at a higher level than one who never sensed temptation. The thoroughly righteous person is the person who by nature simply has no desire to do evil and wants only to do good. The person who controls oneself does so by exerting willpower and struggling to do good (and likewise struggling to avoid doing evil). While their actions resemble one another's, the *tzadik* is on a higher ethical plane. Perhaps introspection and personal experience with others suggest to us that few persons are naturally virtuous.

72

ו:ב אֲבָל הֶחָסִיד — הוּא שֶׁנִּמְשָׁךְ בִּפְעֻלָּתוֹ אַחַר מַה־שֶּׁתְּעִירֵהוּ תַּאֲוָתוֹ וּתְכוּנָתוֹ; וְיַעֲשֶׂה הַטּוֹבוֹת — וְהוּא מִתְאַוֶּה וְנִכְסָף אֲלֵיהֶן. וּבְהַסְכָּמָה מִן הַפִּילוֹסוֹפִים: שֶׁהֶחָסִיד יוֹתֵר חָשׁוּב וְיוֹתֵר שָׁלֵם מִן־הַמּוֹשֵׁל בְּנַפְשׁוֹ. אֲבָל אָמְרוּ: שֶׁהַמּוֹשֵׁל בְּנַפְשׁוֹ כְּחָסִיד בְּעִנְיָנִים רַבִּים; וּמַעֲלָתוֹ לְמַטָּה מִמֶּנּוּ בְּהֶכְרֵחַ, לִהְיוֹתוֹ מִתְאַוֶּה לִפְעֹל הָרַע — וְאַף־עַל־פִּי שֶׁאֵינוֹ עוֹשֶׂה אוֹתוֹ — מִפְּנֵי שֶׁתְּשׁוּקָתוֹ לְרַע הִיא תְּכוּנָה רָעָה בַּנֶּפֶשׁ. וּכְבָר אָמַר שְׁלֹמֹה הַמֶּלֶךְ, עָלָיו הַשָּׁלוֹם, כַּיּוֹצֵא בָזֶה: נֶפֶשׁ רָשָׁע אִוְּתָה רָע (משלי כא, י). וְאָמַר בְּשִׂמְחַת הֶחָסִיד בְּמַעֲשֶׂה הַטּוֹב, וְהִצְטַעֵר מִי שֶׁאֵינוֹ צַדִּיק בַּעֲשִׂיָּתָהּ, זֶה הַמַּאֲמָר: שִׂמְחָה לַצַּדִּיק עֲשׂוֹת מִשְׁפָּט וּמְחִתָּה לְפֹעֲלֵי אָוֶן (שם כא, טו).

6:2a The *tzadik*, on the other hand, does what his or her soul desires. That person does good, wants and indeed yearns to do good. The philosophers all agree that the *tzadik* is more important and on a higher level than the one who controls one's passions. However, they did say that the one who controls one's passions resembles the *tzadik*; [the fact that] he or she is on a lower level follows from his or her desire to do evil, which was not acted upon. That desire suggests an evil quality in the individual's soul. Solomon the king referred to such a case when he wrote, "The soul of the wicked desires evil" [Prov. 21:10]. In the (following) words, Solomon spoke of the joy that the righteous person has in doing good and the sorrow that the unrighteous person feels while doing good: "To do justly is joy to the righteous but ruin to the workers of iniquity" [Prov. 21:15].

From a rabbinic perspective, it would seem that the one who desires to sin and does not is more worthy of reward than the thoroughly righteous *tzadik*, since the rabbis also taught that "according to the suffering is the reward." From a philosopher's perspective, at least as Maimonides reports it, the *tzadik* would be at a higher level because such a person is already on a higher stage of perfection. But Maimonides is not prepared to conclude that the rabbis and philosophers are in conflict with one another. Instead he tries to harmonize the conflicting traditions.

Yetzer Tov/Yetzer Hara

The rabbis, like most of us, wondered why some human beings are good while others are evil. Why indeed does it seem that some people have the impulse to do evil while others have a proclivity toward good? They came to understand through a textual analysis of the word *yatzar*, "formed" "*Adonai*, God *formed* Adam from the dust of the earth" [Gen. 2:7] which here is spelled with two *yods*—when one would expect only one—that each individual has two *yetzers*. God created and formed each human with the inherent potential (they used the term "inclination") to do good or evil. However, this *yetzer* (good or evil) is only in potential. Even the *yetzer hara* (inclination to do evil) was neither absolutely evil nor uncontrollable. The *yetzer hara* was necessary for the human to exist. While uncontrolled, for example, it might lead to lust and adultery, under control (held in balance by the *yetzer tov*), it led an individual to want to marry, have children, raise a family, build a home, and engage in business. According to the rabbis, the study of Torah and the discipline of observing *mitzvot* assisted the individual (through the *yetzer tov*) in the lifelong struggle with one's *yetzer hara*.

Diverse Threads (Shaatnez)

In Leviticus 19:19, the Torah prohibits the wearing of any garment with diverse threads, what is called *kilayim*. Diverse threads may be the explanation for the word that follows in the passage, *shaatnez*. This word, apparently non-Semitic in origin, remains somewhat unclear to us. However, the prohibition is repeated in Deuteronomy 22:11, where *shaatnez* is explained as "wool and flax together."

Although this *mitzvah* is described as one of the ordinances (*chukkim*) to be obeyed without question (Lev. 19:19), the context for the *mitzvah* both in Leviticus and Deuteronomy suggests that the notion of mixing items of different origins lies behind the prohibition of wearing diverse threads. Maimonides (in his *Guide for the Perplexed* III:37) related the prohibition to the vestments worn by the priests engaged in idolatrous worship. Yet, we see this discomfort with mixing in various places in the Torah where it expresses uneasiness (through prohibition) with the "control" by humans of multiple species or generations.

Prohibited Sexual Relations

According to Jewish law, there are three cardinal sins for which one must die and not transgress, even for the sake of saving one's own life. *Giluy arayot* (literally, the uncovering of nakedness) is one of these three transgressions. While it includes adultery or marital infidelity (as determined in the so-called Ten Commandments, or *Aseret Hadibrot*), it also includes other sexual behaviors prohibited by the Torah (Lev. 18 and 20) such as incest. For the sages, *giluy arayot* was extremely dangerous for society. It could cause mass destruction, affecting both the innocent and guilty. Certain biblical figures, such as Esau, were considered to have been guilty of this sin.

זֶהוּ הַנִּרְאֶה מִדִּבְרֵי הַנְּבִיאִים נָאוֹת לְמַה־שֶׁזְּכָרוּהוּ הַפִּילוֹסוֹפִים. וְכַאֲשֶׁר חָקְרְנוּ דִּבְרֵי חֲכָמִים בְּזֶה הָעִנְיָן נִמְצָא לָהֶם: שֶׁהַמִּתְאַוֶּה לַעֲבֵרוֹת וְנִכְסָף אֲלֵיהֶן — הוּא יוֹתֵר חָשׁוּב וְיוֹתֵר שָׁלֵם, מֵאֲשֶׁר לֹא יִתְאַוֶּה אֲלֵיהֶן וְלֹא יִצְטַעֵר בַּהֲנָחָתָן; עַד שֶׁאָמְרוּ: שֶׁכָּל אֲשֶׁר יִהְיֶה הָאָדָם יוֹתֵר חָשׁוּב וְיוֹתֵר שָׁלֵם — תִּהְיֶה תְּשׁוּקָתוֹ לַעֲבֵרוֹת וְהִצְטַעֲרוֹ בַּהֲנָחָתָן יוֹתֵר גָּדוֹל. וְהֵבִיאוּ בְּזֶה הַדְּבָרִים וְאָמְרוּ:

74

„כָּל־הַגָּדוֹל מֵחֲבֵרוֹ יִצְרוֹ גָּדוֹל מִמֶּנּוּ". וְלֹא דַיָּם זֶה, עַד שֶׁאָמְרוּ: שֶׁשְּׂכַר הַמּוֹשֵׁל בְּנַפְשׁוֹ גָּדוֹל לְפִי רֹב צַעֲרוֹ בְּמָשְׁלוֹ בְּנַפְשׁוֹ, וְאָמְרוּ: „לְפוּם צַעֲרָא — אַגְרָא". וְיוֹתֵר מִזֶּה — שֶׁהֵם צִוּוּ לִהְיוֹת הָאָדָם מִתְאַוֶּה לַעֲבֵרוֹת, וְהִזְהִירוּ מִלּוֹמַר: שֶׁאֲנִי בְּטִבְעִי לֹא אֶתְאַוֶּה לְזֹאת הָעֲבֵרָה, וְאַף־עַל־פִּי שֶׁלֹּא אָסְרָה הַתּוֹרָה. וְהוּא אָמְרָם: „רַבָּן שִׁמְעוֹן בֶּן־גַּמְלִיאֵל אוֹמֵר: לֹא יֹאמַר אָדָם: אִי־אֶפְשִׁי לֶאֱכֹל בָּשָׂר בְּחָלָב; אִי־אֶפְשִׁי לִלְבּשׁ שַׁעַטְנֵז: אִי־אֶפְשִׁי לָבוֹא עַל־הָעֶרְוָה — אֶלָּא: אֶפְשִׁי, וּמָה אֶעֱשֶׂה — אָבִי שֶׁבַּשָּׁמַיִם גָּזַר עָלַי".

6:2b It would seem that the prophets agree with the philosophers. When we examined the words of the sages, however, we found that they believed that the one who wanted–even yearned–to sin and did not do so was a better person than one who never wanted to sin. They said, "That person is greater than another whose inclination to evil is greater (and who controls oneself)" [B. Talmud, *Sukkah* 52b]. Moreover, the sages added that such a person would have the greater reward because of the greater difficulty in self-control. Thus, they stated, "According to the suffering so is the reward" [*Pirke Avot* 5:23]. Moreover, the sages maintained that a person should want to transgress, lest someone say, "Even were the Torah not to have prohibited it, because of my nature I would not have wanted to commit this transgression!" As the sages said, "Let no one say, 'I don't want to eat milk and meat together. I don't want to put on diverse threads [*shaatnez*]. I don't want to have prohibited sexual intercourse. I want all these things, but what can I do? My parent in Heaven has prohibited them all'" [*Sifra, Kedoshim Parashata* 9:9].

Maimonides harmonizes the rabbinic view with the view of the philosophers by asserting that the difference between the two views lies in the kind of question put before both. Neither the thoroughly righteous person nor the one who controls oneself is being challenged by the kind of transgression that reason would preclude. Hence the reward is attained by virtue of obedience to the revelation rather than by following the mandates of reason. Thus, reward for the latter is warranted.

Kalam

When philosophy–in the form of the study of Platonic and Aristotelian texts–entered Islamic society, it created problems for Islamic theology. The concepts of God, the actions of God, the human being, and the human task found in these texts differed from those found in the texts of the Koranic tradition. *Kalam* dialectics (*kalam* from the Arabic word for "word" or "speech"), became the theological response to philosophy. The teachers of *Kalam* became known as *Mutakallimun*: dialecticians. They defended theology by adapting some philosophical notions while retaining certain notions of the Islamic tradition. From philosophy, the *Mutakallimun* took the concept of an immaterial Deity. From their Islamic tradition, they took the notion of creation. From philosophy (and from some earlier Islamic thinkers), the *Mutakallimun* derived arguments for free will. *Kalam* treatises tended to be organized into two parts: unity and justice. Unity presented the arguments for creation by which they proved the notion of one God. Justice argued that God was just, because humans were free.

Jewish and Christian thinkers took up the method of *Kalam* as philosophy entered their respective camps. Saadyah Gaon (882-942) was described as one of the *Mutakallimun;* his *Book of Beliefs and Opinions* may be seen as a *Kalam* book. It too deals with the notions of unity and justice. On the other hand, Maimonides opposed the *Kalam*. He devoted a number of chapters in his *Guide for the Perplexed* to the refutation of its views, particularly the argument that whatever could be imagined could be true. Moreover, Maimonides thought that *Kalam* had originated in the Christian world before Islam came upon the scene as a defense of Christianity against philosophy on behalf of "kings ... who protected religion."

Rational Commandments

Although some individual rabbis attempted to provide reasons for some of the commandments, rabbinic Judaism viewed the commandments as decrees of God. It even saw the commandment that prohibited the taking of the mother bird with her babies as a Divine decree rather than an indicator of Divine compassion. Some of the Jewish philosophers, however, sought to divide the categories of rational and nonrational commandments. In particular, Saadyah Gaon (882-942) maintained that while all the commandments were ultimately rational, the rationality of some of the commandments was immediately apparent. He believed that the rationality of other commandments was not so readily apparent; thus, they were to be observed on the basis of tradition. Yehudah HaLevi (1080-1142) argued that the commandments could be divided into those that were rational and those that were not. However, it was precisely those commandments, such as the Sabbath and circumcision, whose rationality was not apparent, that were most important because they were linked to the Jewish people. Any group, even a group of brigands, HaLevi contended, would have to agree on a command purpose in order to maintain itself. Hence rational commandments–which were required by every group–could not reflect a specific Divine purpose. Like others before him, Moses Maimonides (1135-1204) also divided the commandments into rational and nonrational (what he called ritual); however, his stress on thought raised questions as to the efficacy of the observance of commandments, whether they were rational or ritual commandments.

ג:ו וּלְפִי הַמּוּבָן מִפְּשׁוּטֵי שְׁנֵי הַמַּאֲמָרִים בִּתְחִלַּת הַמַּחֲשָׁבָה הֵם סוֹתְרִים זֶה אֶת זֶה — וְאֵין הָעִנְיָן כֵּן; אֲבָל שְׁנֵיהֶם אֱמֶת וְאֵין מַחֲלֹקֶת בֵּינֵיהֶם כְּלָל. וְהוּא: שֶׁהָרָעוֹת אֲשֶׁר הֵן אֵצֶל הַפִּילוֹסוֹפִים רָעוֹת, אֲשֶׁר אָמְרוּ: שְׁמִי שֶׁלֹּא יִתְאַוֶּה אֲלֵיהֶן יוֹתֵר חָשׁוּב מִן־הַמִּתְאַוֶּה אֲלֵיהֶן וְיִכְבֹּשׁ אֶת־יִצְרוֹ מֵהֶן — הֵם הָעִנְיָנִים

הַמְפֻרְסָמִים אֵצֶל כָּל־בְּנֵי אָדָם שֶׁהֵם „רָעוֹת": כִּשְׁפִיכוּת דָּמִים, וּגְנֵבָה, וּגְזֵלָה,
וְאוֹנָאָה, וּלְהַזִּיק לְמִי שֶׁלֹּא הֵרַע לוֹ, וְלִגְמֹל רַע לְמֵיטִיב לוֹ, וְלִבְזוֹת אָב וָאֵם
וְכַיּוֹצֵא בְאֵלּוּ. וְהֵן הַמִּצְווֹת שֶׁאָמְרוּ עֲלֵיהֶן הַחֲכָמִים, זִכְרוֹנָם לִבְרָכָה: „שֶׁאִלּוּ
לֹא נִכְתְּבוּ רְאוּיוֹת הֵן לְכָתֵב". וְיִקְרְאוּ אוֹתָן קְצָת מֵחַכְמֵינוּ הָאַחֲרוֹנִים אֲשֶׁר
חָלוּ חֳלִי הַמְדַבְּרִים: „מִצְווֹת הַשִּׂכְלִיּוֹת".

6:3a At first glance, on a superficial reading, it might seem that the philosophical and rabbinic statements contradict one another. In truth, this is not so, for there is no conflict between them. When the philosophers spoke of evil, when they said that anyone who did not want to do evil was on a higher level than anyone who did [want to do evil] even though that person controlled oneself, they were speaking of those generally accepted evils such as murder, robbery, theft, fraud, harming of someone who never harmed you, hurting someone who helped you, treating your mother and father badly, and other similar vices. These are covered by those *mitzvot* that, according to the Talmud, "were they not already written [in the Torah] they would have to be written" [B. Talmud, *Yoma* 67b]. Later scholars, upon whom the "*Kalam* sickness has fallen" called these "rational commandments."

In this section, Maimonides begins the discussion about the relationship between the revelation of Torah and the individual. He makes the argument that those commandments that are prohibitions would not be prohibited without Torah. Thus, the individual who refrains from doing what is prohibited is indeed on a higher level. On the other hand, the righteous individual would not want to transgress any of the other (positive) commandments.

וְאֵין סָפֵק שֶׁהַנֶּפֶשׁ אֲשֶׁר תִּכְסֹף לְדָבָר מֵהֶם וְתִשְׁתּוֹקֵק אֵלָיו — שֶׁהִיא חֲסֵרָה;
וְשֶׁהַנֶּפֶשׁ הַחֲשׁוּבָה לֹא תִתְאַוֶּה לְאֶחָד מֵאֵלּוּ הָרָעוֹת כְּלָל, וְלֹא תִצְטַעֵר
בְּהִמָּנְעָהּ מֵהֶם. אֲבָל הַדְּבָרִים שֶׁאָמְרוּ עֲלֵיהֶם הַחֲכָמִים, שֶׁהַכּוֹבֵשׁ אֶת־יִצְרוֹ
מֵהֶם הוּא יוֹתֵר חָשׁוּב וּגְמוּלוֹ יוֹתֵר גָּדוֹל — הֵם: „הַתּוֹרוֹת הַשִּׁמְעִיּוֹת", וְזֶה
אֱמֶת; שֶׁאִלְמָלֵא הַתּוֹרָה לֹא הָיוּ רָעוֹת כְּלָל. וּמִפְּנֵי זֶה אָמְרוּ: שֶׁצָּרִיךְ הָאָדָם
שֶׁיַּנִּיחַ נַפְשׁוֹ אוֹהֶבֶת אוֹתָן וְלֹא יִהְיֶה לוֹ מוֹנֵעַ מֵהֶן רַק הַתּוֹרָה.

6:3b There is no doubt that any soul who would want to transgress such *mitzvot* is clearly deficient. A righteous soul would not want to transgress any of these *mitzvot* at all; in no way would it be troubled by not doing so. Those transgressions to which the sages referred, when they said that a person who controls one's inclinations is on a higher level and will receive a greater reward than one who never felt their attraction, are those prohibited by the "revealed commandments." Were it not for the Torah they would not be transgressions! For this reason, one should desire them and know that it is the Torah alone that prohibits them. Therefore, the sages said that one should want to do them and to know that it is only the Torah that prevents that person from acting on one's desire.

Maimonides follows Jewish tradition by explaining that the *chukim* (statutes of the Torah) are arbitrary instructions of God, which one may neither question nor disobey. The *tzadik*, having accepted the notion of a nonrational Divine revelation, would have no difficulty obeying such *mitzvot*. The person who has achieved virtue without revelation would have to struggle to try to understand such commandments and struggle even more to obey them.

וּבְחַן חָכְמָתָם, עֲלֵיהֶם הַשָּׁלוֹם, וּבְמַה־שֶּׁהִמְשִׁילוּ. שֶׁהֵם לֹא אָמְרוּ: „אַל יֹאמַר אָדָם: אִי־אֶפְשִׁי לַהֲרֹג הַנֶּפֶשׁ; אִי־אֶפְשִׁי לִגְנֹב; אִי־אֶפְשִׁי לְכַזֵּב, אֶלָּא: אֶפְשִׁי, וּמָה אֶעֱשֶׂה — אָבִי שֶׁבַּשָּׁמַיִם גָּזַר עָלַי"; אֲבָל הֵבִיאוּ דְבָרִים „שִׁמְעִיִּים" כֻּלָּם: בָּשָׂר בְּחָלָב, וּלְבִישַׁת שַׁעַטְנֵז, וַעֲרָיוֹת. וְאֵלּוּ הַמִּצְוֹת וְכַיּוֹצֵא בָהֶן, הֵן אֲשֶׁר קָרְאָן הַשֵּׁם־יִתְבָּרֵךְ: „חֻקּוֹת". וְאָמְרוּ רַבּוֹתֵינוּ, זִכְרוֹנָם לִבְרָכָה: „חֻקִּים שֶׁחָקַקְתִּי לָךְ — אֵין לְךָ רְשׁוּת לְהַרְהֵר בָּהֶם": וְעוֹבְדֵי כּוֹכָבִים מְשִׁיבִין עֲלֵיהֶם, וְהַשָּׂטָן מְקַטְרֵג בָּהֶם, כְּגוֹן: פָּרָה אֲדֻמָּה וְשָׂעִיר הַמִּשְׁתַּלֵּחַ וְכוּ׳. וַאֲשֶׁר קָרְאוּ אוֹתָן הָאַחֲרוֹנִים: שִׂכְלִיּוֹת, יִקְרָאוּ: מִצְוֹת, כְּפִי מַה שֶּׁבֵּאֲרוּ הַחֲכָמִים.

6:3c Look at the wisdom of the sages and see what an example they gave. They did not say, "Let no person say, 'I don't want to kill anyone. I don't want to steal. I don't want to lie. I want to do all these things, but what can I do? My parent in Heaven prohibits it.'" Instead, they referred to things that were revealed, like [the prohibition against eating] milk and meat, putting on *shaatnez*, and the prohibited sexual acts. These commandments and others like them are called "statutes." To explain them, the sages interpreted the Torah's words, "I am *Adonai*" to mean [God said] 'I have enacted these statutes and you have no right to question them'" [B. Talmud, *Yoma* 67b]. The statutes are those that "the non-Jews derisively ask about" and "Satan mocks" [B. Talmud, *Yoma* 67b]. Among such statutes are the red heifer [Numbers 19] and the scapegoat [Leviticus 16]. What later thinkers called rational, the sages would have called commandments and would have explained them.

While the *chukkim* that Maimonides adduces may seem rather extreme in their unintelligibility, it might be argued that any particular behavior (even Shabbat) might be challenged precisely because it may serve as a marker for separate Jewish identity. One does not maintain specific Jewish identity by refraining, as one should, from murder. One maintains Jewish identity by doing those things that are specific to the Jewish group, even though such activity may not seem "reasonable" or the kind of thing that everybody does. For Judaism, being reasonable is not enough. For the sages, even the rational commandments derive their force from revelation and not from reason. In conclusion, Maimonides harmonizes the two points so that the thoroughly righteous person is described both as one who never has the desire to transgress, as well as one who has a desire to transgress but refrains from doing so out of self-control.

ו:ד　הִנֵּה הִתְבָּאֵר־לְךָ מִכֹּל מַה־שֶּׁאָמַרְנוּ אֵיזוֹ מִן־הָעֲבֵרוֹת יִהְיֶה מִי שֶׁלֹּא יִשְׁתּוֹקֵק אֲלֵיהֶן יוֹתֵר חָשׁוּב מִן־הַמִּשְׁתּוֹקֵק אֲלֵיהֶן וְכוֹבֵשׁ יִצְרוֹ מֵהֶן, וְאֵיזוֹ מֵהֶן יִהְיֶה הָעִנְיָן בְּהֵפֶךְ. — וְזֶה חִדּוּשׁ נִפְלָא בְּהַעֲמִיד שְׁנֵי הַמַּאֲמָרִים; וּלְשׁוֹנָם מוֹרָה עַל־אֲמִתַּת מַה־שֶּׁבֵּאַרְנוּ. וּכְבָר נִשְׁלְמָה כַּוָּנַת זֶה הַפֶּרֶק.

6:4 It is now clear to you from what has been said which kind of transgression puts the person who never wanted to transgress on a higher level than the person who wanted to do so but exercised self-control and did not do so. The reverse case [also holds true]. This is a marvelous new idea in explaining two sets of statements so that their language indicates the truth of what we have stated. We have now completed what we intended to discuss in this chapter.

GLEANINGS

THE COSMIC NATURE OF MITZVOT

It is easy to illustrate the cosmic nature of *mitzvot* on the level of physical reality. The universe is so constructed that, if I wish to survive, I must have adequate oxygen, nourishment, and exercise. God "wants" me to breathe fresh air, ingest healthful foods, and regularly move my muscles. These, therefore, are *mitzvot*.

No less is true in the realm of ethical *mitzvot*. Honesty is a compelling *mitzvah*. Human nature (which is, after all, nature at its highest level of development) is such that in the long run the individual or the social group that consistently flaunts the dictates of honesty risks disaster. The struggle for freedom is a compelling *mitzvah*. Ultimately only those who cherish their own freedom and grant it to others can achieve happiness. To love is a compelling *mitzvah*. Only the person who is capable of giving and receiving love will ever be fulfilled. These things are true, not because we want them to be and not because they were decreed by a human legislature, but because they are ineluctable aspects of reality. Hence the recognition, acceptance, and observance of them constitute *mitzvot*.

(Roland B. Gittelsohn, "Mitzvah without Miracles," *Gates of Mitzvah*.
New York: Central Conference of American Rabbis, 1979)

ROLAND B. GITTELSOHN (1910-1995). *Rabbi, theologian, author, spiritual leader of Temple Israel in Boston, Massachusetts, and founding president of ARZA (Association of Reform Zionists of America).*

RITUAL MITZVOT

Small-*m mitzvot*–the performance of ritual acts–have an aesthetic and affective function. They both beautify and enhance by religious drama the moral values and the ideals of our heritage. They become a structure on which the preservation of our people's tradition and its continuity may rest. We select the *mitzvot* we will perform, we shape our folkways, change our music, revise our prayers, eliminate customs and add other new customs. But *Mitzvah* is not the product of our human social engineering. *Mitzvah* is God's demand issuing in moral and spiritual values. Ceremonial *mitzvot* with their fold associations, their customs, and their symbolic objects and actions are the carrier of the values, the structural framework for the people's task of transmission. But large-*M Mitzvah* is the enduring essence to which the structure of small *m* testifies and pays obeisance.

(Arthur J. Lelyveld, "*Mitzvah*: The Larger Context," *Gates of Mitzvah*.
New York: Central Conference of American Rabbis, 1979)

ARTHUR J. LELYVELD (1913-1996). *Social activist, rabbi, and spiritual leader of Fairmount Temple, Cleveland, Ohio.*

ESSENTIAL MITZVOT

It is incumbent upon us to observe those commandments which adumbrate the essence of Judaism or which can be related to such an essence. Obviously, one cannot in such a brief exposition define what that essence is. One can, however, assert that all the commandments which are corollary to Judaism's ethical monotheism–however that unity is currently interpreted–and to its consequent moral imperatives should be obeyed.

Those that are predicated solely on long-antiquated historic episodes or on exclusively particularistic or outmoded unethical and superstitious notions should be discarded. Reform Judaism has correctly maintained that Judaism is an evolving religion and that consequently there are aspects of Judaism one should accept and others that should be discarded, while in still other areas creative innovation is required. More important than the question of obsequious, abject obeisance to the totality of the 613 commandments is whether such responsible creativity is not essential to the viability and survival of Judaism.

(Maurice N. Eisendrath, "The State of Jewish Belief," *Commentary*, vol. 42, no. 2 [August 1966]: 83)

MAURICE N. EISENDRATH (1902-1973). *An outspoken community leader who addressed many social and political issues. He served the UAHC as president from 1943 until his death.*

DOING MITZVOT *IN ORDER TO KNOW GOD*

Doing Jewish law–at least when we do not see it as the direct command of God–has been a metaphoric way of affirming the *doing* side of the dichotomy, the side that speaks of deed, of action, of human possibility, of the ability to make a difference. Law is *active*; it is something we do. It is an effort to save ourselves and bring salvation to our world.

My feeling now is that in modern Judaism, we have played out that motif for all it's worth. I am not saying that I now believe in a life of being passive, of sitting around and waiting for God's grace, of utter despair about human power to effect lasting change. But more and more in my life, and in the lives of Jews with whom I work, I feel the need for a metaphoric way to say more often: Some things are not in our power, we cannot actually save ourselves, we need to be humble. In some deep sense, we need not justify ourselves, because we are *already* loved–not forgiven for this or that wrong, but fundamentally and unalterably accepted.

The law in one of its secular forms is: Work hard, do well in school, and you will be a success. One can somehow prove one's own worth in the world through action. And now our health-care focus has added another side to legalism: Take care of your body, eat the right food, and exercise, and you will be healthy.

Sometimes it works, and sometimes it doesn't. The world is not as ordered as the legal tradition implies, and the elements of surprise, of paradox, of grace, all seem left out by our notions of self-help and activism. How does Judaism help us to recall that we are *not* in control? How do we play out in our lives the religious message that we are justified by something *beyond* ourselves?

When the law was understood as being God's word, the law itself had that effect. When Jews accepted the "yoke" of the *mitzvot*, they did not believe that they were saving themselves. Rather, they were following instructions that allowed God to save them. But for us, the notion that we embrace halakhah feels like a way of saying: the Jewish people have created something wonderful–a religion of deeds. Yes, we can do something about our lives, to improve our world. But we need to hear the other piece, too–that we are not completely in control. I'm afraid all our constant talking about Jewish law often drowns out that message.

(Nancy Fuchs-Kreimer, "The Power and the Perils of Jewish Practice," *Reconstructionist*, vol. 53, no. 8 [July-August 1988]: 16-17)

NANCY FUCHS-KREIMER (1952-). *Rabbi, director of the Religious Studies Program of the Reconstructionist Rabbinical Association, and former editor of Ra'ayonot, the journal of the Reconstructionist Rabbinical Association (1987-1990).*

SELF-RESTRAINT

If you profess Judaism, you must seek to be just to yourself by self discipline and self control and self development. You dare not spoil the good that is in you, for through being a Jew you dedicate that good to the service of God. You must use in God's cause your power of body, mind and soul. Then you must seek the good of other people, and see that they have the best opportunities for a good life, those indeed which you desire for yourself. The one God, being just, requires you to practice justice yourself, if you would imitate Him, not only for the people you love, but for those from whom you are distant by accident or by choice. There is room in God's world for every man and his right to be here is as good as yours.

God has made His world beautiful, and we have found it possible to spoil it. Through our wilful blindness, even the glory of nature may be wasted on us. Unless we train the eyes of children to see and their ears to hear, beauty makes little appeal to them.

We have all an artistic sense which can be cultivated because it is one of God's gifts which is universal. Let us seek beauty and reverence it, because it contains an element of the divine spirit.

I have spoken about the unity of God as the first principle of Judaism, and shown how it can affect our life as a community and as individuals. In my next letter, I will try to show more fully man's relation to God, and the possible effect of our loyalty to God in making the world progress towards goodness.

As I said at the beginning of my letter, in my view Judaism does not consist in keeping observances, though observances have an important place nevertheless in Jewish life. They will be put in their right place when we find the way of life which is Judaism. In conclusion I would only ask you to consider the difference between the way of life with God and the way of life without Him. Most of us *do* fear to be unworthy of the best we know. Some Jews today are trying to live in defiance of their Judaism. Nevertheless, Judaism is blamed for *their* shortcomings.

We would try to witness to our faith, to show that it is good to know that God is the Lord. Holding that faith we say: "The Lord is with us, we shall not fear."

(Lily Montagu, "Concepts of Judaism," in Lily Montagu: *Sermons, Addresses, Letters, and Prayers*, ed. Ellen M. Umansky. New York: Mellen Press, 1985)

LILY MONTAGU (1873-1963). *A social worker and magistrate who pioneered Liberal Judaism in Britain. She conducted worship services and wrote on religious subjects. With Claude Montefiore, she established the Jewish Religious Union, which sponsored the Liberal Jewish Synagogue (in London), and the World Union for Progressive Judaism.*

LEISURE AS SELF-RESTRAINT

Aristotle believed that the sole purpose of rest was to be able to work again: "We need relaxation because we cannot work continuously. Relaxation is not an end, for it is taken for the sake of activity." Aristotle didn't understand that leisure should have intrinsic meaning and importance and *not* just help us re-charge our engines for the next bout with the world.

Jump with me across the centuries from the ancient pagan criticisms of the Sabbath to our great-grandparents, who came as immigrants to America. Poor and stressed, they lived tenuous existences. Many were tailors and wagonmasters and shoemakers and barkeepers and middle-men—and they longed for the blessed rest of the Sabbath.

But many impoverished workers who emigrated to America left the idea of the Sabbath back home. Upon landing here, they encountered two ideologies that agreed on the importance of work: Socialism, which exalted the worker; and capitalism which venerated hard work. In their new world, the Sabbath was incongruous with the all-consuming work ethos.

The Depression reinforced the modern American obsession with work. Not to work was financially disastrous and psychologically traumatic. (It still is. Therapists note that for men, unemployment is often linked with sexual impotence.)

As anti-Semitism waned after World War Two, corporate barriers began to fall and Jews entered professions previously closed to them. Sabbath observance drastically declined since to celebrate a day of liberation from profession or career, after such a long fight to get that career, was almost unthinkable.

Earlier generations of Jews observed the Sabbath because it was what God wanted them to do. Later generations neglected it, except as nostalgia or ethnic memory. But there was never a time in American culture when the Sabbath was needed more than now. Many people want to break their bondage to career and materialism, yet don't know how to since modernity doesn't provide many models for that struggle. Judaism does–at least for one day.

The Sabbath is more than an obligation, more than candles, wine and religious services. It needs to be reframed so it can be what it was intended to be: A 24-hour protest against materialism, careerism and competition. In his essay entitled "Shabbat as Protest," Canadian Reform Rabbi W. Gunther Plaut wrote, "We must understand that doing nothing, being silent and open to the world, letting things happen inside, can be as important as–and sometimes more important than–what we commonly call 'useful'." The Sabbath is the ultimate statement that the world does not own us.

(Jeffrey K. Salkin, Being God's Partner: How to Find the Hidden Link between Spirituality and Your Work.
Woodstock, Vermont: Jewish Lights Publishing, 1994)

JEFFREY K. SALKIN (1954-). *Rabbi at The Community Synagogue in Port Washington, New York; author.*

EVIL INCLINATION

Nothing is intrinsically evil. If something were, then God who is the Source of All Being could not be present everywhere in creation. If something were intrinsically evil, it would have to derive its reality from a force independent from God.

(Lawrence Kushner, The Book of Words: Talking Spiritual Life, Living Spiritual Talk.
Woodstock, Vermont: Jewish Lights Publishing, 1993)

CHAPTER SEVEN

The Barriers That Exist between God and Humans

The discussion of barriers that impede knowledge is used by Maimonides to suggest a theory of prophecy that diverges from historical Jewish tradition.

Prophecy

It would seem that there are as many theories of prophecy as there are those who have reflected upon it. For the biblical writer, prophecy seems to be a rather straightforward matter: God spoke to specific people and called them to a particular role as spokespersons for God, regardless of whether or not the individual wanted that role. For the rabbis, prophecy was something that occurred in the past. Since the destruction of the Temple, they argued, prophecy was something that no longer occurred. Only children and fools would make a claim to it. For the medieval philosophers, prophecy ultimately became the same as philosophy. However, according to Saadyah Gaon, prophecy took less time than did philosophy. Taking a different perspective, Maimonides claimed that although both prophet and philosopher required the same philosophical training, prophecy was alloyed with imagination. In the modern period, Hermann Cohen perpetuated the medieval notion of prophecy; he maintained that revelation was the creation of reason.

Modern thinkers who saw religion's (and particularly, Judaism's) purpose as the creation of a just society (hence the term "social justice") found support in the words of the prophets. "Let nation not lift up sword against nation" (Isa. 2:4; Mic. 4:3) suggested a model for relations between nations. "Seek justice, relieve the oppressed, judge the fatherless, plead for the widow" (Isa. 1:17) suggested a model for the relation of individuals within nations. It may be argued that the concern of some of the prophets for the poor reflects the egalitarian values of an earlier shepherd tradition. Thus, Amos–the first of the writing prophets–spoke of those who "...sell the righteous for silver and the needy for a pair of shoes" (Amos 2:6) and who "...oppress the poor, that crush the needy" (Amos 4:1). Isaiah spoke of those who "...join house to house,...field to field, until there is no room" (Isa. 5:8).

On the basis of the wilderness experience, it would seem that Amos and Isaiah opposed the Temple cult or, at least, the notion that the sacrificial system was sufficient to gain God's favor. Speaking for God, Amos said, "I hate, I despise your feasts.... Although you offer me burnt-offerings and meal-offerings, I will not accept them.... Did you bring Me sacrifices and offerings in the wilderness forty years, O house of Israel?" (Amos 5:21-22, 25). Isaiah asked,

"When you come to appear before Me, Who required this at your hand?... New moon and sabbath, the holding of convocations–I cannot endure iniquity along with the solemn assembly. Your new moons and your appointed seasons, My soul hates..." (Isa. 1:12-13).

While the Temple cult and ritual generally found favor in the eyes of prophets such as Ezekiel and Malachi, the words of Amos and Isaiah best suited those who viewed religious life to be best expressed by ideas like Amos's "But let justice well up as waters, And righteousness as a mighty stream" (Amos 5:24). It may be argued that modern Jews felt addressed precisely by the role of prophet as critics of societies and dreamers. In the post-modern era, we realize that we may have been wrong. We now once again look upon ritual to complement the prophetic spirit as a necessary part of human affairs in both the religious and civil spheres. Perhaps it is because ritual is so attractive and so much part of the spiritual life that we are again compelled to heed the prophetic call to righteousness and participate in traditional Jewish ritual.

ז:א הַרְבֵּה יִמָּצֵא בַּמִּדְרָשׁוֹת וּבָאַגָּדוֹת, וְיֵשׁ מֵהֶן בַּגְּמָרָא: שֶׁיֵּשׁ מִן־הַנְּבִיאִים מִי שֶׁיִּרְאֶה הַשֵּׁם־יִתְבָּרֵךְ מֵאַחֲרֵי מְחִיצוֹת רַבּוֹת; וּמֵהֶם, מִי שֶׁיִּרְאֵהוּ מֵאַחֲרֵי מְחִיצוֹת מוּעָטוֹת — לְפִי קָרְבָתָם אֶל הַשֵּׁם־יִתְבָּרֵךְ וּלְפִי מַעֲלָתָם בַּנְּבוּאָה. עַד שֶׁאָמְרוּ: מֹשֶׁה רַבֵּנוּ, עָלָיו הַשָּׁלוֹם, רָאָה הַשֵּׁם־יִתְבָּרֵךְ מֵאַחֲרֵי מְחִיצָה אַחַת בְּהִירָה, כְּלוֹמַר: מַזְהִירָה. וְהוּא אָמְרָם: „הִסְתַּכֵּל בָּאַסְפַּקְלַרְיָא הַמְּאִירָה". וְ„אַסְפַּקְלַרְיָא" — שֵׁם הַמַּרְאָה הַנַּעֲשָׂה מִגּוּף הַמַּזְהִיר כְּשֶׁהֵם וּזְכוּכִית, כְּמוֹ שֶׁהִתְבָּאֵר בְּסוֹף כֵּלִים.

7:1 There are many statements in the *Midrash*, in the *Aggadah*, and in the *Gemara* as well that some prophets saw God (so to speak) behind many partitions, while other prophets saw God behind few partitions. It seems that the difference lies in the relation of some prophets to God and the level of their prophecy. The sages spoke of Moses seeing God through only one clear partition when they said that Moses looked through a clear glass (*aspacklaria*) (B. Talmud, *Yevamot* 49b). The word *aspacklaria* refers to an object that is transparent–like crystal or glass–as is explained at the end of tractate *Kelim* in the Mishnah.

Maimonides simply elucidates a list of intellectual and moral vices, all of which create barriers between the individual and God. This listing helps us to understand the role of the prophet in Maimonidean thought.

ז:ב וְהַכַּוָּנָה בְּזֶה הָעִנְיָן מַה־שֶּׁאֹמַר לְךָ, וְהוּא שֶׁאֲנַחְנוּ בֵּאַרְנוּ בַּפֶּרֶק הַשֵּׁנִי: שֶׁהַמַּעֲלוֹת, מֵהֶן — מַעֲלוֹת שִׂכְלִיּוֹת, וּמֵהֶן — מַעֲלוֹת הַמִּדּוֹת. וְכֵן הַפְּחִיתֻיּוֹת, מֵהֶן — פְּחִיתֻיּוֹת שִׂכְלִיּוֹת: כְּסִכְלוּת וּמִעוּט הַהֲבָנָה, וְדֹחַק הַתְּבוּנָה; וּמֵהֶן —

85

פְּחִיתֻיּוֹת הַמִּדּוֹת: כְּרֹב הַתַּאֲוָה, וְהַגַּאֲוָה, הָרֹגֶז, וְהַכַּעַס, וְהָעַזּוּת, וְאַהֲבַת הַמָּמוֹן וְהַדּוֹמֶה לָהֶן, וְהֵן רַבּוֹת מְאֹד. וּכְבָר זָכַרְנוּ הַסֵּדֶר בִּידִיעָתָן בַּפֶּרֶק הָרְבִיעִי. וְאֵלּוּ הַפְּחִיתֻיּוֹת כֻּלָּן — הֵן מְחִיצוֹת הַמַּבְדִּילוֹת בֵּין הָאָדָם וּבֵין הַשֵּׁם־יִתְבָּרֵךְ. מַאֲמַר הַנָּבִיא מְבָאֵר זֶה: כִּי אִם־עֲוֹנֹתֵיכֶם הָיוּ מַבְדִּילִים בֵּינֵכֶם לְבֵין אֱלֹהֵיכֶם (ישעיה נט, ב). יֹאמַר: שֶׁעֲווֹנֹתֵינוּ — וְהֵן אֵלּוּ „הָרָעוֹת", כְּמוֹ שֶׁזָּכַרְנוּ — הֵן הַמְּחִיצוֹת הַמַּבְדִּילוֹת בֵּינֵינוּ וּבֵינוֹ יִתְבָּרֵךְ.

7:2 In chapter 2, we had explained that the virtues are either intellectual or moral and that the vices are either intellectual or moral. The intellectual vices are stupidity, ignorance, and the unwillingness to understand. Among the moral vices are lust, pride, anger, arrogance, and the love of money. There are many such vices. We have already mentioned their order in chapter 4. Each one of these moral vices sets up a barrier between the individual and God, even as the prophet stated, "But your iniquities have separated you and your God" [Isa. 59:2]. The iniquities of which the prophet spoke are the aforementioned moral vices. They are the barriers between God and us.

According to Maimonides, prophecy requires the would-be prophet to possess specific moral and intellectual virtues. For Maimonides, God can only convey prophecy to those persons who have prepared themselves to be prophets.

ז:ג וְדַע, שֶׁכָּל־נָבִיא לֹא נִתְנַבֵּא אֶלָּא אַחַר שֶׁיִּהְיוּ לוֹ כָּל־הַמַּעֲלוֹת הַשִּׂכְלִיּוֹת, וְרֹב מַעֲלוֹת הַמִּדּוֹת וְהַחֲזָקוֹת שֶׁבָּהֶן, וְהוּא אָמְרָם: „אֵין הַנְּבוּאָה שׁוֹרָה, אֶלָּא עַל־חָכָם, גִּבּוֹר וְעָשִׁיר". וְ„חָכָם" — הוּא כּוֹלֵל כָּל־הַמַּעֲלוֹת הַשִּׂכְלִיּוֹת בְּלִי סָפֵק. וְ„עָשִׁיר" — הוּא מִמַּעֲלוֹת הַמִּדּוֹת, רְצוֹנִי לוֹמַר: הַהִסְתַּפְּקוּת, מִפְּנֵי שֶׁהֵם קוֹרְאִים הַמִּסְתַּפֵּק — עָשִׁיר. וְהוּא אָמְרָם בְּגֶדֶר הֶעָשִׁיר: „אֵיזֶהוּ עָשִׁיר? — הַשָּׂמֵחַ בְּחֶלְקוֹ", רְצוֹנוֹ לוֹמַר: שֶׁיַּסְפִּיק לוֹ בְּמַה־שֶּׁהִמְצִיא לוֹ זְמַנּוֹ, וְלֹא יִכְאַב בְּמַה־שֶּׁלֹּא הִמְצִיא לוֹ. וְכֵן „גִּבּוֹר" — הוּא גַם־כֵּן בְּמַעֲלוֹת הַמִּדּוֹת, רְצוֹנִי לוֹמַר: שֶׁיַּנְהִיג כֹּחוֹתָיו כְּפִי הַדַּעַת וְהָעֵצָה, כְּמוֹ שֶׁבֵּאַרְנוּ בַּפֶּרֶק הַחֲמִישִׁי, וְהוּא אָמְרוּ: „אֵיזֶהוּ גִבּוֹר? — הַכּוֹבֵשׁ אֶת־יִצְרוֹ".

7:3a You should know that a prophet prophesied only when he had achieved the intellectual virtues and most of the important moral virtues. This is what the sages meant when they said, "Prophecy rests only on a person who is wise, strong, and rich [B. Talmud, *Shabbat* 92a; *Nedarim* 38a]. The term "wise" encompasses all the intellectual virtues without any doubt. The term "rich" refers to moral qualities, particularly self-sufficiency. Such a person is called "rich" as the sages said in defining the rich person, "Who is rich? The one who rejoices in one's portion" [*Pirke Avot* 4:1]. Such a person is satisfied with what one has at a particular time. That person is not troubled by what he or she does not have. "Strong" also refers to ethical qualities. Such a person will conduct his or her life according to knowledge and according to counsel, as we have already explained in chapter 5. That is the meaning of the statement, "Who is strong? The person who controls one's inclinations" [*Pirke Avot* 4:1].

Prophets are humans. They may exhibit moral and intellectual flaws. When they do, they are separated from God and therefore cannot prophesy.

וְאֵין מִתְּנָאֵי הַנָּבִיא שֶׁיִּהְיוּ אֶצְלוֹ כָּל־מַעֲלוֹת הַמִּדּוֹת, עַד שֶׁלֹּא תַפְחִיתֵהוּ פְחִיתוּת — שֶׁהֲרֵי שְׁלֹמֹה הַמֶּלֶךְ, עָלָיו הַשָּׁלוֹם, הֵעִיד עָלָיו הַכָּתוּב: בְּגִבְעוֹן נִרְאָה יְיָ אֶל־שְׁלֹמֹה (מלכים־א ג, ה), וּמָצִינוּ לוֹ פְּחִיתוּת מִדּוֹת, וְהִיא: רֹב הַתַּאֲוָה, בְּבֵאוּר בְּהַרְבּוֹת נָשִׁים, וְזֶה מִפְּעֻלוֹת תְּכוּנַת רֹב הַתַּאֲוָה. וְאָמַר מְבֹאָר: הֲלֹא עַל־אֵלֶּה חָטָא שְׁלֹמֹה (נחמיה יג, כו). וְכֵן דָּוִד הַמֶּלֶךְ, עָלָיו הַשָּׁלוֹם, נָבִיא אָמַר: לִי דִּבֶּר צוּר יִשְׂרָאֵל (שמואל־ב כג, ג) — וּמָצָאנוּ אוֹתוֹ: בַּעַל־אַכְזָרִיּוּת. אַף־עַל־פִּי שֶׁלֹּא שִׁמֵּשׁ בָּהּ כִּי אִם בְּעוֹבְדֵי גִלּוּלִים וּבַהֲרִיגַת הַכּוֹפְרִים, וְהָיָה רַחֲמָן לְיִשְׂרָאֵל; אֲבָל בָּא בְּבֵאוּר בְּ„דִבְרֵי הַיָּמִים", שֶׁהַשֵּׁם־יִתְבָּרֵךְ לֹא הִרְשָׁהוּ לִבְנוֹת בֵּית־הַמִּקְדָּשׁ, וְלֹא הָיָה רָאוּי בְּעֵינָיו לָזֶה לְרֹב מַה־שֶּׁהָרַג. אָמַר: אַתָּה לֹא־תִבְנֶה בַיִת לִשְׁמִי כִּי דָמִים רַבִּים שָׁפַכְתָּ אַרְצָה לְפָנָי (דברי הימים־א כב, ח). וּמָצָאנוּ אֵלִיָּהוּ, זָכוּר לַטּוֹב, מִדַּת הָרַגְזָנוּת. וְאַף־עַל־פִּי שֶׁשִּׁמֵּשׁ בָּהּ בַּכּוֹפְרִים וַעֲלֵיהֶם הָיָה כוֹעֵס, אֲבָל אָמְרוּ הַחֲכָמִים: שֶׁהַשֵּׁם־יִתְבָּרֵךְ לְקָחוֹ וְאָמַר לוֹ, שֶׁאֵינוֹ רָאוּי לִמְשֹׁל בִּבְנֵי אָדָם וְלִהְיוֹת לָהֶם לְכֹהֵן, מִי שֶׁיֵּשׁ לוֹ קִנְאָה כְּמוֹ שֶׁיֵּשׁ לוֹ — כִּי יְמִיתֵם. וְכֵן מָצִינוּ בִשְׁמוּאֵל — שֶׁפָּחַד מִשָּׁאוּל; וּבְיַעֲקֹב — שֶׁפָּחַד מִפְּגִישַׁת עֵשָׂו. אֵלּוּ הַמִּדּוֹת וְכַיּוֹצֵא בָהֶן — הֵן מְחִיצוֹת בֵּין הַשֵּׁם־יִתְבָּרֵךְ עִם הַנְּבִיאִים, עֲלֵיהֶם הַשָּׁלוֹם. וּמִי שֶׁיֵּשׁ לוֹ שְׁתֵּי מִדּוֹת, אוֹ שָׁלֹשׁ מֵהֶן בִּלְתִּי מְמֻצָּעוֹת — כְּמוֹ שֶׁבֵּאַרְנוּ בַּפֶּרֶק הָרְבִיעִי — נֶאֱמַר בּוֹ: שֶׁרָאָה הַשֵּׁם־יִתְבָּרֵךְ מֵאַחַר שְׁתֵּי מְחִיצוֹת, אוֹ שָׁלֹשׁ.

7:3b It is not required that a prophet possess every ethical quality and that he or she be free from every flaw. We can see this in the case of Solomon the King, [who was a prophet] of whom it was written, "In Gibeon,

87

Adonai appeared to Solomon in a dream by night" [I Kings 3:5]. It is clear that Solomon had many moral flaws, one of which was lust: that psychic quality that caused him to increase the number of his wives. Scripture explicitly states this flaw: "Did not Solomon, king of Israel, sin by these things?" [Neh. 13:26]. David the King was also a prophet, as indicated by the verse, "The God of Israel said, 'The Rock of Israel spoke to me...'" [I Sam. 23:3]. Yet we find that he was cruel. Although he was kind to Israel, he was cruel to idolaters and killed heretics. Because of the many people whom David had slain, God considered him unworthy to build the Temple and did not permit him to do so. Thus we read, "But the word of *Adonai* came to me, saying... 'You shall not build a house for My name, because you have shed much blood on the earth in My sight'" [I Chron. 22:8]. We also find that Elijah the prophet was an angry man. Although his anger was directed toward heretics–according to the sages–God took him, telling him that because of his anger, he was unworthy to rule or to serve as a priest, for he might have put his people at risk [B. Talmud, *Sanhedrin* 113b]. We find that Samuel feared Saul and Jacob feared meeting Esau. These ethical lapses may be viewed as barriers between the prophets and God. One suffering from two or three of these lapses would hardly be a person of the "mean" described in chapter four. Such a person might be described as seeing God through two or three barriers.

Preparation for prophecy is both ethical and intellectual. To attain the intellectual virtues, one must proceed through the philosopher's curriculum of logic, mathematics, physics, and metaphysics. A deficiency in the intellectual virtues will preclude prophecy. A deficiency in the ethical virtues may not. Prophecy may be possible even were the would-be prophet to exhibit the ethical vice of anger.

ז:ד וְלֹא תַרְחִיק הֱיוֹת חֶסְרוֹן קְצָת הַמִּדּוֹת מְמַעֵט מִמַּדְרֵגַת הַנְּבוּאָה — שֶׁאֲנַחְנוּ מָצִינוּ קְצָת פְּחִיתוּת הַמִּדּוֹת יִמְנְעוּ הַנְּבוּאָה לְגַמְרִי, כַּכַּעַס. אָמְרוּ: „כָּל־הַכּוֹעֵס, אִם נָבִיא הוּא — נְבוּאָתוֹ מִסְתַּלֶּקֶת מִמֶּנּוּ". וְהֵבִיאוּ רְאָיָה מֵאֱלִישָׁע שֶׁנִּסְתַּלְּקָה מִמֶּנּוּ הַנְּבוּאָה כְּשֶׁכָּעַס — עַד שֶׁהֵסִיר כַּעֲסוֹ, וְהוּא אָמְרוּ: וְעַתָּה קְחוּ לִי מְנַגֵּן (מלכים־ב ג, טו).

7:4 Some moral lapses will diminish the ability to prophesy. Other [moral lapses], like anger for example, will totally [keep a person from prophesy]. The sages said that when a prophet becomes angry, he loses his ability to prophesy [B. Talmud, *Pesachim* 66b]. The prophet Elisha provided the basis of their statement; when he became angry, he lost his ability to prophesy until his anger passed. That is the meaning of the verse concerning Elisha, "'But now bring me a minstrel.' And it came to pass, when the minstrel played, that the hand of *Adonai* came upon him" [II Kings 3:15].

Certain other things, such as anguish, may also preclude prophecy. Maimonides cites the example of Jacob in anguish over the disappearance of Joseph.

ז:ה וּבַעֲבוּר הָאֲנָחָה וְהַדְּאָגָה שֶׁל יַעֲקֹב אָבִינוּ, עָלָיו הַשָּׁלוֹם, כָּל־יְמֵי הִתְאַבְּלוֹ עַל־יוֹסֵף — נִסְתַּלְּקָה מִמֶּנּוּ רוּחַ הַקֹּדֶשׁ, עַד שֶׁנִּתְבַּשֵּׂר בְּחַיָּיו. אָמַר: וַתְּחִי רוּחַ יַעֲקֹב אֲבִיהֶם (בראשית מה, כז). וְאָמַר הַמְתַרְגֵּם: „וּשְׁרַת רוּחַ נְבוּאָה עַל־יַעֲקֹב אֲבוּהוֹן". וּלְשׁוֹן הַחֲכָמִים: „אֵין הַנְּבוּאָה שׁוֹרָה לֹא מִתּוֹךְ עַצְלוּת וְלֹא מִתּוֹךְ עַצְבוּת — אֶלָּא מִתּוֹךְ שִׂמְחָה".

7:5 Anguish might preclude prophecy, as was the case with Jacob, who, mourning his lost son Joseph, had the Holy Spirit taken from him. It came back only when he heard the news that Joseph was alive. Thus, we read, "...the spirit of Jacob their father revived" [Gen. 45:27]. The *Targum* [on Gen. 45:27] interprets the verse, "And the spirit of prophecy rested on Jacob their father." According to the sages, prophecy does not descend during [a mood of] languor or sadness but only through joy [B. Talmud, *Shabbat* 30b; *Pesachim* 117a].

For Moses ben Maimon, Moses ben Amram was the greatest prophet (and therefore philosopher) of all. Yet even he was limited by his human nature. Commenting on Exodus 33:18ff., Maimonides notes that Moses was told that he could not see God's face. Maimonides understands this to mean that Moses could not know the true nature of God, since his intellect–like all human beings who are alive–was encased in the matter of his body. It is matter, claims Maimonides, in all its forms and permutations, that is the ultimate barrier of true knowledge. Moses came as close as is humanly possible to this knowledge.

ז:ו וְכַאֲשֶׁר יָדַע מֹשֶׁה רַבֵּנוּ, עָלָיו הַשָּׁלוֹם, שֶׁלֹּא נִשְׁאֲרָה לוֹ מְחִיצָה שֶׁלֹּא הֵסִיר אוֹתָהּ, וְכִי נִשְׁלְמוּ בּוֹ מַעֲלוֹת הַמִּדּוֹת כֻּלָּן וְהַמַּעֲלוֹת הַשִּׂכְלִיּוֹת כֻּלָּן — בִּקֵּשׁ לְהַשִּׂיג מַהוּת הַשֵּׁם־יִתְבָּרֵךְ עַל־אֲמִתַּת מְצִיאוּתוֹ — אַחַר שֶׁלֹּא נִשְׁאַר לוֹ מוֹנֵעַ — וְאָמַר: הַרְאֵנִי נָא אֶת־כְּבוֹדֶךָ (שמות לג, יח). וְהוֹדִיעוֹ הַשֵּׁם־יִתְבָּרֵךְ: שֶׁאִי־אֶפְשָׁר לוֹ זֶה, בִּהְיוֹתוֹ שֵׂכֶל נִמְצָא בְּחֹמֶר, רְצוֹנוֹ לוֹמַר: מֵאֲשֶׁר הוּא אָדָם,

וְהוּא אָמְרוֹ: כִּי לֹא־יִרְאַנִי הָאָדָם וָחָי (שָׁם, כ). הִנֵּה לֹא נִשְׁאֲרָה לוֹ בֵּינוֹ וּבֵין הַשָּׂגַת הַקָּדוֹשׁ־בָּרוּךְ־הוּא עַל־אֲמִתַּת מְצִיאוּתוֹ אֶלָּא מְחִיצָה אַחַת בִּהְירָה — וְהוּא הַשֵּׂכֶל הָאֱנוֹשִׁי שֶׁאֵינוֹ נִבְדָּל. וְגָמַל אֵלָיו יִתְבָּרֵךְ חֶסֶד בְּתֵת לוֹ מִן־הַהַשָּׂגָה — אַחַר שֶׁשָּׁאֲלָהּ — יוֹתֵר מִמַּה־שֶׁהָיָה אֶצְלוֹ קֹדֶם שְׁאֵלָתוֹ, וְהוֹדִיעוֹ: שֶׁתַּכְלִית הַהִיא אִי־אֶפְשָׁר לוֹ, מִפְּנֵי שֶׁהוּא בַּעַל גָּשֶׁם. וְכִנָּה אֲמִתַּת הַהַשָּׂגָה בִּ"רְאִיַת פָּנִים" — כִּי הָאָדָם כְּשֶׁיִּרְאֶה פְּנֵי חֲבֵרוֹ, תִּהְיֶה אָז בְּנַפְשׁוֹ חֲקוּקָה צוּרָתוֹ עַד שֶׁלֹּא יִתְעָרֵב לוֹ עִם זוּלָתוֹ, אֲפִלּוּ בְּשָׁעָה שֶׁאֵינוֹ רוֹאֶה אוֹתוֹ. אֲבָל כְּשֶׁיִּרְאֶה אֲחוֹרָיו — אַף־עַל־פִּי שֶׁהוּא מַכִּירוֹ בָּרְאִיָּה הַהִיא — פְּעָמִים יְסֻפַּק עָלָיו וְיִתְעָרֵב לוֹ עִם זוּלָתוֹ. כֵּן הַשָּׂגָתוֹ יִתְבָּרֵךְ עַל־הָאֱמֶת — הִיא: יְדִיעַת הַשֵּׁם־יִתְבָּרֵךְ מֵאֲמִתַּת מְצִיאוּתוֹ מַה־שֶׁלֹּא יִשְׁתַּתֵּף בְּמְצִיאוּת הַהִיא זוּלָתוֹ מִן־הַנִּמְצָאוֹת; עַד שֶׁיִּמְצָא בְנַפְשׁוֹ מְצִיאוּתוֹ חֲזָקָה וְנִבְדֶּלֶת עַל־מַה־שֶׁמָּצָא בְנַפְשׁוֹ מִמְּצִיאוּת שְׁאָר הַנִּמְצָאוֹת. וְאִי־אֶפְשָׁר לָאָדָם זֶה הַשִּׁעוּר מִן הַהַשָּׂגָה — אֶלָּא שֶׁהוּא, עָלָיו הַשָּׁלוֹם, הִשִּׂיג לְמַטָּה מִזֶּה מְעָט. וְהוּא אֲשֶׁר כִּנָּה וְאָמַר: וְרָאִיתָ אֶת־אֲחֹרָי (שמות לג, כג).

7:6 Only when Moses knew that he had perfected himself in every moral and intellectual virtue, and removed every impediment so that there were no barriers between God and himself, did he seek to know the true essence of God. Thus, Moses said, "Show me, I pray, Your glory" [Exod. 33:18]. God then informed him that that was impossible, because Moses' intellect was encased in matter as a human being. That is the meaning of the phrase "... for humans shall not see Me and live" [Exod. 33:20]. Only one clear barrier remained between God and Moses in the apprehension of the true nature of God: the fact that the human intellect is not separate [from matter while one is alive]. God graciously rewarded Moses by telling him what he had not known before he asked: as long as he had a body, what he sought was impossible for him to achieve. Scripture uses the term "seeing of the Face" to indicate true apprehension. When one sees the face of another person, that person's image is fixed in your mind and one does not mix that person with someone else [even when he does not see the person]. However, when one sees the back of another person, even though he may be acquainted with that person, he may be in doubt as to the identity of that person and may even confuse that person with someone else. So it is with the apprehension of God. The true knowledge of God is the awareness that nothing else among all other existing things participates in the Divine existence. One would find that God's

90

existence is totally different from the existence of anything else. No human being can fully comprehend this. Moses, however, comprehended something of this, as the verse suggests, "...and you shall see My back" [Exod. 33:23].

The book promised by Maimonides in the following paragraph was never written.

ז:ז וַאֲנִי עָתִיד לְהַשְׁלִים זֶה הָעִנְיָן בְּסֵפֶר הַנְּבוּאָה.

7:7 In the future, I will complete the discussion of this matter in a book on prophecy.

In this final section, Maimonides compares his rabbinical colleagues to the prophets and their ability to prophesy, noting that all humans, whether prophet or rabbi, are flawed by virtue of their being human. Moses, too, was human and therefore limited, but Moses was unparalleled. Maimonides returns to this theme of those things that are barriers to true knowledge in his *Guide for the Perplexed*. From the first chapter to the last in the *Guide*, in many different ways, Maimonides seeks to lead his reader away from attributing corporeality to the Deity because of its entailed notion of matter. In the *Guide* I:54 and III:54, Maimonides returns to the verses in Exodus 33:18ff. to argue that the knowledge of God is derived from a study of God's ways, which are God's actions manifested in reality. Nevertheless, the complete knowledge of God is available only after one's death, when the final impediment of matter has been removed (*Guide* III:51).

ז:ח וְכַאֲשֶׁר יָדְעוּ חֲכָמִים, זִכְרוֹנָם לִבְרָכָה, שֶׁשְּׁנֵי הַמִּינִים הָאֵלּוּ מִן הַפְּחִיתִיוֹת, רְצוֹנִי לוֹמַר: הַשִּׂכְלִיּוֹת וְהַמִּדּוֹת, הֵם אֲשֶׁר יַבְדִּילוּ בֵּין הַשֵּׁם־יִתְבָּרֵךְ וּבֵין הָאָדָם, וּבָהֶן הוּא יִתְרוֹן מַעֲלוֹת הַנְּבִיאִים, אָמְרוּ עַל־קְצָתָם בְּמַה־שֶּׁרָאוּ מֵחָכְמָתָם וּמִדּוֹתֵיהֶם: רְאוּיִים הֵם שֶׁתִּשְׁרֶה שְׁכִינָה עֲלֵיהֶם כְּמֹשֶׁה רַבֵּנוּ, עָלָיו הַשָּׁלוֹם. וְלֹא יֵעָלֵם מִמְּךָ עִנְיַן הַדִּמְיוֹן — שֶׁהֵם דִּמּוּ אוֹתָם בּוֹ, לֹא שֶׁהֶשְׁווּם אֵלָיו חָלִילָה. וְכֵן אָמְרוּ עַל־אֲחֵרִים: כִּיהוֹשֻׁעַ בִּן־נוּן, עַל־הַצַּד אֲשֶׁר זָכַרְנוּ. וְזֶה עִנְיָן אֲשֶׁר כֻּוַּנּוּ לְבָאֵר בְּזֶה הַפֶּרֶק.

7:8 The sages, seeing that most of the prophets had those intellectual and ethical defects, to some degree, that usually separate a person from God and yet they still prophesied, proposed that some of their own number [the thirty disciples of Hillel] whose wisdom and virtues they knew of, should also have had the Divine spirit rest upon them in the same manner as Moses [B. Talmud, *Sukkah* 28a; *Baba Batra* 134a]. The comparison [between Moses and the thirty disciples] that the sages made should not mislead you; they did not (God forbid!) equate the disciples to Moses. They spoke the same way in comparing others to Joshua. This is what we intended to explain in this chapter.

GLEANINGS

NATURAL PROPHECY

Nature and nature's God speak with myriads of voices, but only the gifted few hear their messages. What to us may seem but an ordinary landscape, appears enriched upon the canvass, with the artist's genius conveying truth that we, unaided, might never have recognized. While we hear nothing but empty sounds, the ear of the composer may perceive in them, the message of music. Thus nature spoke to a Mozart in an idiom all his own, which he translated into luminous symphonies. Similarly, nature's mysterious laws disclosed themselves to a Newton, a Darwin, and Edison, or an Einstein. These messages of beauty and of truth may come suddenly as inspirations, which men of genius subsequently check and develop and express in rational terms for all men to understand.

So it is with religion. Suddenly, like a flash of lightning, a great vision lights up within the mind of a prophet, such as ordinary men would not sense by themselves and which they may even reject and combat when they hear it. Nonetheless, the inspiration or revelation of the religious genius is of greatest significance for the people, investing human life with new meaning and promise. The prophets reveal God to men, and thus lead men from bondage to spiritual freedom.

(Samuel S. Cohon, *Religious Affirmations*. Los Angeles: 1983)

THE RELIGIOUS GENIUS OF PROPHECY

Talent may be practiced, it may even be acquired by laborious application; genius is a free gift, a gift of grace, a mark of consecration stamped upon man, that can never be acquired, if it be not in the man. Talent, therefore, can not overcome impediments and obstacles if they present themselves with overwhelming force, it can not thrive under unfavorable circumstances. Genius, on the other hand, advances its conquering force against the most untoward conditions, it opens a way, it must expand its force, for it is a living impulse, a power that is stronger than its possessor, a touch of the energy dispersed into nature but condensed in him, linking him with the Spirit of all spirits who manifests Himself to him by higher illumination. Talent propagates the knowledge which has been stored up, perfects it also now and then, and makes it the common property of all. Genius enriches humanity with new truths and perceptions, it gives the impulse to all great things that have come and are still to come to pass in this world.

(Abraham Geiger, *Judaism and Its History in Two Parts*, trans. Charles Newburgh. New York: The Bloch Publishing Co., 1911)

PROPHECY AS THE VOICE OF GOD

The voice of God as it manifests in the imagination has an existence separate from the imagination, but it is also shaped by the particular imagination which apprehends it. Its apprehension is proportionately imperfect according to the fallibility of humans. Some humans, by virtue of their extraordinary spiritual preparation and/or by the inexplicable gift of God, have transcended the limits of their imagination. These prophets hear the voice of God as it *is*—outside the particularity of their imagination.

(Ira F. Stone, *Seeking the Path to Life: Theological Meditations on God and the Nature of People, Love, Life and Death.* Woodstock, Vermont: Jewish Lights Publishing, 1992)

PROPHETIC INSPIRATION

There is a certain danger in attributing to religious experience the decisive religious value. Religion can no more be built on it than it can be built on mere prayer; it is only a means of becoming aware of religion. For the religious experience is not yet religion itself. The religious life will never be able to dispense with this experience, for in it faith raises itself, if not to its summit, then to a sacred height. Yet man lives neither for nor on his emotional moods. "To indulge in pious reveries is easier than to do what is right," and in the past men have had slight difficulty in reconciling pious reveries with deeds that were not right. Such moods of religious emotion may mislead one to suppose that they in themselves already constitute complete religion.

Judaism teaches that religion must not be a mere internalized experience, even of the most intense kind, but rather the very fulfillment of life. Though this may seem a mere verbal distinction, it is really a distinction within the soul. Only the right deed places man in the presence of God at all times and only it can be demanded of him at all times. Through it alone can man reach that deep inner unity with God, as well as that other unity with his fellow men. If the ideal embraces everybody and imposes its demand upon all, then men are brought together into a community of God. In the pious deed is the sustaining foundation of the confession of faith. It provides the secure religious foundation, common and equal to all, for the love of God and the trust in God. We cannot truly believe in what we do not practice. He who has not become sure of God by *doing* good, will not achieve a lasting realization of God's being through a mere inner experience. It is through man's deed that God reveals himself in life. "We will do and we will hear" (Exod. 24:7), says the old phrase in the account of the revelation in Exodus, with a meaning which overflows the vessel of its words. And as the Talmud later expresses it, "Take the commandments of God to your heart, for then you will know God, and you will have discovered his ways." Knowledge too proceeds from the will–from the will for the good.

Judaism also has its Word, but it is only one word–"to do." "The word is very nigh unto thee, in thy mouth, and in thy heart, that thou mayest do it" (Deut. 30:14). The deed becomes proof of conviction. Judaism too has its doctrine, but it is a doctrine of behavior, which must be explored in action in order that it may be fulfilled. Hence there is no doctrine in Judaism other than the expression of the divine *command*. "The secret things belong to the Lord our God: but those things which are revealed belong unto us and our children for ever that we may *do* all the words of this law" (Deut. 29:28).

(Leo Baeck, *The Essence of Judaism.* New York: Schocken Books, 1948)

SINAI AND PROPHECY

Entry into the covenant at Sinai is the root experience of Judaism, the central event that established the Jewish people. Given the importance of this event, there can be no verse in the Torah more disturbing to the feminist than Moses' warning to his people in Exodus 19:15, "Be ready for the third day; do not go near a woman." For here, at the very moment that the Jewish people stands at Sinai ready to receive the covenant—not now the covenant with individual patriarchs but with the people as a whole—at the very moment when Israel stands trembling waiting for God's presence to descend upon the mountain, Moses addresses the community only as men. The specific issue at stake is ritual impurity: An emission of semen renders both a man and his female partner temporarily unfit to approach the sacred (Lev. 15:16-18). But Moses does not say, "Men and women do not go near each other." At the central moment of Jewish history, women are invisible. Whether they too stood there trembling in fear and expectation, what they heard when the men heard these words of Moses, we do not know. It was not their experience that interested the chronicler or that informed and shaped the Torah.

Moses' admonition can be seen as a paradigm of what I have called "the profound injustice of Torah itself." In this passage, the Otherness of women finds its way into the very center of Jewish experience. And although the verse hardly can be blamed for women's situation, it sets forth a pattern recapitulated again and again in Jewish sources. Women's invisibility at the moment of entry into the covenant is reflected in the content of the covenant which, in both grammar and substance, addresses the community as male heads of household. It is perpetuated by the later tradition, which in its comments and codifications takes women as objects of concern or legislation but rarely sees them as shapers of tradition and actors in their own lives.

It is not just a historical injustice that is at stake in this verse, however. There is another dimension to the problem of the Sinai passage without which it is impossible to understand the task of Jewish feminism today. Were this passage simply the record of a historical event long in the past, the exclusion of women at this critical juncture would be troubling, but also comprehensible for its time. The Torah is not just history, however, but also living memory. The Torah reading, as a central part of the Sabbath and holiday liturgy, calls to mind and recreates the past for succeeding generations. When the story of Sinai is recited as part of the annual cycle of Torah readings and again as a special reading for Shavout, women each time hear ourselves thrust aside anew, eavesdropping on a conversation among men and between men and God. As Rachel Adler puts it, "Because the text has excluded her, she is excluded again in this yearly re-enactment and will be excluded over and over, year by year, every time she rises to hear the covenant read." If the covenant is a covenant with all generations (Deut. 29:13ff), then its reappropriation also involves the continual reappropriation of women's marginality.

This passage in Exodus is one of the places in the Tanakh where women's silence is so deeply charged, so overwhelming, that it can provoke a crisis for the Jewish feminist. As Rachel Adler says, "We are being invited by Jewish men to re-covenant, to forge a covenant which will address the inequalities of women's position in Judaism, but we ask ourselves, "Have we ever had a covenant in the first place? Are women Jews?" This is a question asked at the edge of a deep abyss. How can we ever hope to fill the silence that shrouds Jewish women's past? If women are invisible from the first moment of Jewish history, can we hope to become visible now? How many of us will fight for years to change the institutions in which we find ourselves only to achieve token victories? Perhaps we should put our energy elsewhere, into the creation of new communities where we can be fully present and where our struggles will not come up against walls as old as our beginnings.

(Judith Plaskow, *Standing Again at Sinai*. New York: Harper and Row, 1990)

REVELATION AND PROPHECY

What Does an Independent God Reveal?

In the existentialistic theologies of Rosenzweig and Buber, God has independent reality and can therefore provide something to human beings that they cannot acquire on their own. Yet both thinkers so respect science that they seek to explain the divine input as not blatantly clashing with its findings. They do this by reinterpreting God's revelation by analogy with interpersonal communication.

The shortness of Rosenzweig's life prevented his taking this analogy much beyond a description of revelation as love, a relationship that commands imperatively if essentially nonverbally. Buber explained this same experience of obligation and aspiration as resulting from the I–thou relationship. Two aspects of this situation impinge critically on Buber's doctrine of revelation: command without regulation and God's gift of presence.

The former notion arises from a curious fact about interpersonal intimacy: The meaning born between the partners transcends anything they did or said together. In reflection, it must be called ineffable. Yet it was real and, in its own way, commanding; the relationship will not be the same if we do not act on it. What exactly we must now do depends on us, and in filling in the details of our duty we testify to the nature of our relationship. That being so, what was given us in the revelation–meeting can strictly only be called "presence." The other gave us not rules but self and with it the empowerment of the I-thou relationship. So, too, God "speaks" and "commands" by being there with us; and we, heavy with the meaning we have come to know, then create the acts or write the accounts that will carry this truth into our lives. Religious practices and texts arise entirely from the human side of the relationship but do so in living response to encounters with the real God. They remain sacred as long as they authentically reflect or renew our relationship with God.

It remains to be added that an act is involved here. God must give presence or, if you prefer, become present. Without the Other, there is no genuine encounter, and nothing we might do can force it into being: If we cannot produce it on demand even with people, how much the less might we do so with God? When it happens that we occasionally find God before us–mostly as indirect participant in other I-thou meetings but also in direct, "person-to-person" encounter–that is a gift. God, not normally present to us in this way, has appeared and, in so doing, has given us revelation.

(Eugene B. Borowitz, *Renewing the Covenant: A Theology for the Postmodern Jew.* Philadelphia: The Jewish Publication Society, 1991)

THINGS THAT SEPARATE GOD FROM PEOPLE

Both Judaism and feminism offer us visions of a life that is *integrated*. When we think of ourselves as coming in separable pieces that can be pulled out or pushed under as the moment or context changes, we deny our wholeness. When we see our "separate parts" as a unity, however, and recognize the fullness of our personhood, that experience is deeply spiritual.

Thinking of ourselves as separable denies the interrelationship among our various aspects. I might characterize myself, for example, as Jewish, feminist, anarchist, political scientist. But those identities are not simply additive—each affects, and is part of, the others and of my understanding of myself. Our ability to experience a sense of our full selves depends, in some crucial respects, on *not* making those distinctions. And our ability not to make them depends on the existence of communities that will *support* the full range of our beings.

We need to look differently at what we mean by "community." We tend to think of communities as based on *same-ness*—held together by what we have in common. As a consequence, any recognition of diversity is seen as a threat to the unity of the community.

As American Jews have long been aware, however, there is also a sense in which our communities consist of a multitude of smaller communities. *Aspects* of ourselves are nourished by different groups or communities, each of which contributes to our development, and each of which deserves some "recognition" in that larger community of which we are a part.

Within the context of the feminist movement, for example, we are coming to see that there is probably no such thing as *woman*. Each of us is rooted in the particular cultural, ethnic, or religious communities in which she grew up and to which she is, to some extent, connected. To ask of one another that we discard those identities in the name of an abstract *womanhood* is to deny the richness of our particular lives. Similarly, as Jews within American culture, we have resisted the denial of our particularities in the name of abstract *Americanism*.

We need to begin to think similarly about the Jewish community itself. If the Jewish community is to meet the needs of *all* of its members, it cannot continue to see itself (and to act) as a monolithic whole, as if all Jews were alike. Our communities must recognize our individuality and our rootedness in *other* communities that also nurture aspects of our identities. Paradoxically then, if we are to feel fully integrated as persons, we need to feel our roots in multiple communities. Any community which is to nurture that wholeness must actively welcome diversity into its very definition.

We must think about how to structure our communities so that *all* Jews—women as well as men, singles as well as married, gays or lesbians as well as heterosexuals, the young and old as well as the middle-aged—will feel comfortable and welcome. Such a recognition of diversity—that takes seriously its implications for programming, education, liturgy, and community organization—will allow each of us to realize our full sense of self within the context of the community.

(Martha Ackelsberg, "Rabbis Are People Too: Politics, Spirituality, and the Jewish Community," *Reconstructionist*, vol. 52, no. 1 [September 1986]: 21-22)

MARTHA ACKELSBERG (1946-). *Professor of government and of women's studies at Smith College, where she is also a member of the Committee on Jewish Studies. She was a founding member of Ezrat Nashim (the first women's organization in recent years to argue for equality for women in Judaism) and of B'not Esh, a Jewish feminist spirituality collective.*

CHAPTER EIGHT

On Being Human

As moderns, we may not be willing to accept Maimonides' corporeal theory of the temperaments for example, the idea that the person [with a dry physical structure would be apt to learn]. However, his insight into the relationship between nurture and nature reflects our modern understanding of human development. Regardless of the potential inherent in the individual, that potential will never be realized if it is never activated. However, those not born with the potential may, with a great deal of struggle, reach a similarly high level of achievement.

ח:א אִי אֶפְשָׁר שֶׁיִּוָּלֵד הָאָדָם מִתְּחִלַּת עִנְיָנוֹ בְּטֶבַע בַּעַל מַעֲלָה, וְלֹא בַעַל חִסָּרוֹן, כְּמוֹ שֶׁאִי־אֶפְשָׁר שֶׁיִּוָּלֵד הָאָדָם בְּטֶבַע בַּעַל מְלָאכָה מִן־הַמְּלָאכוֹת. אֲבָל אֶפְשָׁר לָאָדָם שֶׁיִּוָּלֵד בְּטֶבַע מוּכָן לְמַעֲלָה אוֹ לְחִסָּרוֹן, בִּהְיוֹת פְּעֻלַּת הָאַחַת מֵהֶן יוֹתֵר קַלָּה עָלָיו מִפְּעֻלַּת הָאַחֶרֶת. וְהַמָּשָׁל בּוֹ: כְּשֶׁיִּהְיֶה הָאָדָם מִזְגוֹ נוֹטֶה אֶל הַיֹּבֶשׁ וְיִהְיֶה עֶצֶם מֹחוֹ זַךְ, וְהַלֵּחוּת בּוֹ מְעַטָּה — יֵקַל עָלָיו לִגְרֹס וְלִזְכֹּר, וּלְהָבִין הָעִנְיָנִים יוֹתֵר מִבַּעַל לֵחָה לְבָנָה רַב־הַלֵּחוּת בַּמֹּחַ. אֲבָל אִם יֻנַּח הָאִישׁ הַהוּא הַמּוּכָן בְּמִזְגוֹ אֶל זֹאת הַמַּעֲלָה מִבִּלְתִּי לְמֹד כְּלָל, וְלֹא יְעוֹרֵר כֹּחוֹתָיו — יִשָּׁאֵר סָכָל בְּלִי סָפֵק. וְכֵן כְּשֶׁיְּלַמְּדוּ זֶה הֶעָב הַטֶּבַע, רַב־הַלֵּחוּת — יֵדַע וְיָבִין, אֲבָל בְּקֹשִׁי. וְעַל־זֶה הַמִּין בְּעַצְמוֹ יִמָּצֵא אִישׁ שֶׁמֶּזֶג לִבּוֹ יוֹתֵר חַם מִמַּה־שֶּׁצָּרִיךְ — יִהְיֶה גִּבּוֹר, רְצוֹנִי לוֹמַר: מוּכָן לִגְבוּרָה. אִם יְלַמְּדוּהוּ הַגְּבוּרָה — יִהְיֶה גִּבּוֹר בִּמְהֵרָה בְּלִי סָפֵק. וְאַחֵר, מֶזֶג לִבּוֹ יוֹתֵר קַר מִמַּה־שֶּׁצָּרִיךְ וְהוּא מוּכָן לְצַד הַמֹּרֶךְ וְהַפַּחַד, וּכְשֶׁיְּלַמְּדוּהוּ וְיַרְגִּילוּהוּ — יְקַבְּלֵם מְהֵרָה. וְאִם יְכַוְּנוּ בּוֹ הַגְּבוּרָה — לֹא יָשׁוּב גִּבּוֹר רַק בְּקֹשִׁי גָדוֹל, אֲבָל יָשׁוּב כְּשֶׁיַּרְגִּילוּהוּ בְּלִי סָפֵק.

8:1 No person is ever born perfected in every virtue or corrupted by every vice any more than any person is born as a particular kind of artisan. One may be born with a tendency toward some virtue or some vice, so that it is easier for that person to act on the one or the other. For example, were a person's physical structure to be on the dry side, then one's brain matter would be clearer, less moist. Such a person would find it easier to study, to remember, and to understand than would a person whose somatic structure was less dry and whose brain, therefore, was more moist. However, if a person inclined by nature to study were not so motivated and were not to study at all, then without any doubt, that person would remain ignorant. On the other hand, were the person with the moist nature to receive instruction and study, s/he would learn and understand, albeit with difficulty. Similarly, one may find a person whose temperament is abnormally hot. Such a person would be inclined to be a hero and with proper training would rapidly become one. Another person might possess an abnormally cold temperament. Such a person would be inclined to be a coward; it would take much to make that person a hero. However, even such a person could be trained to be a hero, although it would take great dedication and great exertion.

Maimonides anticipates a critique of his understanding of the human psyche. Whether the challenge comes from astrology or some other area, he argues that the individual has free will to act and is not prevented from acting by an external force. Without free will, there would be no point to a system of positive and negative *mitzvot*.

ח:ב וְאָמְנָם בֵּאַרְתִּי לְךָ זֶה, שֶׁלֹּא תַחְשֹׁב הַשִּׁגְעוֹנוֹת אֲשֶׁר יִשְׁקְרוּ בָהֶם חַכְמֵי הַכּוֹכָבִים — אֲמִתִּיוֹת. כִּי יַחְשְׁבוּ שֶׁמּוֹלַד הָאָדָם יְשִׂימֵהוּ בַּעַל מַעֲלָה, אוֹ בַעַל חֶסָרוֹן; וְשֶׁהָאִישׁ מֻכְרָח עַל-הַמַּעֲשִׂים הָהֵם בְּהֶכְרֵחַ. אָמְנָם אֲנִי יוֹדֵעַ, שֶׁהַדָּבָר הַמֻּסְכָּם עָלָיו מִתּוֹרָתֵנוּ וּמִפִּילוֹסוֹפֵי יָוָן, כְּמוֹ שֶׁאִמְּתוּהוּ טַעֲנוֹת הָאֱמֶת: שֶׁפְּעֻלּוֹת הָאָדָם כֻּלָּן מְסוּרוֹת לוֹ אֵין מַכְרִיחַ אוֹתוֹ בָּהֶן, וְלֹא מֵבִיא אוֹתוֹ זוּלַת עַצְמוֹ — כְּלָל, שֶׁיַּטֵּהוּ לְצַד מַעֲלָה, אוֹ לְצַד חֶסָרוֹן — אֶלָּא-אִם-כֵּן תִּהְיֶה לוֹ הֲכָנַת הַמִּזְגִּים לְבַד, כְּמוֹ שֶׁבֵּאַרְנוּ: שֶׁיֵּקַל לוֹ עִנְיָן, אוֹ יִכְבַּד; אֲבָל שֶׁיִּתְחַיֵּב, אוֹ יִהְיֶה-בּוֹ נִמְנָע — אֵין זֶה כְּלָל. וְאִלּוּ הָיָה הָאָדָם מֻכְרָח עַל-פְּעֻלּוֹתָיו — יִהְיוּ בְּטֵלוֹת מִצְווֹת הַתּוֹרָה וְאַזְהָרוֹתֶיהָ וְהָיָה הַכֹּל שֶׁקֶר גָּמוּר, אַחַר שֶׁאֵין בְּחִירָה לָאָדָם בְּמַה-שֶּׁיַּעֲשֶׂה.

8:2a I have made the point of explaining this to you so that you should not think that the asinine arguments of the astrologers are correct. They wrongly think that the astrological situation at the moment of birth determines a person's life by fixing permanently certain benefits and/or defects. There is general agreement to the contrary–whether we look at our Torah or we look at the proofs presented by the Greek philosophers–that every human being can control his/her actions;

nothing external impels a person to act in any particular manner. Although one's somatic structure may make it easier or more difficult, moving toward virtue or vice is up to the individual. Were a person to be compelled to or inhibited from acting, the entire system of Torah *mitzvot*, both positive and negative, would be nullified and everything [related to it] would be utterly false.

Continuing his line of reasoning, Maimonides argues that were a person not to have free will–the ability to choose and to act upon one's choice–then learning would be of no value. Moreover, no persons could be held responsible for any of their actions. The notion of free will and its adjacent responsibility for one's actions seems to be at risk in much of modern society. Nature and/or nurture is blamed for many things as if people were forced from within or from without to do what they do. Whether in the airy theoretical realm of academe or the earthy realm of the criminal court, the argument is made that either one's genes or one's environment determines human action. The individual, it is argued, has little choice in the matter.

וְכֵן הָיָה מִתְחַיֵּב בִּטּוּל הַלִּמּוּד וְהַהִתְלַמְּדוּת, וְלִמּוּד כָּל־מְלֶאכֶת־מַחֲשֶׁבֶת. הָיָה כָּל־זֶה הֶבֶל וּלְבַטָּלָה, אַחַר שֶׁהָאָדָם אִי־אֶפְשָׁר לוֹ כְּלָל — מִפְּנֵי הַגּוֹרֵם הַמַּכְרִיחַ אוֹתוֹ מֵחוּץ זוּלָתוֹ, לְפִי דַעַת הָאוֹמְרִים זֶה — שֶׁלֹּא יַעֲשֶׂה הַפֹּעַל הַפְּלוֹנִי, וּמִבְּלִי שֶׁיֵּדַע הַחָכְמָה הַפְּלוֹנִית, וְשֶׁלֹּא תִהְיֶה לוֹ הַמִּדָּה הַפְּלוֹנִית. וְהָיָה הַגְּמוּל וְהָעֹנֶשׁ גַּם־כֵּן עָוֶל גָּמוּר: הֵן מִמֶּנּוּ קְצָתֵנוּ לִקְצָתֵנוּ, הֵן מֵהַשֵּׁם־יִתְבָּרֵךְ לָנוּ. שֶׁזֶּה שִׁמְעוֹן שֶׁהָרַג לִרְאוּבֵן — אַחַר שֶׁזֶּה מֻכְרָח שֶׁיַּהֲרֹג, וְזֶה מֻכְרָח שֶׁיֵּהָרֵג — לָמָּה נַעֲנֹשׁ שִׁמְעוֹן? וְאֵיךְ יִתָּכֵן גַּם־כֵּן עָלָיו יִתְבָּרֵךְ, צַדִּיק וְיָשָׁר הוּא, שֶׁיַּעֲנִישֵׁהוּ עַל פֹּעַל שֶׁאִי־אֶפְשָׁר לוֹ שֶׁלֹּא יַעֲשֵׂהוּ; וַאֲפִלּוּ הִשְׁתַּדֵּל שֶׁלֹּא יַעֲשֵׂהוּ לֹא הָיָה יָכוֹל?

8:2b If a person had no choice in any action, then education of any kind would be purposeless. Even the study of a trade would be senseless if, as those who hold this view think, some external factor could prevent a person from entering that trade. If such a factor could prevent the learning of a particular science or the achieving of a particular [moral] quality, then reward and punishment would be totally unjust, whether carried out by us or by God. If Simon killed Reuben because Simon was destined to be a murderer and Reuben was destined to be murdered, why should Simon be punished? Why would God, who is righteous and just, punish a person for doing what, no matter the exertion, that person could not help doing?

Maimonides will argue that people are responsible for their actions. To believe otherwise is blasphemous. Torah offers the individual the choice of doing *mitzvot*, which, in turn, offers the individual life.

וְהָיוּ בְּטֵלוֹת גַּם־כֵּן הַהֲכָנוֹת כֻּלָּן עַד סוֹפָן: מִבְּנוֹת בָּתִּים, וְכִנּוּס הַמָּמוֹן, וְלִבְרֹחַ בְּעֵת הַפַּחַד, וְזוּלָתָם מִן־הַדּוֹמִים לָהֶם — כִּי אֲשֶׁר נִגְזַר שֶׁיִּהְיֶה, אִי־אֶפְשָׁר מִבִּלְתִּי הֱיוֹתוֹ? — וְזֶה כֻּלּוֹ שֶׁקֶר גָּמוּר וּכְנֶגֶד הַמֻּשְׂכָּל וְהַמֻּרְגָּשׁ; וַהֲרִיסוּת חוֹמַת הַתּוֹרָה; וְלִגְזֹר עַל הַשֵּׁם־יִתְבָּרֵךְ בְּעָוֶל, חָלִילָה לוֹ מִמֶּנּוּ. אָמְנָם, הָאֱמֶת אֲשֶׁר אֵין סָפֵק בּוֹ, שֶׁפְּעֻלּוֹת הָאָדָם כֻּלָּן מְסוּרוֹת לוֹ: אִם יִרְצֶה — יַעֲשֶׂה; וְאִם לֹא יִרְצֶה — לֹא יַעֲשֶׂה, מִבִּלְתִּי הֶכְרֵחַ שֶׁיַּכְרִיחֵהוּ עָלָיו — וּמִפְּנֵי זֶה רָאוּי לְצַוּוֹתוֹ. אָמַר: רְאֵה נָתַתִּי לְפָנֶיךָ הַיּוֹם אֶת־הַחַיִּים וְאֶת־הַטּוֹב, אֶת־הַבְּרָכָה וְאֶת־הַקְּלָלָה — וּבָחַרְתָּ בַּחַיִּים (דברים ל, טו־יט), וְשָׁם הַבְּחִירָה לָנוּ בָּהֶם. וְחִיֵּב הָעֹנֶשׁ לְמִי שֶׁיַּמְרֶה; וְהַגְּמוּל לְמִי שֶׁיַּעֲבֹד: אִם תִּשְׁמְעוּ; וְאִם לֹא תִשְׁמְעוּ. וְחִיֵּב הַלִּמּוּד וְהַהִתְלַמְּדוּת: וְלִמַּדְתֶּם אֹתָם אֶת־בְּנֵיכֶם (שם יא, יט) וּלְמַדְתֶּם אֹתָם וּשְׁמַרְתֶּם לַעֲשֹׂתָם (שם ה, א), וְכָל־מַה־שֶּׁבָּא בְּלִמּוּד הַמִּצְווֹת.

8:2c Every human activity, whether it is building houses, accumulating money, escaping from danger, or anything else, would make no sense if everything were predestined and if it were impossible to make any changes. Such a view is absolutely false! It goes against reason and experience. It would destroy the purpose of the Torah and would impute injustice to God. The truth, without a doubt, is that each person controls his/her actions. Whatever a person wants to do, that person can do; likewise, whatever a person does not want to do, that person need not do. No outside force compels any action. Therefore, it makes sense that each person is charged with the performance of *mitzvot*. Thus, it is written, "See, I have set before you today life and good and death and evil...therefore choose life so that you may live..." [Deut. 30:15, 19]. Choice is joined to life. Punishment, then, is fitting for the person who rebels, and reward is fitting for the person who obeys. This is the meaning of the biblical phrases "If you will hearken..." and "if you will not hearken." Teaching and studying are required, as it is written, "And you will teach them [to] your children" [Deut. 11:19] and "...that you may learn them, and observe to do them" [Deut. 5:1]. Indeed, everything is included in the study of the *mitzvot*.

The discussion of free will brings Maimonides further into an examination of determinism or fatalism. Because we have free will, he argues, we can also direct the outcome of future events. They are not predetermined. Not even God can compel us to do something–even were that something a *mitzvah* that would bring us blessing.

וְחַיָּב גַּם־כֵּן הַהֲכָנוֹת כֻּלָּן, כְּמוֹ שֶׁכָּתוּב בַּתּוֹרָה: כִּי תִבְנֶה בַּיִת חָדָשׁ וְעָשִׂיתָ מַעֲקֶה לְגַגֶּךָ וְלֹא תָשִׂים דָּמִים בְּבֵיתֶךָ (דברים כב, ח); פֶּן־יָמוּת בַּמִּלְחָמָה (שם כ, ה־ז); בַּמֶּה יִשְׁכָּב; (שמות כב, יז); לֹא יַחֲבֹל רֵחַיִם וָרָכֶב (דברים כד, ו), וְהַרְבֵּה בַּתּוֹרָה וּבַנְּבִיאִים מִזֶּה הָעִנְיָן, רְצוֹנִי לוֹמַר: הַהֲכָנוֹת. אֲבָל מַה־שֶּׁנִּמְצָא לַחֲכָמִים, עֲלֵיהֶם הַשָּׁלוֹם, וְהוּא אָמְרָם: „הַכֹּל בִּידֵי שָׁמַיִם חוּץ מִיִּרְאַת שָׁמַיִם" — הִיא גַּם־כֵּן אֱמֶת, וְנוֹטֶה לְצַד מַה־שֶּׁזְּכַרְנוּ. אֶלָּא שֶׁהַרְבֵּה פְּעָמִים יִטְעוּ בּוֹ בְּנֵי אָדָם וְיַחְשְׁבוּ קְצָת פְּעֻלּוֹת הָאָדָם הַבָּאוֹת לִבְחִירָתוֹ, שֶׁהוּא מֻכְרָח עֲלֵיהֶם: כְּזִוּוּג פְּלוֹנִי, אוֹ הֱיוֹת הַמָּמוֹן בְּיָדוֹ — וְזֶה בִּלְתִּי אֱמֶת. כִּי זֹאת הָאִשָּׁה אֲשֶׁר לְקָחָהּ בִּכְתֻבָּה וְקִדּוּשִׁין וְהִיא כְשֵׁרָה לוֹ, וּלְקָחָהּ לוֹ לִפְרִיָּה וְרִבְיָה, וְהִיא מִצְוָה — וְהַשֵּׁם־יִתְבָּרֵךְ לֹא יִגְזֹר בַּעֲשִׂיַּת הַמִּצְוָה. וְאִם יְהֵא בַּנִּשּׂוּאִין אִסּוּר, הִיא עֲבֵרָה.

8:2d Preparations for future events are also under our control, as indicated by the Torah's directive "When you build a new house, then you should make a parapet for your roof so that you do not bring blood on your house, if anyone falls off of it" [Deut. 22:8] and the statement "... lest he die in the battle" [Deut. 20:5, 6, 7]. The same sense of control of the future is also indicated in the statement "... where will he sleep?" [Exod. 22:25] and in the statement "No one shall take the mill or the upper millstone as a pledge for [it is equivalent to] taking a person's life as a pledge" [Deut. 24:6]. There are many examples of this kind elsewhere in the Torah and in the Prophets. However, the statement of the rabbis that "everything is in the hands of Heaven except for the fear of Heaven" [B. Talmud, *Berakhot* 33a; *Megillah* 25a; *Niddah* 16b] is also true and relates to what we have mentioned. However, some people have occasionally misunderstood this rabbinic statement. Such people thought that there were certain activities that might seem freely chosen but were really predestined, like a particular marital match or the achievement of some financial success. This is simply not true! For example, marrying the right person for the right reasons in the right way involves the performance of *mitzvot*, yet God cannot compel any person to perform any *mitzvah*. Were a marriage to be forbidden for some reason and yet take place, then those who married would have committed a sin.

As with a *mitzvah*, so with *averah*. God cannot compel us to sin. While modern science may attempt to explain a variety of things that take place in nature, Maimonides argues that only the things not under our control (like the fall of rain or how tall we become) are under God's direction.

וְהַשֵּׁם לֹא יִגְזֹר בַּעֲשִׂיַּת הָעֲבֵרָה. וְכֵן זֶה אֲשֶׁר גָּזַל מָמוֹן פְּלוֹנִי, אוֹ גְּנָבוֹ מִמֶּנּוּ, אוֹ הוֹנָה אוֹתוֹ וְכִחֵשׁ בּוֹ וְנִשְׁבַּע עָלָיו בְּשֶׁקֶר — אִם נֹאמַר, שֶׁהַשֵּׁם־יִתְבָּרֵךְ גָּזַר עַל־זֶה שֶׁיַּגִּיעַ זֶה הַמָּמוֹן לְיָדוֹ, וְשֶׁיֵּצֵא מִיַּד זֶה הָאַחֵר — כְּבָר גָּזַר בָּעֲבֵרָה? וְאֵין הָעִנְיָן כֵּן. אֲבָל כָּל פְּעֻלּוֹת הָאָדָם מְסוּרוֹת לוֹ וּתְלוּיוֹת בִּבְחִירָתוֹ — בָּהֵן בְּלֹא סָפֵק יִמָּצְאוּ הַמִּצְווֹת וְהָעֲבֵרוֹת. כִּי כְּבָר בֵּאַרְנוּ בַּפֶּרֶק הַשֵּׁנִי: שֶׁמִּצְווֹת הַתּוֹרָה וְאַזְהָרוֹתֶיהָ הֵן בַּפְּעֻלּוֹת אֲשֶׁר לָאָדָם בָּהֵן בְּחִירָה שֶׁיַּעֲשֵׂם, אוֹ שֶׁלֹּא יַעֲשֵׂם. וּבְזֶה הַחֵלֶק מִן־הַנֶּפֶשׁ תִּמָּצֵא יִרְאַת שָׁמַיִם, וְאֵינָהּ בִּידֵי שָׁמַיִם — אֲבָל נִמְסְרָה לִבְחִירַת הָאָדָם, כְּמוֹ שֶׁבֵּאַרְנוּ. אִם־כֵּן מַהוּ אָמְרָם: "הַכֹּל בִּידֵי שָׁמַיִם"? אָמְנָם יִרְצוּ בוֹ הָעִנְיָנִים הַטִּבְעִיִּים, אֲשֶׁר אֵין בְּחִירָה לָאָדָם בָּהֶם, כְּגוֹן: בִּהְיוֹתוֹ אָרֹךְ, אוֹ קָצָר; אוֹ רֶדֶת הַמָּטָר, אוֹ עֲצִירָה, אוֹ הֶפְסֵד הָאֲוִיר, אוֹ זַכּוּתוֹ וְכַיּוֹצֵא בָהֶם מִכָּל־מַה־שֶּׁבָּעוֹלָם — זוּלַת תְּנוּעַת הָאָדָם וּמְנוּחָתוֹ.

8:2e However, God does not compel anyone to sin. If someone stole money, robbed someone, or struck someone, and then, swearing falsely, denied doing it, and we were to say that God had decreed that the money was to be conveyed from one to the other, then we would have to say that God had decreed that a transgression take place. That just can't be true. Undoubtedly, every person's actions are controllable by that person, dependent only on his/her choice. Hence, one can speak of *mitzvot* and *averot*. We have already explained in chapter 2 that the positive and negative *mitzvot* assume our ability to act or refrain from acting. Consequently, "the fear of Heaven" is to be found in the part of the human soul not in "the hands of Heaven," specifically in our ability to choose. So one may ask, what did the rabbis mean by "Everything is in power of Heaven"? By "everything," they meant those things of nature that are not under our control, like being tall or short, having or not having abundant rainfall, having polluted or clean air, and all other things in nature unrelated to human activity.

Because we are free, we are responsible for our actions, whether for good or for evil. God does not decide for us. We decide whether we perform *mitzvot* or commit *averot*. It is therefore appropriate for us to atone for our sins, because we are responsible for them.

ח:ג וְאָמְנָם זֶה הָעִנְיָן אֲשֶׁר בֵּאֲרוּ חֲכָמִים, שֶׁהַמִּצְווֹת וְהָעֲבֵרוֹת אֵינָן בִּידֵי שָׁמַיִם
וְלֹא בִּרְצוֹנוֹ, אֲבָל בִּרְצוֹן הָאָדָם — נִמְשְׁכוּ בָזֶה אַחַר דִּבְרֵי יִרְמְיָהוּ, עָלָיו
הַשָּׁלוֹם, וְהוּא אָמְרוֹ: מִפִּי עֶלְיוֹן לֹא תֵצֵא הָרָעוֹת וְהַטּוֹב (איכה ג, לח).
שֶׁ„הָרָעוֹת״ — הֵם: הַמַּעֲשִׂים הָרָעִים, וְ„הַטּוֹב״ — הֵם: הַמַּעֲשִׂים הַטּוֹבִים.
וְאָמַר: שֶׁהַשֵּׁם־יִתְבָּרֵךְ אֵינוֹ גּוֹזֵר עַל־הָאָדָם לַעֲשׂוֹת רַע, אוֹ טוֹב. וְאַחַר שֶׁהָעִנְיָן
כֵּן — רָאוּי לָאָדָם לְהִתְאוֹנֵן וְלִבְכּוֹת עַל מַה־שֶּׁעָשָׂה מִן הַחֲטָאִים וְהָעֲבֵרוֹת,
אַחַר שֶׁפָּשַׁע בִּרְצוֹנוֹ, וְאָמַר: מַה־יִּתְאוֹנֵן אָדָם חַי, גֶּבֶר עַל־חֲטָאָיו (שם, לט).
וְאַחַר־כָּךְ שָׁב וְאָמַר: שֶׁרְפוּאוֹת זֶה הַחֳלִי בְּיָדֵינוּ. כִּי כְמוֹ שֶׁפָּשַׁעְנוּ בִּבְחִירָתֵנוּ
— כֵּן לָנוּ לָשׁוּב מִמַּעֲשֵׂינוּ הָרָעִים; וְאָמַר אַחַר־כָּךְ: נַחְפְּשָׂה דְרָכֵינוּ וְנַחְקֹרָה
וְנָשׁוּבָה עַד ה׳, נִשָּׂא לְבָבֵנוּ אֶל־כַּפָּיִם, אֶל־אֵל בַּשָּׁמָיִם (שם, מ־מא).

8:3 The sages made it clear that the performance of *mitzvot* and the commission of transgressions were not in the "hands of Heaven," under Divine control. Rather, they were under human control. Here they followed the statement of Jeremiah that "out of the mouth of the Most High proceeds not evil nor good" [Lam. 3:38]. By "good" Jeremiah meant good deeds, and by "evil" he meant evil deeds. Thus he proclaimed that God does not decree that a person must do good or evil. It is therefore fitting that a person should mourn and weep for the sins and transgressions that have been committed as a result of following one's own will. Scripture consequently states, "Why does a living person complain, a strong person because of his [or her] sins" [Lam. 3:39]. Jeremiah tells us that the cure for the affliction is in our own hands: just as we sinned by choice, we can repent by choice. He says, "Let us search and try our ways, and return to *Adonai*. Let us lift up our heart with our hands to God in the heavens" [Lam. 3:40-41].

Maimonides relates human will to the Divine will. He will argue that the Divine will is changeless and eternal. His view differs from the view of the *Mutakallimun*, who argued that the Divine will operates from moment to moment. Their view of the Divine followed from their denial of any metaphysical structure in the universe. Maimonides' view suggests that the Divine will is unrelated to the human will.

ח:ד אֲבָל הַמַּאֲמָר הַמְפֻרְסָם אֵצֶל בְּנֵי אָדָם, וְגַם יִמָּצְאוּ מִמֶּנּוּ בְּדִבְרֵי הַחֲכָמִים
וּבְדִבְרֵי הַנְּבִיאִים גַּם־כֵּן, וְהוּא: שֶׁיְּשִׁיבַת הָאָדָם וְקִימָתוֹ, וְכָל־תְּנוּעוֹתָיו בִּרְצוֹן
הַשֵּׁם־יִתְבָּרֵךְ וְחֶפְצוֹ — הוּא מַאֲמָר אֲמִתִּי עַל־צַד אֶחָד, וְהוּא: כְּמִי שֶׁהִשְׁלִיךְ
אֶבֶן עַל־הָאֲוִיר וְיָרְדָה לְמַטָּה, שֶׁאָמַרְנוּ בָהּ: שֶׁבִּרְצוֹן הַשֵּׁם־יִתְבָּרֵךְ יָרְדָה

„לְמַטָּה", וְהוּא מַאֲמָר אֲמִתִּי: שֶׁהַשֵּׁם־יִתְבָּרֵךְ רָצָה שֶׁתִּהְיֶה הָאָרֶץ כֻּלָּהּ בַּמֶּרְכָּז;
וּמִפְּנֵי זֶה בְּכָל־עֵת שֶׁיַּשְׁלִיכוּ חֵלֶק מִמֶּנָּה לְמַעְלָה, יִתְנוֹעֵעַ אֶל הַמֶּרְכָּז. וְכֵן
כָּל־חֵלֶק מֵחֶלְקֵי הָאֵשׁ מִתְנוֹעֵעַ לְמַעְלָה בָּרָצוֹן שֶׁקָּדַם לִהְיוֹת מִתְנוֹעֵעַ לְמַעְלָה.
לֹא שֶׁהַשֵּׁם־יִתְבָּרֵךְ רָצָה בְּעֵת שֶׁהִתְנוֹעֵעַ זֶה הַחֵלֶק מִן־הָאָרֶץ, שֶׁיִּתְנוֹעֵעַ לְמַטָּה.
וּבָזֶה חוֹלְקִים הַמְדַבְּרִים. כִּי שָׁמַעְתִּי אוֹמְרִים: שֶׁהָרָצוֹן בְּכָל־דָּבָר עֵת אַחַר עֵת
תָּמִיד. וְלֹא כֵן נַאֲמִין אֲנָחְנוּ. אַךְ הָרָצוֹן הָיָה בְּשֵׁשֶׁת יְמֵי בְרֵאשִׁית, שֶׁיִּמָּשְׁכוּ
הַדְּבָרִים כֻּלָּם עַל־טִבְעָם תָּמִיד, כְּמוֹ שֶׁאָמַר: מַה־שֶּׁהָיָה הוּא שֶׁיִּהְיֶה,
וּמַה־שֶּׁנַּעֲשָׂה הוּא שֶׁיֵּעָשֶׂה, וְאֵין כָּל־חָדָשׁ תַּחַת הַשָּׁמֶשׁ (קהלת א, ט).

8:4a A popular notion, found even among the words of the prophets and statements of the sages, is that everything a person does, whether sitting, standing, or any other action, is due to the will of God. From one aspect, the notion is true. [For example,] were a person to throw a stone into the air, it would fall to the earth. One could say that the stone fell by the will of God. The statement would be true; God does want the world to come to the center. If you throw something up, it moves toward the center. [This is Maimonides' view of gravity.] One may equally say that when flames ascend, they follow God's pre-eternal will; it is not that God willed it at the moment. Similarly, what fell toward the earth did so following God's pre-eternal will; it is not that God willed it at the moment that it fell. The *Mutakallimun* differ here, for I have heard them say that the Divine will operates moment to moment at all times. We, on the other hand, believe that the Divine will operated through the six days of creation and that things follow their own nature from then on. This is what Kohelet meant when he said, "What has been is what will be, and what has been done will be done. And there is nothing new under the sun" (Eccles.1:9).

The notion of a "pre-eternal" Divine will, which Maimonides ascribes to the rabbis, is one that sets miracles in the natural order, having been designed by Divine will to appear at future moments.

וּמִפְּנֵי זֶה הֻצְרְכוּ הַחֲכָמִים לוֹמַר: כִּי כָּל־הַמּוֹפְתִים הַיּוֹצְאִים חוּץ לַטֶּבַע אֲשֶׁר
הָיוּ, וְגַם אֲשֶׁר עֲתִידִים לִהְיוֹת מֵאֲשֶׁר יָעַד בָּהֶם הַכָּתוּב — כֻּלָּם קָדַם בָּהֶם
הָרָצוֹן בְּשֵׁשֶׁת יְמֵי בְרֵאשִׁית; וְהוּשַׂם בְּטֶבַע הַדְּבָרִים אָז שֶׁיִּתְחַדֵּשׁ בָּהֶם
מַה־שֶּׁיִּתְחַדֵּשׁ. וְכַאֲשֶׁר יִתְחַדֵּשׁ הַדָּבָר בְּעֵת הַצֹּרֶךְ יַחְשְׁבוּ הָרוֹאִים בּוֹ שֶׁעַתָּה
נִתְחַדֵּשׁ — וְאֵין הַדָּבָר כֵּן. וּכְבָר הִרְחִיבוּ בְּזֶה הָעִנְיָן הַרְבֵּה בְּמִדְרַשׁ קֹהֶלֶת

וְזוּלָתוֹ, וּמַאֲמָרָם בְּזֶה הָעִנְיָן: „עוֹלָם כְּמִנְהָגוֹ נוֹהֵג". וְתִמְצָאֵם, עֲלֵיהֶם הַשָּׁלוֹם,
תָּמִיד בְּכָל־דִּבְרֵיהֶם בּוֹרְחִים מִתֵּת הָרָצוֹן בְּדָבָר אַחַר דָּבָר, וּבְעֵת אַחַר עֵת.
וְעַל־זֶה הַצַּד יֵאָמֵר בָּאָדָם כְּשֶׁיָּקוּם וְיֵשֵׁב: שֶׁבִּרְצוֹן הַשֵּׁם־יִתְבָּרֵךְ קָם וְיָשַׁב,
רוֹצֶה לוֹמַר: שֶׁהוּשַׂם בְּטִבְעוֹ בִּתְחִלַּת בְּרִיאָתוֹ שֶׁיָּקוּם וְיֵשֵׁב בִּבְחִירָתוֹ; לֹא
שֶׁהוּא רוֹצֶה עַתָּה בְּעֵת קוּמוֹ שֶׁיָּקוּם, אוֹ שֶׁלֹּא יָקוּם, כְּמוֹ שֶׁלֹּא רוֹצֶה עַתָּה
בִּנְפִילַת הָאֶבֶן הַזֹּאת שֶׁתִּפֹּל.

8:4b The sages were moved to argue that all the miracles that occurred–or that Scripture promised would occur–were all established by God's pre-eternal will during the six days of creation. Certain marvels were set into nature to appear at a particular time. When one appeared, the onlookers would think that it had been created at that moment, although that was not true. The sages discussed the matter at some length in the *midrash* on Ecclesiastes. The summary of their views is contained in the statement "The world continues in its accustomed way [*haolam k'minhago nohayg*]" (B. Talmud, *Avodah Zarah* 54b). You will find that the sages avoided ascribing the Divine will operating in different things from moment to moment. From this point of view, one may say that a person's standing and sitting follows the Divine will. In other words, one stands and sits because the ability to stand and sit at will is set into one's very nature. It is not that an individual stands or sits because God wills the person to stand or sit at a particular moment. This is the same as God's not willing at a particular moment that the rock thrown upward will fall or not fall.

Maimonides concludes this section with a broad statement that forms the basis for his entire argument: God created the human being to be an autonomous actor.

וּכְלַל הַדָּבָר שֶׁנַּאֲמִין בּוֹ, הוּא: כִּי כְּמוֹ שֶׁרָצָה הַשֵּׁם־יִתְבָּרֵךְ שֶׁיִּהְיֶה הָאָדָם
נִצָּב־הַקּוֹמָה, רְחַב הֶחָזֶה, בַּעַל אֶצְבָּעוֹת — כֵּן רָצָה שֶׁיִּתְנוֹעֵעַ וְיָנוּחַ מֵעַצְמוֹ,
וְיַעֲשֶׂה פְּעֻלּוֹת בִּבְחִירָתוֹ: אֵין מַכְרִיחַ לוֹ עֲלֵיהֶם, וְלֹא מוֹנֵעַ מֵהֶם, כְּמוֹ
שֶׁיִּתְבָּאֵר בַּתּוֹרָה הָאֲמִתִּית, הַמְבָאֶרֶת זֶה הָעִנְיָן בְּאָמְרָהּ: הֵן הָאָדָם הָיָה כְּאַחַד
מִמֶּנּוּ לָדַעַת טוֹב וָרָע (בראשית ג, כב). וּכְבָר בֵּאֵר הַתַּרְגוּם בְּפֵרוּשׁ, שֶׁהָרָצוֹן בּוֹ:
„מִמֶּנּוּ לָדַעַת טוֹב וָרָע" — רוֹצֶה לוֹמַר: שֶׁהוּא הָיָה אֶחָד בָּעוֹלָם, רְצוֹנִי לוֹמַר:
מִין שֶׁאֵין כָּמוֹהוּ מִין אַחֵר שֶׁיִּשְׁתַּתֵּף עִמּוֹ בְּזֶה הָעִנְיָן אֲשֶׁר נִמְצָא בוֹ, וְהוּא:
שֶׁמֵּעַצְמוֹ וּמִנַּפְשׁוֹ יֵדַע הַטּוֹב וְהָרָע וְיַעֲשֶׂה אֵיזֶה מֵהֶם שֶׁיִּרְצֶה, וְאֵין מוֹנֵעַ לוֹ
מֵהֶם. וְאַחַר שֶׁהוּא כֵן, אֶפְשָׁר שֶׁיִּשְׁלַח יָדוֹ וְיִקַּח מִזֶּה וְאָכַל וָחַי לְעוֹלָם (שם).

105

8:4c In summary, we believe that just as God willed that human beings [are three dimensional] stand erect, have a broad body, and have fingers, so God willed that humans should be able to move and stop on their own and perform various acts voluntarily. God never compels any person to do anything, nor does God prevent anyone from doing anything. The true Torah has explained all of this by the statement "Behold, the human has become as one of us, to know good and evil" [Gen. 3:22]. The *Targum* interpreted this to mean, [taking the Hebrew *mimenu* as "from him" rather than as "one of us,"] "from oneself knowing good and evil." In other words, the human is "one" [unique] in the world, a totally unique species who is able–on one's own and through one's own soul–to know good and evil and be able to choose, without any hindrance, one or the other. If that is the case, we understand the next part of the verse, "...lest he put forth his hand and take also of the tree of life and eat, and live forever" [Gen. 3:22].

Since each person is able to choose between good and evil, we need to be taught the difference between good and evil so that we can make the proper choice. Just as we are able to choose, we are able to make a different choice and change our actions.

וְאַחַר שֶׁיִּתְחַיֵּב זֶה בִּמְצִיאוּת הָאָדָם, רְצוֹנִי לוֹמַר: שֶׁיַּעֲשֶׂה בִּבְחִירָתוֹ פְּעֻלוֹת הַטּוֹב וְהָרַע כַּאֲשֶׁר יִרְצֶה, אִם־כֵּן יִתְחַיֵּב לְלַמְּדוֹ דַּרְכֵי הַטּוֹב וְהָרָע, וְשֶׁיְּצַוֵּהוּ וְיַזְהִירֵהוּ וְיַעֲנִישֵׁהוּ וְיִגְמְלֵהוּ — וְיִהְיֶה כָּל־זֶה יָשָׁר. וְכֵן רָאוּי לוֹ לְהַרְגִּיל עַצְמוֹ בִּפְעֻלּוֹת הַטּוֹבוֹת, עַד שֶׁיִּהְיוּ לוֹ הַמַּעֲלוֹת; וְיִתְרַחֵק מִן־הַפְּעֻלּוֹת הָרָעוֹת, עַד שֶׁיָּסוּרוּ מִמֶּנּוּ הַפְּחִיתֻיּוֹת, אֲשֶׁר הֵן נִמְצָאוֹת אִתּוֹ. וְלֹא יֹאמַר שֶׁהֵן בְּעִנְיָן שֶׁאֵינָן יְכוֹלוֹת לְהִשְׁתַּנּוֹת — כִּי כָל־עִנְיָן אֶפְשָׁר לְהִשְׁתַּנּוֹת מִן־הַטּוֹב אֶל הָרַע וּמִן־הָרַע אֶל הַטּוֹב, וְהַכֹּל בִּבְחִירָתוֹ. וּמִפְּנֵי זֶה הָעִנְיָן זָכַרְנוּ כָּל־מַה־שֶּׁזָּכַרְנוּ מֵעִנְיַן הַמִּצְווֹת וְהָעֲבֵרוֹת.

8:4d It is in the nature of the human being to be able to choose to do good or evil. It is therefore necessary to teach each person the ways of good and evil, to give positive and negative *mitzvot*, and [to warn the individual about] reward and punishment. It is most fitting and proper that each person be accustomed to do good deeds in order to achieve virtue and keep far from evil deeds to remove the vices. One should not think that these [virtues or vices] cannot be changed; everything amenable to choice can be changed from good to evil and from evil to good. That is why we said what we did about the positive and negative *mitzvot*.

Maimonides will wrestle with those Torah verses that seem to suggest Divine determinism and will harmonize them with his own view. The verse (Gen. 15:13) in which Abraham was told that his descendants would be enslaved in Egypt did not compel any individual Egyptian to mistreat the Israelites. The verse merely contained a general prediction. We moderns, knowing what we know about the Holocaust, may reflect on the guilt of individual Nazis in a demonic society.

ח:ה וְהִנֵּה נִשְׁאַר עָלֵינוּ לְבָאֵר דָּבָר אֶחָד מִזֶּה הָעִנְיָן, וְהוּא: שֵׁשׁ מִפְּסוּקִים יַחְשְׁבוּ בָּהֶם בְּנֵי הָאָדָם, שֶׁהַשֵּׁם-יִתְבָּרֵךְ יִגְזֹר בְּמֶרִי, וְשֶׁהַשֵּׁם-יִתְבָּרֵךְ יַכְרִיחַ עָלָיו — זֶה שֶׁקֶר, וּצְרִיכִים אָנוּ לְבָאֲרָם, כִּי הַרְבֵּה מִבְּנֵי הָאָדָם הִתְבַּלְבְּלוּ בָהֶם. וּמִזֶּה מַה-שֶּׁנֶּאֱמַר לְאַבְרָהָם: וַעֲבָדוּם וְעִנּוּ אֹתָם אַרְבַּע מֵאוֹת שָׁנָה (בראשית טו, יג), אָמְרוּ: "הֲלֹא תִרְאֶה שֶׁגָּזַר עַל-הַמִּצְרִיִּים שֶׁיַּחְמְסוּ זֶרַע אַבְרָהָם — וְלָמָה עֲנָשָׁם, הֲלֹא בְהֶכְרֵחַ, בִּגְזֵרַת הַשֵּׁם-יִתְבָּרֵךְ יִתְעַלֶּה הִשְׁתַּעְבְּדוּ בָהֶם, כְּמוֹ שֶׁגָּזַר עֲלֵיהֶם? וְהַתְּשׁוּבָה לְאֵלּוּ: שֶׁזֶּה הָעִנְיָן דּוֹמֶה כְּאִלּוּ אָמַר הַשֵּׁם-יִתְבָּרֵךְ: שֶׁהַנּוֹלָדִים לֶעָתִיד יִהְיֶה מֵהֶם מוֹרֵד, וְעוֹבֵד, וְחָסִיד, וְרָע — וְזֶה אֲמִתִּי. וְלֹא מִפְּנֵי זֶה הַמַּאֲמָר הִתְחַיֵּב פְּלוֹנִי הָרַע לִהְיוֹת רָע; וְלֹא פְּלוֹנִי הַצַּדִּיק לִהְיוֹת צַדִּיק עַל-כָּל פָּנִים. אֲבָל כָּל-מִי שֶׁיִּרְצֶה מֵהֶם לִהְיוֹת רַע — יִהְיֶה בִּבְחִירָתוֹ; וְאִלּוּ הָיָה רוֹצֶה לִהְיוֹת צַדִּיק — הָיָה יָכוֹל, וְאֵין מוֹנֵעַ לוֹ. וְכֵן כָּל-צַדִּיק וְצַדִּיק אִלּוּ הָיָה רוֹצֶה לִהְיוֹת רַע, לֹא הָיָה מוֹנֵעַ לוֹ מִזֶּה. כִּי הַדְּבָרִים שֶׁאָמַר הַקָּדוֹשׁ-בָּרוּךְ-הוּא, לֹא אֲמָרָם עַל-אִישׁ יָדוּעַ, עַד שֶׁיֹּאמַר: "כְּבָר נִגְזַר עָלָיו"; וְאָמְנָם בָּאוּ הַדְּבָרִים לַכְּלָל, וְנִשְׁאַר כָּל-אִישׁ וָאִישׁ בִּבְחִירָתוֹ בְּעִקַּר יְצִירָתוֹ. וְכֵן כָּל-אִישׁ וָאִישׁ מִן-הַמִּצְרִיִּים אֲשֶׁר חָמְסוּ וְעִנּוּ אוֹתָם, הָיָה בִּבְחִירָתוֹ שֶׁלֹּא יַחְמְסֵם אִלּוּ הָיָה רוֹצֶה, כִּי לֹא נִגְזַר עַל-הָאִישׁ בִּפְרָט שֶׁיַּחְמְסֵם.

8:5 There remains for us to explain those biblical verses that have suggested that God decrees that some people must sin. Even though this is a false notion, we should still explain these verses because they have confused so many people. Among these verses is what was said to Abraham, "Know for sure that your offspring will be a stranger in a land that is not theirs and will serve them; and they will afflict them four hundred years..." [Gen. 15:13]. [Reading this verse,] some people have said, "You see, God decreed that the Egyptians would deal violently with the seed of Abraham." To answer such people, one could make the argument that were God to announce that among the people to be born in the future there would be one who was a rebel, one who was obedient, one who was pious, and one who was wicked, and while that might be true, it would not compel the one who would be wicked to be wicked nor the one who would be obedient to be obedient. Whoever wanted to be wicked would so choose; if one wanted to be righteous, there is nothing to stop a person from becoming righteous. If a righteous person wanted to become wicked, there is nothing to stop that person from becoming wicked. What God declared [in the Torah] was not directed to any specific person [to prevent someone] from saying that God decreed something specific for that person. The statement dealt with generalities; each individual by nature retained the power of choice. Any Egyptian who had oppressed and hurt the Israelites could have refrained had that person wanted to do so, since it was not decreed that any particular individual had to act in such a manner.

Maimonides will also wrestle with the verse (Deut. 31:16) that predicts that the Israelites would go astray after the death of Moses. For Maimonides, such a prediction compelled no individual Israelite to go astray, any more than the prescribed punishments of the Torah required that any Israeite act so as to deserve them. Punishment exists precisely because individuals are free to act in such a manner as to avoid them.

ח:ו וְזֹאת הַתְּשׁוּבָה בְּעַצְמָהּ נָשִׁיב עַל־אָמְרוֹ: הִנְּךָ שֹׁכֵב עִם־אֲבֹתֶיךָ וְקָם הָעָם הַזֶּה וְזָנָה אַחֲרֵי אֱלֹהֵי נֵכָר (דברים לא, טז). שֶׁאֵין הֶפְרֵשׁ בֵּין זֶה, וּבֵין אָמְרוֹ: „כָּל־מִי שֶׁיַּעֲבֹד עֲבוֹדַת כּוֹכָבִים — יֵעָשֶׂה בּוֹ כַּךְ וָכָךְ". שֶׁאִם לֹא יִמָּצֵא לְעוֹלָם מִי שֶׁיַּעֲבֹד אוֹתָהּ, תִּהְיֶה הַהַפְחָדָה לְבַטָּלָה; וְיִהְיוּ הַקְּלָלוֹת כֻּלָּן לְבַטָּלָה. וְכֵן הָעֳנָשִׁים אֲשֶׁר בַּתּוֹרָה. אֵין לָנוּ לוֹמַר, כַּאֲשֶׁר מָצָאנוּ דִין סְקִילָה בַּתּוֹרָה — שֶׁזֶּה שֶׁחִלֵּל שַׁבָּת הָיָה מֻכְרָח לְחַלֵּל; וְלֹא מִפְּנֵי הַקְּלָלוֹת שֶׁבָּאוּ בַתּוֹרָה, נֹאמַר: שֶׁאֲשֶׁר עָבְדוּ עֲבוֹדַת כּוֹכָבִים וְחָלוּ עֲלֵיהֶם הַקְּלָלוֹת הָהֵן, שֶׁנִּגְזַר עֲלֵיהֶם לְעָבְדָהּ — אֲבָל בִּבְחִירָתוֹ עֲבָדָהּ כָּל־מִי שֶׁעֲבָדָהּ וְחָל עָלָיו הָעֹנֶשׁ, כְּמוֹ שֶׁנֶּאֱמַר: גַּם־הֵמָּה בָּחֲרוּ בְּדַרְכֵיהֶם וְגוֹ' (ישעיה סו, ג) גַּם־אֲנִי אֶבְחַר בְּתַעֲלוּלֵיהֶם וּמְגוּרֹתָם אָבִיא לָהֶם (שם, ד).

8:6 We could apply the same argument to God's statement to Moses, "Behold, you are about to sleep with your ancestors; and this people will rise up and go astray after the foreign gods of the land . . ." [Deut. 31:16]. There is no difference between this statement and someone saying, "If someone worships idols, then God will do such and such." If no one ever worships idols, then the warning is nullified. All the curses and all the punishments described in the Torah would be without purpose [were freedom denied]. For example, what would be the

---

purpose of the law prescribing stoning as punishment for desecrating the Sabbath were a person forced to do so? It was not the curses in the Torah against the idolaters that destined those who worshiped idols to be destroyed. Rather, it was their free choice that doomed them, as it is written, "Accordingly as they have chosen their ways, And their soul delights in their abominations; Even so I will choose their mockings, And will bring their fears upon them…" [Isa. 66:3-4].

The philosopher now comes to one of the most difficult challenges to his claim in the entire Torah. He must face the challenge of the verses dealing with Pharoah. Were he and the Egyptians punished at the Re(e)d Sea for actions over which they had no control? The Torah did state that God had hardened Pharoah's heart! Maimonides argues that Pharoah had chosen and acted on his own. God merely hardened Pharoah's resolve. He and his soldiers freely sinned and were punished.

ח:ז אֲבָל אָמְרוֹ: וְחִזַּקְתִּי אֶת-לֵב-פַּרְעֹה (שמות יד, ד), וְאַחַר-כָּךְ עָנְשׁוֹ וֶהֱמִיתוֹ — יֵשׁ בּוֹ מָקוֹם לְדַבֵּר וְיַעֲלֶה מִמֶּנּוּ בְּיָדֵנוּ שֹׁרֶשׁ גָּדוֹל. וְהִסְתַּכֵּל מַאֲמָרִי בָּזֶה הָעִנְיָן וְשִׂים אֵלָיו לִבְּךָ, וְחַבֵּר אוֹתוֹ עַל-דִּבְרֵי זוּלָתִי — וּבְחַר לְךָ הַטּוֹב. וְהוּא אֶצְלִי: שֶׁפַּרְעֹה וְסִיעָתוֹ אִלּוּ לֹא הָיָה לָהֶם חֵטְא אֶלָּא שֶׁלֹּא שִׁלְּחוּ יִשְׂרָאֵל, הָיָה הָעִנְיָן מְסֻפָּק עַל-כָּל-פָּנִים — שֶׁהֲרֵי הַקָּדוֹשׁ-בָּרוּךְ-הוּא מְנָעָם מִלְּשַׁלֵּחַ אוֹתָם, כְּמוֹ שֶׁנֶּאֱמַר: כִּי-אֲנִי הִכְבַּדְתִּי אֶת-לִבּוֹ וְאֶת-לֵב עֲבָדָיו (שמות י, א). וְאֵיךְ הָיָה מְבַקֵּשׁ מֵהֶם לְשַׁלְּחָם, וְהֵם מֻכְרָחִים שֶׁלֹּא לְשַׁלְּחָם? וְאֵיךְ עָנְשָׁם אַחַר-כָּךְ כַּאֲשֶׁר לֹא שִׁלְּחָם — וְזֶה נִרְאֶה עָוֶל בְּלֹא סָפֵק, וְסוֹתֵר כָּל-מַה-שֶּׁהִקְדַּמְנוּ הַצָּעָתוֹ? — אֶלָּא שֶׁאֵין הָעִנְיָן כֵּן. אֲבָל פַּרְעֹה וְסִיעָתוֹ מָרוּ בִּבְחִירָתָם בְּלִי הֶכְרֵחַ, וְחָמְסוּ הַגֵּרִים אֲשֶׁר הָיוּ בְּתוֹכָם וְעִוְּלוּ עֲלֵיהֶם עָוֶל גָּמוּר, כַּאֲשֶׁר נֶאֱמַר בְּבֵאוּר: וַיֹּאמֶר אֶל-עַמּוֹ: הִנֵּה עַם בְּנֵי יִשְׂרָאֵל וְגוֹ' הָבָה נִתְחַכְּמָה לוֹ (שם א, ט-י) — וְזֹאת הַפְּעֻלָּה הָיְתָה מֵהֶם בִּבְחִירָתָם מִבְּלִי הַכְרֵחַ, רַק בְּרֹעַ לְבָבָם.

8:7a The passage "And I will harden Pharaoh's heart and he shall follow after them" [Exod. 14:4], followed by a description of Pharaoh's punishment and death, requires some discussion; it contains an important principle. Reflect carefully on what I have written on this matter. Compare it to what others have written and choose what is best. Had Pharaoh and his associates sinned only by not sending out the Israelites, then the matter [of God's justice] would be extremely problematic, for God had prevented Pharaoh from sending them out, as it is written, "…for I have hardened his heart, and the heart of his servants…" [Exod. 10:1].

How could God ask them to send them out when they were prevented from doing so? How could God punish them, indeed, kill all of them, afterward for not sending them out? Without a doubt, it would seem to be a gross injustice. It would contradict all that we have already discussed. However, it is not as it seems. Pharaoh and his associates had chosen freely to treat harshly the strangers who were in their midst; they acted most unjustly, as Scripture attests, "And he [Pharaoh] said, 'Behold, the Israelites are too many and too mighty for us; come, let us deal wisely with them . . . '" [Exod. 1:9-10]. And that's what Pharaoh and his people did, acting freely, without compulsion, motivated solely by the evil in their hearts.

God's real punishment of the Egyptians is explained by Maimonides. He tells the reader that the Egyptians were prevented from repenting. Had they repented, they would have been able to prevent their own destruction. Repentance, Maimonides suggests, can save all.

וְהָיָה עֹנֶשׁ הַשֵּׁם־יִתְבָּרֵךְ לָהֶם עַל־זֶה לְמָנְעָם מֵהַתְּשׁוּבָה, עַד שֶׁיָּחוּלוּ עֲלֵיהֶם מֵהָעֳנָשִׁים מַה־שֶּׁהָיָה רָאוּי לָהֶם מִן־הַדִּין. וּמְנִיעָתָם מֵהַתְּשׁוּבָה הִיא — שֶׁלֹּא יְשַׁלְּחֵם. וּכְבָר בֵּאֵר לוֹ הַשֵּׁם־יִתְבָּרֵךְ זֶה הָעִנְיָן וְהוֹדִיעוֹ: שֶׁאִלּוּ הָיָה רוֹצֶה לְהוֹצִיאָם לְבָד, הָיָה מְאַבֵּד אוֹתוֹ וְסִיעָתוֹ וְהָיוּ יוֹצְאִים מְהֵרָה מֵאֵין אָחוֹר. אָמְנָם, רָצָה עִם הוֹצִיאוֹ אוֹתָם לְעָנְשָׁם עַל־מַה־שֶּׁקָּדַם מֵחֲמַת שִׁעְבּוּדָם, כְּמוֹ שֶׁהִבְטִיחַ וְאָמַר: וְגַם אֶת־הַגּוֹי אֲשֶׁר יַעֲבֹדוּ דָּן אָנֹכִי וְאַחֲרֵי־כֵן יֵצְאוּ בִּרְכֻשׁ גָּדוֹל (בראשית טו, יד) — וְאִי־אֶפְשָׁר לְעָנְשָׁם אִלּוּ הָיוּ עוֹשִׂים תְּשׁוּבָה; וְעַל־כֵּן נִמְנְעוּ מֵהַתְּשׁוּבָה וְהֶחֱזִיקוּ בָהֶם. וְהוּא אָמְרוֹ: כִּי עַתָּה שָׁלַחְתִּי אֶת־יָדִי וָאַךְ אוֹתְךָ וְאֶת־עַמְּךָ בַּדָּבֶר וַתִּכָּחֵד מִן־הָאָרֶץ. וְאוּלָם בַּעֲבוּר זֹאת הֶעֱמַדְתִּיךָ בַּעֲבוּר הַרְאֹתְךָ אֶת־כֹּחִי וּלְמַעַן סַפֵּר שְׁמִי בְּכָל־הָאָרֶץ (שמות ט, טו־טז).

8:7b God's punishment was the prevention of their repentance so that they would receive suitable punishment. It was their inability to repent that prevented them from sending out the Israelites. God explained this to Pharaoh and told him that if God merely wanted to take out the Israelites, God could have destroyed Pharaoh and his people. Then the Israelites could have left without delay. However, God wanted to take the Israelites out of Egypt and also to punish the Egyptians for having enslaved them, as God had promised, saying, ". . . and also that nation, whom they will serve, will I judge; and afterward they will come out with great substance" [Gen. 15:14]. It would have been impossible to punish the Egyptians had they repented. Therefore, they were kept from repenting and they kept on sinning. That is the meaning of the statement, "Surely now I have put forth My hand, and smitten you and your people with pestilence, and you have been cut off from the earth. But in very deed for this cause have I made you to stand, to show you My power, and that My name may be declared throughout all the earth" [Exod. 9:15-16].

Maimonides will have difficulty relating the biblical text and the rabbinic interpretation that God can prevent repentance. If Pharoah was free to sin but not free to repent, then the notion of free will is affected. Were one to say that God knew that the sinner would not repent, then that Divine knowledge was a factor in the sinner's inability to repent. Maimonides attempts to escape the problem by claiming that we mortals have neither Divine knowledge nor understand Divine justice. In truth, however, that solution creates other problems. The rabbis believed that the punishment of sins took place primarily in the next world. So Maimonides reflects on the rabbinic notion that the punishment may take place in the next world and adds that the punishment may take place in this world and/or in the next.

ח:ח וְאֵין לְדַקְדֵּק עָלֵינוּ אִם נֹאמַר: שֶׁהַשֵּׁם־יִתְבָּרֵךְ יַעֲנֹשׁ הָאָדָם וְיִמְנָעֵהוּ מֵהַתְּשׁוּבָה וְלֹא יַעַזְבֵהוּ לִבְחֹר בִּתְשׁוּבָה — כִּי הוּא יִתְבָּרֵךְ יֵדַע הַחַטָּאִים, וּלְפִי חָכְמָתוֹ וְיָשְׁרוֹ יִהְיֶה שִׁעוּר הָעֹנֶשׁ: פְּעָמִים בָּעוֹלָם־הַבָּא לְבָד; וּפְעָמִים בָּעוֹלָם־הַזֶּה לְבָד; וּפְעָמִים בִּשְׁנֵיהֶם. וְעָנְשׁוֹ בָּעוֹלָם־הַזֶּה חָלוּק: פְּעָמִים יַעֲנֹשׁ בְּגוּף, פְּעָמִים בְּמָמוֹן, וּפְעָמִים בִּשְׁנֵיהֶם. וְכַאֲשֶׁר יְבַטְּלוּ קְצָת תְּנוּעוֹת בְּנֵי אָדָם שֶׁהֵם בִּבְחִירָתוֹ עַל־צַד הָעֹנֶשׁ: כְּבִטּוּל יָדוֹ מִן־הַמְּלָאכָה שֶׁלֹּא יָכוֹל לַעֲשׂוֹת בָּהּ מְאוּמָה, כְּמוֹ שֶׁעָשָׂה לְיָרָבְעָם בֶּן־נְבָט; אוֹ לְסַמֵּא עֵינָיו מִן־הָרְאוֹת, כְּמוֹ שֶׁעָשָׂה לְאַנְשֵׁי סְדוֹם, הַנֶּאֱסָפִים עַל פֶּתַח לוֹט — כֵּן יְבַטֵּל מִמֶּנּוּ בְּחִירַת הַתְּשׁוּבָה, עַד שֶׁלֹּא יִתְעוֹרֵר אֵלֶיהָ כְּלָל וְיָמוּת בְּחֶטְאוֹ. וְלֹא נִתְחַיֵּב לָדַעַת חָכְמָתוֹ, עַד שֶׁנֵּדַע לָמָּה עָנַשׁ זֶה בְּזֶה הַמִּין מִן־הָעֹנֶשׁ וְלֹא עֲנָשׁוֹ בְּמִין אַחֵר, כְּמוֹ שֶׁלֹּא נֵדַע מֶה הָיְתָה הַסִּבָּה לִהְיוֹת לְזֶה הַמִּין זֹאת הַצּוּרָה, וְלֹא הָיְתָה לוֹ צוּרָה אַחֶרֶת. אֲבָל הַכְּלָל: כִּי כָּל־דְּרָכָיו חֶסֶד וּמִשְׁפָּט, וַיַעֲנִישׁ הַחוֹטֵא כְּפִי חֶטְאוֹ, וְיִגְמֹל הַמֵּיטִיב כְּפִי הַטָבָתוֹ.

8:8 One should not find fault with our saying that God may punish someone by preventing that person from repenting or allowing that person to choose repentance. God knows the sinners and God prescribes punishment according to the dictates of God's wisdom and justice, sometimes in this world, sometimes in the next, and sometimes in both worlds. Punishment in this world may be either physical or monetary or both. Sometimes the punishment will affect a person's ability to control the body. Thus, for example, that person will not be able to use his or her hands in his or her craft so that he or she becomes unable to earn a living. This happened to Jeroboam ben Nevat. One may be punished by becoming blind, as occurred to those people of Sodom who gathered around the door of the place where Lot was staying. The ability to choose repentance may be lost completely. If nothing moves a person to repentance, the sinner will die in his/her sin. We are not meant to understand the wisdom of God. We may not know why God punished one person in one way and another person in another way. We just don't know why a particular species has a particular form. [All we need know is] the general principle that all God's ways are steadfast love and justice, that God punishes the sinner according to one's sin and rewards the one who does good according to one's goodness.

The relationship between repentance and change is similar to the rabbinic notion that sin begins as a thread that one can easily break. If no repentance occurs and one persists in the sin, then sin becomes like a string that becomes harder to break. If no repentance occurs and one persists in the sin, then sin becomes a cord that becomes still harder to break until sin becomes a habit that no one can break. Habit becomes a major factor in change and in repentance. Thus, one might interpret such habit in the lives of sinners as equivalent to God's preventing such sinners from repenting. As a demonstration of Divine power, Maimonides argues that God gave Pharaoh the opportunity to repent (to change his mind). When he did not do so, God told him that he would die as a punishment.

ח:ט וְאִם תֹּאמַר: לָמָּה בִּקֵּשׁ מִמֶּנּוּ לְשַׁלַּח אֶת־יִשְׂרָאֵל פַּעַם אַחַר פַּעַם, וְהוּא נִמְנָע מִלְּשַׁלְּחָם? וְלָמָּה לֹא בָּאוּ עָלָיו הַמַּכּוֹת וְהוּא עוֹמֵד בְּמִרְדּוּ עַל־עַקְשׁוּתוֹ — כְּמוֹ שֶׁאָמַרְנוּ: שֶׁעָנְשׁוֹ מֵהַשֵּׁם־יִתְבָּרֵךְ הוּא: שֶׁיַּעֲמֹד עַל־עַקְשׁוּתוֹ — וְלֹא הָיָה מְבַקֵּשׁ מִמֶּנּוּ לְבַטֵּל מַה־שֶּׁאִי־אֶפְשָׁר לוֹ לַעֲשׂוֹתוֹ? וְזֶה גַם כֵּן הָיָה לַחָכְמָה מֵהַשֵּׁם יִתְבָּרֵךְ, שֶׁיּוֹדִיעֵהוּ: שֶׁהַשֵּׁם־יִתְבָּרֵךְ יְבַטֵּל בְּחִירָתוֹ כְּשֶׁיִּרְצֶה לְבַטְּלָהּ. וְאָמַר לוֹ: "הִנְנִי מְבַקֵּשׁ מִמְּךָ שֶׁתְּשַׁלְּחֵם, וְאִם תְּשַׁלְּחֵם — תִּהְיֶה נִצּוֹל; רַק יָדַעְתִּי שֶׁאַתָּה לֹא תְשַׁלְּחֵם — עַד שֶׁתָּמוּת". וְהָיָה הוּא צָרִיךְ שֶׁיּוֹדֶה לְשַׁלְּחָם, עַד שֶׁיֵּרָאֶה הֵפֶךְ דִּבְרֵי הַנָּבִיא שֶׁאָמַר, שֶׁהוּא יִהְיֶה נִמְנָע לְהוֹדוֹת — וְלֹא הָיָה יָכוֹל. וְהָיָה בָּזֶה אוֹת גָּדוֹל וּמְפֻרְסָם אֵצֶל בְּנֵי־אָדָם, כְּמוֹ שֶׁכָּתוּב: וּלְמַעַן סַפֵּר שְׁמִי בְּכָל־הָאָרֶץ (שמות ט, טז), שֶׁהַשֵּׁם־יִתְבָּרֵךְ אֶפְשָׁר שֶׁיַּעֲנַשׁ שֶׁיְּמָנְעֵהוּ שֶׁיְּמָנְעֵהוּ בִּחִירַת פְּעֻלָּה אַחַת; וְיוֹדִיעֵהוּ בָּזֶה, שֶׁלֹּא יוּכַל לִמְשֹׁךְ נַפְשׁוֹ וְלַהֲשִׁיבָהּ אֶל הַבְּחִירָה הַהִיא.

8:9 One might ask why did God ask Pharaoh, time after time, to send forth the Israelites while he refused each time to do so and why the plagues kept coming to smite him while he persisted in his rebellion. It is as we have said, that God punished him by having him remain stubborn. God did not ask Pharaoh without reason to do something that he would not do. Following Divine wisdom, God informed him that his ability to choose had been taken away. God said to Pharaoh, "I asked you to send them [the Israelites]. Had you done so, you would have been saved. Now you will send them out, but you will die." It was necessary that Pharaoh [finally] agree to send them out so that Pharaoh might seem to disprove the words of the prophet [Moses] who said that he could not so agree. [In truth] he [Pharaoh] had no power of choice. This became a great and widely known marvel among all peoples, as it is written, "I have made you stand, to show you My power, and that My name may be declared throughout all the earth" [Exod. 9:16]. God may punish by making a person unable to make a particular choice and by making that person aware that such is the case and that s/he can do nothing about it.

Like Pharaoh, the king of Sihon died as a result of his own sins. Lest people wonder the same thing about this king as they did about Pharaoh, Maimonides reminds us of the prophecy of Isaiah.

וְעַל־זֶה הַצַּד בְּעַצְמוֹ הָיָה עֹנֶשׁ סִיחוֹן מֶלֶךְ חֶשְׁבּוֹן. כִּי לְמַה־שֶּׁקָּדַם מִמְּרְיוֹ אֲשֶׁר **ח:י** לֹא הֻכְרַח עָלָיו, עֲנָשׁוֹ יִתְבָּרֵךְ שֶׁמְּנָעוֹ (מֵהַעֲבִיר יִשְׂרָאֵל בִּגְבוּלוֹ) מֵהָפִיק רְצוֹן יִשְׂרָאֵל, עַד שֶׁנִּלְחֲמוּ עִמּוֹ וַהֲרָגוּהוּ. וְהוּא אָמְרוֹ: וְלֹא אָבָה סִיחוֹן מֶלֶךְ חֶשְׁבּוֹן הַעֲבִרֵנוּ בּוֹ, כִּי־הִקְשָׁה יְיָ אֱלֹהֶיךָ אֶת־רוּחוֹ וְאִמֵּץ אֶת־לְבָבוֹ וְגוֹ' (דברים ב, ל). וַאֲשֶׁר הֵבִיא לִהְיוֹת עִנְיַן זֶה הַפָּסוּק קָשֶׁה עַל־הַמְפָרְשִׁים כֻּלָּם — מִפְּנֵי שֶׁחָשְׁבוּ, כִּי לֹא נֶעֱנַשׁ סִיחוֹן אֶלָּא שֶׁלֹּא הִנִּיחַ אֶת יִשְׂרָאֵל עָבַר בִּגְבוּלוֹ. וְאָמְרוּ: אֵיךְ עֲנָשׁוֹ — וְהוּא מֻכְרָח, כִּי הִקְשָׁה ה' אֶת־רוּחוֹ וְאִמֵּץ אֶת־לְבָבוֹ? כְּמוֹ שֶׁחָשְׁבוּ רַבִּים שֶׁלֹּא נֶעֱנַשׁ פַּרְעֹה וְעַמּוֹ, אֶלָּא מִפְּנֵי שֶׁלֹּא שִׁלְּחוּ יִשְׂרָאֵל מֵאַרְצָם — וְאֵין הָעִנְיָן כֵּן, אֶלָּא כְּמוֹ שֶׁבֵּאַרְנוּ. וּכְבָר בֵּאֵר הַשֵּׁם־יִתְבָּרֵךְ עַל־יְדֵי יְשַׁעְיָה הַנָּבִיא, שֶׁהוּא יִתְבָּרֵךְ יַעֲנִישׁ קְצָת הַמּוֹרְדִים: שֶׁיִּמָּנַע מֵהֶם הַתְּשׁוּבָה וְלֹא יַעֲזֹב הַבְּחִירָה בְּיָדָם בְּאָמְרוֹ: הַשְׁמֵן לֵב־הָעָם הַזֶּה וְאָזְנָיו הַכְבֵּד וְעֵינָיו הָשַׁע פֶּן־ יִרְאֶה בְעֵינָיו וּבְאָזְנָיו יִשְׁמָע, וּלְבָבוֹ יָבִין — וָשָׁב וְרָפָא לוֹ (ישעיהו ו, י).

8:10a Such was the punishment of Sihon, king of Heshbon. He had refused without reason to allow Israel to pass through his border. Hence, he was punished by not being allowed to gain favor from them. This ultimately led to war and his own death. This is the meaning of "But Sihon king of Heshbon would not let us pass by him, for *Adonai* your God hardened his spirit and made his heart obstinate, so that God might deliver him into your hand..." [Deut. 2:30]. This verse has always been difficult for many commentators, who assumed that the sole reason that Sihon was punished was because he did not permit Israel to pass through his border. They wondered how God could punish Sihon if he had been compelled to act as he did, if God had hardened his spirit and made his heart obstinate. This is the same [erroneous] way of thinking as those people who thought that Pharaoh and his associates were punished only because they did not send Israel out of Egypt. The matter, however, is as we have stated it. God has already explained through Isaiah that God had punished some rebels by making it impossible for them to repent and thus taking their ability to choose from them. This is what is meant by "Make the heart of this people fat and make their ears heavy and shut their eyes lest they–seeing with their eyes and hearing with their ears, understanding with their heart–return and be healed" [Isa. 6:10].

Following on the heels of Isaiah, Maimonides reminds us of prophecies of Elijah and Hosea. In both cases, God meted out a similar punishment to the people who had sinned. Because they freely sinned, God prevented them from being able to repent. When Maimonides suggests to the reader that it is simple and requires no further explanation, he is implying that it is a complex matter that can only be understood by a small group of people.

וְזֶה הַדָּבָר פָּשׁוּט אֵין צֹרֶךְ לְפָרֵשׁ; אֲבָל הוּא מַפְתֵּחַ לְמַנְעוּלִים רַבִּים. וְעַל־זֶה הָעִקָּר הוֹלְכִים דִּבְרֵי אֵלִיָּהוּ, זָכוּר לַטּוֹב, בְּאָמְרוֹ עַל־הַכּוֹפְרִים מֵאַנְשֵׁי דוֹרוֹ: וְאַתָּה הֲסִבֹּתָ אֶת־לִבָּם אֲחֹרַנִּית (מלכים־א יח, לז). רְצוֹנוֹ לוֹמַר: כַּאֲשֶׁר חָטְאוּ בִרְצוֹנָם, הָיָה עָנְשָׁם עֲלֵיהֶם מֵאִתְּךָ שֶׁתָּסֵב לִבָּם אֲחֹרַנִּית מִדֶּרֶךְ הַתְּשׁוּבָה, וְלֹא תַנִּיחַ לָהֶם הַבְּחִירָה, וְלֹא רָצוּ לְהַנִּיחַ הַחֵטְא הַהוּא. וְהִתְמִידוּ מִפְּנֵי זֶה עַל־כְּפִירָתָם, בְּאָמְרוֹ: חֲבוּר עֲצַבִּים אֶפְרָיִם הַנַּח־לוֹ (הושע ד, יז). רְצוֹנוֹ לוֹמַר: שֶׁהוּא מִתְחַבֵּר אֶל הָעֲצַבִּים בִּבְחִירָתוֹ וְאוֹהֵב אוֹתָם — עָנְשֵׁהוּ שֶׁיֻּנַּח עַל־אַהֲבָתָם, וְזֶה עִנְיַן „הַנַּח־לוֹ". וְזֶהוּ מִן־הַפֵּרוּשִׁים הַטּוֹבִים לְמִי שֶׁיָּבִין דַּקּוּת הָעִנְיָנִים.

114

8:10b This matter is so simple that it needs no [further] explanation, but it is the key to many locks. The words of Elijah contain the same principle when he spoke about those people of his generation who were heretics. He said, "Hear me, *Adonai*, hear me, so that this people may know that You, *Adonai* are God, for You did turn their heart backward" [I Kings 18:37]. What Elijah meant was that because the people purposely sinned, Divine punishment should be the turning of their hearts away from the path of repentance. God will not allow them to choose; the people will not be able to stop sinning, and they will continue in their heresy, as it says, "Ephraim is joined to idols. Let him alone" [Hos. 4:17]. He meant that Ephraim had freely chosen to be joined to the idols and to love them; his punishment would be that he would remain in love with them. That is the meaning of "Let him alone." This is a very good interpretation for those who understand the subtlety of the matter.

Maimonides will interpret the prophet's plaint (Isa. 63:17) as referring to the pangs of exile and not to the problems of repentance. The prophet pleads with God to save the people from being dominated by pagans, whose success may lead (Jewish) fools to believe in the gods of the pagans, thus profaning the name of God.

ח:יא אָמְנָם, מַאֲמַר יְשַׁעְיָה הַנָּבִיא, עָלָיו הַשָּׁלוֹם, שֶׁאָמַר לָמָּה תַתְעֵנוּ יְיָ מִדְּרָכֶיךָ תַּקְשִׁיחַ לִבֵּנוּ מִיִּרְאָתֶךָ (ישעיה סג, יז) — אֵינוֹ מִזֶּה הָעִנְיָן כְּלָל, וְאֵינוֹ נִתְלֶה בְּדָבָר מִמֶּנּוּ. וְאָמְנָם עִנְיַן אֵלּוּ הַדְּבָרִים כְּפִי מַה־שֶּׁבָּא לְפָנָיו וּלְאַחֲרָיו: שֶׁהַנָּבִיא הַהוּא הָיָה מִתְרָעֵם עַל־גָּלוּתֵנוּ וְגֵרוּתֵנוּ, וְהֶפְסֵק מֶמְשַׁלְתֵּנוּ, וְתִגְבֹּרֶת הָאֻמּוֹת עָלֵינוּ, וְאָמַר עַל־זֶה דֶּרֶךְ תְּפִלָּה: ה׳ אֱלֹהֵי יִשְׂרָאֵל! כְּשֶׁיִּרְאוּ יִשְׂרָאֵל תִּגְבֹּרֶת הַכּוֹפְרִים — יִתְעוּ מִדֶּרֶךְ הָאֱמֶת וְיִטְעֶה לִבָּם מִיִּרְאָתֶךָ, וּכְאִלּוּ הָיִיתָ אַתָּה הַסִּבָּה לַסְּכָלִים הָאֵלֶּה לָצֵאת מִדֶּרֶךְ הָאֱמֶת. כְּמוֹ שֶׁאָמַר מֹשֶׁה רַבֵּנוּ, עָלָיו הַשָּׁלוֹם: וְאָמְרוּ הַגּוֹיִם אֲשֶׁר־שָׁמְעוּ אֶת־שִׁמְעֲךָ לֵאמֹר: מִבִּלְתִּי יְכֹלֶת יְיָ וְגו׳ (במדבר יד, טו־טז). וּמִפְּנֵי זֶה אָמַר אַחַר זֶה: שׁוּב לְמַעַן עֲבָדֶיךָ שִׁבְטֵי נַחֲלָתֶךָ (ישעיה סג, יז). רְצוֹנוֹ לוֹמַר: עַד שֶׁלֹּא יִהְיֶה בָּעִנְיָן חִלּוּל שִׁמְךָ הַגָּדוֹל.

8:11 The statement of Isaiah, "*Adonai*, why do You make us err from Your ways and harden our heart from Your fear?" [Isa. 63:17] does not fit into the previously mentioned category, nor does it relate to it in any way. Rather, the statement relates to the context in Isaiah in terms of what preceded it and what followed. The prophet complains about our exile, our fate, the loss of our polity, and the dominion of the nations over us. He speaks in the form of a prayer, saying, "*Adonai* when Israel

shall see the victory of the heretics, they will be led away from the path
of truth and their hearts will go astray from reverence to You. It will be
as if You are the cause of these fools going away from the path of truth."
Isaiah's statement is much like Moses' statement, "...then the nations
that have heard of Your fame will speak, saying: 'Because *Adonai* was not
able to bring this people into the land that God swore to them,
therefore God has slain them in the wilderness" [Num. 14:15-16].
Isaiah then continued, "Return for Your servant's sake, the tribes of
Your inheritance" [Isa. 63:17]. It is as if Isaiah had prayed, "Do so
before Your great name is profaned."

Such folly, Maimonides tells us, occurred in the time of Malachi, the last of the prophets.
Malachi responded to the Israelites in exile, promising them that in the future, God would
demonstrate the true belief. Malachi warned them that they should be concerned with doing
good in the eyes of *Adonai Tzevaot*, the Lord of the Hosts.

ח:יב וּכְמוֹ שֶׁבֵּאֵר בִּתְרֵי־עָשָׂר מַאֲמַר הַנִּמְשָׁכִים אַחַר אֱמֶת, הַמְנֻצָּחִים מִן־הָעוֹבְדֵי־
כּוֹכָבִים בִּזְמַן הַגָּלוּת, אֲשֶׁר מִסַּפֵּר דִּבְרֵיהֶם: כָּל עֹשֵׂה רָע טוֹב בְּעֵינֵי יְיָ וּבָהֶם
הוּא חָפֵץ, אוֹ אַיֵּה אֱלֹהֵי הַמִּשְׁפָּט?! (מלאכי ב, יז). וְסִפֵּר מִדִּבְרֵיהֶם הַמּוּבָן
מֵאֹרֶךְ הַגָּלוּת: אֲמַרְתֶּם שָׁוְא עֲבֹד אֱלֹהִים, וּמַה־בֶּצַע כִּי שָׁמַרְנוּ מִשְׁמַרְתּוֹ וְכִי
הָלַכְנוּ קְדֹרַנִּית מִפְּנֵי יְיָ צְבָאוֹת; וְעַתָּה אֲנַחְנוּ מְאַשְּׁרִים זֵדִים (שם ג, יד־טו).
וְהִבְטִיחָנוּ שָׁם, שֶׁהוּא יִתְבָּרֵךְ עָתִיד לְבָאֵר הָאֱמֶת, וְאָמַר בָּזֶה: וְשַׁבְתֶּם וּרְאִיתֶם
בֵּין צַדִּיק לְרָשָׁע וְגוֹ' (שם, יח).

8:12 Malachi, the last of the minor prophets, recounted the views of those
Israelites living in the Exile who having been defeated by the idolaters
[adopted their views]. They said, "Everyone who does evil is good in
the sight of *Adonai*, and God delights in them," or "Where is the God of
Justice?" [Mal. 2:17]. The prophet, knowing that it was the length of
the exile that was speaking, quoted them, "You have said: 'It is vain to
serve God. And what profit is it that we have kept God's charge and that
we have walked mournfully because of *Adonai Tzevaot*? And now we
call the proud happy; yea, they that work wickedness are built up. Yea,
they try God and are delivered'" [Mal. 3:14-15]. Malachi then
responded, promising them that God would in the future declare the
truth, "Then shall you again discern between the righteous and the
wicked, between the one who serves God and the one who does not
serve God" [Mal. 3:18].

Maimonides will again remind the reader not to be misled by those biblical verses that seem to suggest that God controls human behavior and interferes with free will. The reader should again read his explanation of those verses and keep in mind the principles that each person has the ability to pursue virtue and avoid vice.

ח:יג אֵלּוּ הַפְּסוּקִים הַמְסֻפָּקִים בַּתּוֹרָה וּבַמִּקְרָא שֶׁיֵּרָאֶה מֵהֶם, שֶׁהַשֵּׁם־יִתְבָּרֵךְ יַכְרִיחַ עַל־הָעֲבֵרוֹת — וְהִנֵּה בֵּאַרְנוּ עִנְיָנָם בְּלֹא סָפֵק, וְהוּא בֵּאוּר אֲמִתִּי עִם טוֹב הַתְבּוֹנְנוּת. וְנִשְׁאַרְנוּ עַל־שָׁרְשֵׁינוּ: שֶׁבִּרְשׁוּת הָאָדָם הִיא הַמִּצְוָה וְהָעֲבֵרָה, וְהוּא הַבּוֹחֵר בְּפִעֳלוֹתֵיהֶן: מַה־שֶׁיִּרְצֶה לַעֲשׂוֹתוֹ — יַעֲשֶׂה; וּמַה־שֶׁלֹּא יִרְצֶה לַעֲשׂוֹתוֹ — לֹא יַעֲשֶׂה; רַק אִם יַעֲנִישֵׁהוּ הַשֵּׁם־יִתְבָּרֵךְ עַל־חֶטְאוֹ שֶׁיְּבַטֵּל רְצוֹנוֹ, כְּמוֹ שֶׁבֵּאַרְנוּ. וְשֶׁקִּנְיָן הַמַּעֲלוֹת וְהַפְּחִיתוּת בְּיָדוֹ, וּמִפְּנֵי זֶה — צָרִיךְ לוֹ שֶׁיִּשְׁתַּדֵּל לִקְנוֹת לְנַפְשׁוֹ הַמַּעֲלוֹת — שֶׁאֵין לוֹ מֵעִיר זוּלָתוֹ שֶׁיְּעִירֵהוּ עֲלֵיהֶן. וְהוּא אָמְרָם בְּמוּסָרֵי זֹאת הַמַּסֶּכְתָּא: אִם אֵין אֲנִי לִי — מִי לִי?

8:13   There are some verses in the Torah and elsewhere in the Bible that would seem to suggest that God forces people to commit transgressions. Without a doubt, we have explained these verses. Careful reflection will show that our explanation is correct. We maintain our position that the power to perform *mitzvot* and to refrain from transgression is given to every human being. A person can choose to do or not do whatever s/he wishes to do. God may punish a sinner by removing his/her ability to choose. Otherwise, the attainment of virtue or vice is in each person's power. Each person should attempt to attain the virtues. No one else can do it for him/her. That is the meaning of the famous phrase in this tractate, "If I am not for myself, who will be for me?" [*Pirke Avot* 1:14].

God's knowledge of future events will be among the last topics that Maimonides will discuss. Such knowledge is related to the notion of Divine determinism. Knowledge for us seems to entail such determinism. When we say that we know, we often mean that we can predict what will happen. If we know that there is a law of gravity, we can predict that if we drop something, it will fall. Maimonides raises a number of questions about Divine knowledge. Does such knowledge entail that certain actions will occur? What does that knowledge embrace? Could the Divine essence, which is simple, relate to a composite of Divine knowledge? If Divine knowledge is simple, how can it embrace individuals? Maimonides answers these questions by asserting that Divine knowledge is unlike human knowledge, just as anything that we might attribute to the Deity is different from anything that we comprehend. To make sure that people understand what he wants to say, Maimonides makes the argument simple.

ח:יד וְלֹא נִשְׁאַר מִזֶּה הָעִנְיָן אֶלָּא דָּבָר אֶחָד שֶׁצָּרִיךְ לְדַבֵּר בּוֹ מְעַט עַד שֶׁתִּשְׁלַם כַּוָּנַת
זֶה הַפֶּרֶק. וְאַף-עַל-פִּי שֶׁלֹּא הָיָה בְדַעְתִּי לְדַבֵּר בּוֹ כְּלָל, אֲבָל הַצֹּרֶךְ הֱבִיאַנִי אֶל
זֶה — וְהוּא: יְדִיעַת הַשֵּׁם-יִתְבָּרֵךְ הָעֲתִידוֹת. שֶׁהִיא הַטַּעֲנָה אֲשֶׁר יִטְעֲנוּ עָלֵינוּ
בָּהּ הַחוֹשְׁבִים: שֶׁהָאָדָם מֻכְרָח עַל-הַמִּצְוָה וְעַל-הָעֲבֵרָה, וְשֶׁכָּל-פְּעֻלּוֹת הָאָדָם
אֵין לוֹ בְּחִירָה בָּהֶן, אַחַר שֶׁבְּחִירָתוֹ תְּלוּיָה בִּבְחִירַת הָאֱלֹהִים. וַאֲשֶׁר גָּרַם
לְזֹאת הָאֱמוּנָה — הוּא: שֶׁיִּשְׁאַל הַשּׁוֹאֵל: זֶה הָאִישׁ, יָדַע בּוֹ הַבּוֹרֵא אִם יִהְיֶה
צַדִּיק אוֹ רָשָׁע, אוֹ לֹא יָדַע? וְאִם תֹּאמַר יָדַע — יִתְחַיֵּב מִזֶּה שֶׁיִּהְיֶה מֻכְרָח
עַל-הָעִנְיָן הַהוּא אֲשֶׁר יָדְעוּ הַשֵּׁם-יִתְבָּרֵךְ טֶרֶם הֱיוֹתוֹ; אוֹ תִהְיֶה יְדִיעָתוֹ בִּלְתִּי
אֲמִתִּית. וְאִם תֹּאמַר: שֶׁלֹּא יָדַע מִקֹּדֶם — יִתְחַיְּבוּ מִזֶּה הַרְחָקוֹת עֲצוּמוֹת,
וְיֵהָרְסוּ חוֹמוֹת נִשְׂגָּבוֹת בְּעִנְיַן הַדָּת. לָכֵן שְׁמַע מִמֶּנִּי מַה-שֶּׁאֹמַר לְךָ וְהִסְתַּכֵּל בּוֹ
מְאֹד — כִּי הוּא הָאֱמֶת בְּלֹא סָפֵק. וְזֶה: כְּבָר הִתְבָּאֵר בְּחָכְמַת הָאֱלֹהוּת, רְצוֹנִי
לוֹמַר: מַה-שֶּׁאַחַר הַטֶּבַע, שֶׁהַשֵּׁם-יִתְבָּרֵךְ אֵינוֹ יוֹדֵעַ בְּ„מַדָּע", וְלֹא חַי בְּ„חַיִּים",
עַד שֶׁיִּהְיֶה הוּא וְהַמַּדָּע שְׁנֵי דְבָרִים, כָּאָדָם וִידִיעָתוֹ. שֶׁהָאָדָם — בִּלְתִּי הַמַּדָּע,
וְהַמַּדָּע — בִּלְתִּי הָאָדָם; וְכֵיוָן שֶׁכֵּן הוּא — הֵם שְׁנֵי דְבָרִים. וְאִלּוּ הָיָה הַשֵּׁם-
יִתְבָּרֵךְ יוֹדֵעַ בְּמַדָּע, הָיָה מִתְחַיֵּב מִזֶּה הָ„רִבּוּי", וְהָיוּ הַנִּמְצָאִים „הַקַּדְמוֹנִים"
רַבִּים: ה' יִתְבָּרֵךְ, וְהַמַּדָּע אֲשֶׁר בּוֹ יֵדַע, וְהַחַיִּים אֲשֶׁר בָּהֶם הוּא חַי, וְהַיְכֹלֶת
אֲשֶׁר בָּהּ יָכוֹל, וְכֵן כָּל-תְּאָרָיו יִתְבָּרֵךְ. וְאָמְנָם זָכַרְתִּי לְךָ תְּחִלָּה טַעֲנָה קְרוֹבָה
וְקַלָּה לְהָבִין אוֹתָהּ וּלְהַשְׂכִּילָהּ לֶהָמוֹן — כִּי הַטְּעָנוֹת וְהָרְאָיוֹת אֲשֶׁר יַתִּירוּ זֶה
הַסָּפֵק הֵן חֲזָקוֹת מְאֹד וּמוֹפְתִיּוֹת אֲמִתִּיּוֹת. וְהִתְבָּאֵר: שֶׁהוּא יִתְבָּרֵךְ שְׁמוֹ —
תְּאָרָיו, וּתְאָרָיו — הוּא, עַד שֶׁיֵּאָמֵר עָלָיו: שֶׁהוּא הַמַּדָּע, וְהוּא הַיּוֹדֵעַ, וְהוּא
הַיָּדוּעַ; וְהוּא הַחַי, וְהוּא הַחַיִּים, וְהוּא הַמַּמְשִׁיךְ לְעַצְמוֹ הַחַיִּים. וְכֵן שְׁאָר
הַתְּאָרִים. וְאִלּוּ הָעִנְיָנִים קָשִׁים, וְלֹא תְקַוֶּה לַהֲבִינָם הֲבָנָה שְׁלֵמָה מִשְּׁתֵּי שׁוּרוֹת
אוֹ שָׁלֹשׁ מִדְּבָרַי; וְאָמְנָם, יַעֲלֶה בְיָדְךָ מֵהֶם סִפּוּר דְּבָרִים לְבָד.

8:14 There remains only one matter to fulfill the purpose of this chapter. I had not meant to speak of it at all, but necessity has brought me to do so. The matter deals with God's knowledge of future events. It is related to the view of those who think that a person is destined to perform a particular *mitzvah* or commit a particular sin and, indeed, that no person is free to act in any way, that his/her choice is dependent on the choice of God. This belief is generated by the questions: Does the Creator know or does God not? Does God know whether this person will be righteous or wicked or does God not? If you say that God knows, then it would follow that the particular person is compelled to become either righteous or wicked. Either that is so or what God knows would not be true knowledge. If you say that God does not know the future, then

118

great difficulties would arise and faith would be affected [literally, "many high walls would be destroyed"]. Therefore, reflect carefully on what I am about to tell you and consider it well. The truth has already been made clear in the science of theology, specifically in metaphysics, that God does not know by [what we consider] knowledge nor is God's life like our life. God's knowledge is not separate from God as our knowledge is separate from us. A person is not the same as knowledge, nor is knowledge the same as a person. The two are different. If God knew by [what we understand as] knowledge, then there would necessarily be multiplicity in God. There would then be many eternal elements existing along with God, particularly knowledge by which God knows and life by which God lives and potency by which God is able to act. So it would be with all the Divine attributes. However, I am going to mention to you a simple and easy argument so that you can understand and make it clear to the masses. The kinds of argument and the means of proof that can deal with this problem are compelling and they are true: God and God's attributes are one and the same. One can say of God that God is knowledge, God is the Knower, and God is the known. God lives, and God is Life. God includes in God's essence life and all the other attributes. These are difficult matters to understand. You cannot hope to fully comprehend them easily [literally, "in two or three lines of my words"]. At first, all you can get are the words themselves.

For Maimonides, God's perfection is beyond our understanding. God's essence, God's will, and God's knowledge are one and the same. As he suggests here (and will state in *Guide for the Perplexed*), to truly know God, one would have to be God.

ח:טו וְלָזֶה הָעִקָּר הַגָּדוֹל לֹא הִתִּיר הַלָּשׁוֹן הָעִבְרִי לוֹמַר: „חֵי ה' צְבָאוֹת", כְּמוֹ שֶׁאוֹמְרִים: „חֵי פַרְעֹה" (בראשית מב, טו), „חֵי נַפְשְׁךָ" (שמואל־א א, טו). רְצוֹנִי לוֹמַר: שֵׁם מְצֹרָף. כִּי הַמְצֹרָף וְהַמִּצְטָרֵף אֵלָיו שְׁנֵי דְבָרִים חֲלוּקִים, וְלֹא יִצְטָרֵף הַדָּבָר לְעַצְמוֹ. וּלְפִי שֶׁחַיֵּי הַשֵּׁם הֵם — עַצְמוֹ, וְעַצְמוֹ — חַיָּיו, וְאֵינוֹ דָבָר אַחֵר זוּלָתוֹ — לֹא הִזְכִּירוּהוּ בְּצֵרוּף, אַךְ אָמַר: חַי יְיָ צְבָאוֹת (מלכים־א יח, טו); חַי יְיָ אֲשֶׁר עָשָׂה לָנוּ אֶת־הַנֶּפֶשׁ הַזֹּאת (ירמיה לח, טז). הַכַּוָּנָה בָּזֶה: שֶׁהוּא וְחַיָּיו דָּבָר אֶחָד. וּכְבָר הִתְבָּאֵר כֵּן בַּסֵּפֶר הַנִּקְרָא: „מַה־שֶׁאַחַר הַטֶּבַע" — שֶׁאֵין יְכֹלֶת בְּדַעְתֵּנוּ לְהָבִין מְצִיאוּתוֹ יִתְבָּרֵךְ עַל־הַשְּׁלֵמוּת, וְזֶה — לִשְׁלֵמוּת מְצִיאוּתוֹ וְחֶסְרוֹן דַּעְתֵּנוּ; וְשֶׁאֵין לִמְצִיאוּתוֹ סִבּוֹת, שֶׁיִּוָּדַע בָּהֶן; וְשֶׁקְּצָרָה דַעְתֵּנוּ מֵהַשִּׂיגוֹ,

כִּקְצֹר אוֹר הָרָאוּת מֵהַשִּׂיג אוֹר הַשֶּׁמֶשׁ, שֶׁאֵינוֹ לְחֻלְשַׁת אוֹר הַשֶּׁמֶשׁ, אֲבָל
לִהְיוֹת אוֹר הַשֶּׁמֶשׁ יוֹתֵר מֵאוֹר הָרָאוּת שֶׁיִּרְצֶה לְהַשִּׂיגוֹ. וּכְבָר דִּבְּרוּ בְּזֶה הָעִנְיָן
הַרְבֵּה וְהֵם כֻּלָּם מַאֲמָרִים אֲמִתִּים מְבֹאָרִים. וְרָאוּי מִפְּנֵי זֶה — שֶׁלֹּא נֵדַע
גַּם־כֵּן „דַּעְתּוֹ", וְשֶׁלֹּא תְכִילֵהוּ דַעְתֵּנוּ כְּלָל, אַחַר שֶׁהוּא — דַּעְתּוֹ, וְדַעְתּוֹ —
הוּא. וְזֶה הָעִנְיָן נִפְלָא מְאֹד, וְהוּא: אֲשֶׁר נִבְצְרָה מֵהֶם אֲמִתָּתוֹ. וְאָמְרוּ: שֶׁהֵם
יָדְעוּ שֶׁמְּצִיאוּתוֹ יִתְבָּרֵךְ עַל־הַשְּׁלֵמוּת אֲשֶׁר הִיא עָלָיו לֹא תֻשַּׂג, וּבִקְשׁוּ לְהַשִּׂיג
יְדִיעָתוֹ עַד שֶׁיֵּדָעוּהָ — וְזֶה מַה־שֶּׁאִי־אֶפְשָׁר: שֶׁאִלּוּ תָּכִיל דַּעְתֵּנוּ מַדָּעוֹ, הָיְתָה
מְכִילָה מְצִיאוּתוֹ — אַחַר שֶׁהַכֹּל דָּבָר אֶחָד. שֶׁהַשָּׂגָתוֹ עַל־הַשְּׁלֵמוּת — הִיא:
שֶׁיֻּשַּׂג כְּמוֹ שֶׁהוּא בִּמְצִיאוּתוֹ, וּמִן־הַיְדִיעָה, וְהַיְכֹלֶת, וְהַחַיִּים, וְהָרָצוֹן, וְזוּלַת זֶה
מִתְאָרָיו הַנִּכְבָּדִים. הִנֵּה כְּבָר בֵּאַרְנוּ, שֶׁהַמַּחֲשָׁבָה בְּהַשָּׂגַת יְדִיעָתוֹ — סִכְלוּת
גְּמוּרָה; אֶלָּא שֶׁאֲנַחְנוּ נֵדַע, שֶׁהוּא יִתְבָּרֵךְ „יוֹדֵעַ", כְּמוֹ שֶׁנֵּדַע שֶׁהוּא „נִמְצָא".
וְאִם יִשְׁאָלֵנוּ שׁוֹאֵל: אֵיךְ הוּא מַדָּעוֹ? נֹאמַר לוֹ: אֲנַחְנוּ לֹא נַשִּׂיג זֶה, כְּמוֹ שֶׁלֹּא
נַשִּׂיג מְצִיאוּתוֹ אֶל הַשְּׁלֵמוּת. וּכְבָר הִרְחִיק כָּל־מִי שֶׁיִּשְׁתַּדֵּל לָדַעַת אֲמִתַּת
יְדִיעָתוֹ יִתְבָּרֵךְ וְנֶאֱמַר לוֹ: הַחֵקֶר אֱלוֹהַּ תִּמְצָא, אִם עַד־תַּכְלִית שַׁדַּי תִּמְצָא?
(אִיּוֹב יא, ז).

8:15 To exemplify this principle [that God and the Divine attributes are the same] the Hebrew language does not say, "the life of *Adonai Tzevaot*" as it does say, "the life of Pharaoh" [Genesis 42:15] or "the life of your soul," [I Samuel 1:15] that is, to grammatically treat the word "life" when applied to God as a construct requiring an absolute, and therefore as two separate things [e.g., life *and* Pharaoh]. One cannot join anything to the essence of God, because the life of God *is the essence of God* and God's essence *is God's life*. They are not two separate things. Thus "life" and "*Adonai*" are not used in a construct-absolute relation: "*Adonai Tzevaot* lives" [I Kings 18:15] and "*Adonai* who made this soul for us" [Jeremiah 38:16]. Again, this is to indicate that God and God's life are the same thing. It also has been explained in Aristotle's *Metaphysics* that our intellect is unable fully to comprehend the essence of God. This is due to the perfection of God's existence and the deficiency of our intellects. God's existence does not present the kinds of causes that would be intelligible to us, so we cannot fully comprehend God with our minds any more than our sense of sight can fully perceive the sun. It is not that the sun is weak. Rather, its light is too strong for our eyes. Many have spoken about this, and much that is true has been written about it. It follows then that we do not know how God's knowledge operates, particularly because God is God's knowledge and God's knowledge is God. This notion is wondrous and beyond our understanding. God's knowledge is knowledge in its ultimate perfection. To comprehend such knowledge is beyond our capacity, for to comprehend it would be to comprehend God because God and God's knowledge are the same. The same would be true with the comprehension of any of the Divine attributes, because they and God are the same. All we can know is that God exists and that God knows. Should one ask us how is God, God's knowledge, we would have to answer that we can no more comprehend this than we can fully comprehend God's existence. To the one who would attempt to learn the true quality of God's knowledge, we would respond in the words of Job, "Can you find out the deep things of God? Can you reach the purpose of the Almighty?" [Job 11:7].

For Maimonides, the conclusion is simple and straightforward. Humans beings are free to choose, free to act, and therefore free to pursue virtue or vice. Because we are free, we can be commanded (instructed). The *mitzvot* were given because we are able to respond to them. We can act, but we cannot understand the Deity. Our task is to study Torah and obey the *mitzvot*.

ח:טז וְהָבֵן כָּל-מַה-שֶּׁאָמַרְנוּ: שֶׁפְּעֻלּוֹת הָאָדָם מְסוּרוֹת אֵלָיו; וּבִרְשׁוּתוֹ לִהְיוֹת צַדִּיק אוֹ רָשָׁע, מִבִּלְתִּי הַכְרָחַת הַשֵּׁם יִתְבָּרֵךְ עָלָיו עַל-אֶחָד מִשְּׁנֵי הָעִנְיָנִים. וּמִפְּנֵי זֶה הָיָה רָאוּי הַצִּוּוּי, וְהַלִּמּוּד, וְהַהֲכָנָה, וְהַגְּמוּל, וְהָעֹנֶשׁ — וְאֵין בְּכָל-זֶה סָפֵק. אָמְנָם, תֹּאַר יְדִיעָתוֹ יִתְבָּרֵךְ וְהַשָּׂגָתוֹ לְכָל-הַדְּבָרִים — דַּעְתֵּנוּ קְצָרָה לְהַשִּׂיגוֹ, כְּמוֹ שֶׁבֵּאַרְנוּ. וְזֶהוּ כְּלָל מַה-שֶּׁכִּוַּנּוּ אֵלָיו בְּזֶה הַפֶּרֶק. וּכְבָר הִגִּיעָה הָעֵת לִפְסֹק הַדְּבָרִים הֵנָּה, וְאַתְחִיל בְּפֵרוּשׁ הַמַּסֶּכְתָּא הַזֹּאת, אֲשֶׁר הִקְדַּמְנוּ לָהּ אֵלּוּ הַפְּרָקִים.

8:16 Understand all that we have said about human activity being under human control and that every person has the freedom to be either righteous or wicked and that God in no way compels anyone to be one or the other. It is because of human freedom that there can be *mitzvot*, study, and understanding–and also reward and punishment. There is no doubt about any of this. As we have explained, we are unable to understand the operation of God's knowledge or God's apprehension of existing things. This is what we intended in this chapter. It is now the time to conclude these words of introduction and to begin the explanation of this tractate.

GLEANINGS

OBEYING WORD OF GOD

In Judaism, personal religion assumes the form of obedience to the commands of God. These *mitzvot* or commands were conceived as divinely revealed in the *Torah*, the Law. While the modern man finds it difficult to regard the Pentateuch as a supernaturally revealed code and to see in it, or even in the Talmud, an all-sufficient chart of life for all ages, he recognizes that the sense of duty underlying the concept of *mitzvah* remains pivotal also in modern Judaism. Kant taught us that, from religion's point of view, our duties are divine commands. Moving beyond Kant, we extend religion further than the confines of our moral duties. Non-rational and non-moral elements enter into its sphere. Whether they are dictated by pedagogical considerations or by psychological motives, deeds required by religion for its proper functioning, must represent, for us, divine commands. This resource of religion has been lost by many Jewish liberals, and must be recovered if religion is to have power in our lives.

(Samuel S. Cohon, Religious Affirmations. Los Angeles:1983)

THE HOLINESS OF GOD

The holiness of God implies an absolute standard of love, truth and righteousness. May not man's holiness be attained in the effort he makes to approach this standard, disciplining himself to obedience, even at the cost of material self-advancement and convenience? Jewish teaching gives us a Holy God transcending, and immeasurably excelling the human ideal; but it also suggests kinship with that ideal. 'Be holy for the Lord your God is holy.' The power of direct communion constitutes one of the glories of our faith; but without the sense of kinship the language of prayer, whether articulate or unexpressed, would fail us and, what is more important, there would be little room for human aspiration. Indeed, much of the joy and hope in human life lies in the "infinite pain of finite hearts which yearn." This yearning is conditioned by faith in the kinship of God. In one of his sermons, Professor [Benjamin] Jowett explains that God's holiness means the Spirit which is altogether above the world and yet has an affinity with goodness and truth in the world. It implies separation as well as elevation, dignity as well as innocence.

(Lily Montagu, "Jewish Self-Identity," in Lily Montagu: Sermons, Addresses, Letters, and Prayers,
ed. Ellen Umansky. New York: Mellon Press, 1985)

ATTACHING ONESELF TO GOD

What difference will it make to the individual if he tries consciously in his life to attach himself to God? He will find authority for his moral life in the commands of God instead of in the conventions of Society. He will not dare to juggle with truth to advance his own petty purposes. Truth belongs to God. It is God who reveals it to man. Every now and then a lie would seem to be very useful; without religion a man sees no reason to turn away from it. Religion makes us responsible to God for the conduct of our lives–without religion we should be justified in eating and drinking and being merry for life would seem to be fleeting and it would not matter very much whether we used it well or ill. It would seem to be ours to do with as we like. But religion makes this attitude impossible. Man is a spiritual animal. If he pays no heed to the divine within himself, he loses the privileges of his manhood. There is no tangible reward for virtue:

> "The wages of sin is death; if the wages of virtue
>   be dust,"
> "Would she have heart to endure for the life of
>   the worm and the fly?
> "She desires no isles of the blest, no quiet seats
>   of the just,
> "To rest in a golden grove, or to bask in a summer
>   sky;"
> "Give her the ways of going on and not to die!"

The just reward lies in this that we can realize the possibilities of a complete life if we develop, instead of crushing, the divine element which is in every human life. We ignore that divine element at our peril. I said that religion makes life better. If we believe in God, if we think that He has sent us into the world to work with Him and for Him to create goodness and joy, then surely life *does* become better. We dare not fail God. There are many things besides lying we *cannot* do. It is because we recognize our allegiance to God that we can love and go on loving even when we are disappointed and misunderstood. We can be just, even when our neighbour's weaknesses are apparent to us; we can be merciful even when we have the power to injure another life. We can put honor, social service, purity, before all else in the world and overcome our unworthy desires, control our passions, combat our selfish inclinations. We can do these things; indeed we must; for in no other way can we serve God. Then again when we are doing our best measuring it in the light of God, we shall know our insufficiency and our feebleness and feel eternity in our hearts and recognize that we can go on striving for ever.

(Lily Montagu, "The Nature of True Religion", in *Lily Montagu: Sermons, Addresses, Letters, and Prayers*, ed. Ellen Umansky. New York: Mellon Press, 1985)

REWARD AND PUNISHMENT

Hope for reward for the good that we do and fear of punishment for our misdeeds is the language in which we express the conflict between life and death in the human soul. Hope for reward embodies our desire to live without sin. Fear of punishment reflects our experience of the inevitable failure of that hope and our acceptance of the fact that such a failure has consequences. Reward and punishment are ancillary to the free will which defines our very mortality. Without reward and punishment, we must posit a world in which the transcendence of mortality is impossible. This would be a world without ultimate reward. Transcendence would not depend on our activities in this world and would be dispensed by an arbitrary God. Both of these possibilities run counter to the experience of God in the imagination of the people Israel.

Some in our tradition fear that human striving to imitate God is somehow debased if performed in anticipation of some kind of reward and punishment. But this misconstrues the

Jewish experience of the divine. Logically, God's commandments must have consequences. And nothing indicates that these consequences will not be played out in this world to help us reduce moments-of-death in life, and in the next world so that we can appreciate life without death. To strive to reap the benefits of life without death and to strive to be chastened by punishment are among the highest yearnings available to us.

(Ira F. Stone, *Seeking the Path to Life: Theological Meditations on God And the Nature of People, Love, Life And Death.* Woodstock, Vermont: Jewish Lights Publishing, 1992)

FREE WILL

Judaism teaches that my free will is basic to my existence. It teaches that I as an individual have the capacity, the power, the right to make moral decisions, between good and evil, between right and wrong—and I have the power to carry them out in the real world, with others, against others, come what may. The exercise of my will is the beginning of Jewish living.

In order to exercise my will, I must believe in me. I must believe in my I-ness, in my capacities, in my freedom. This is not easy to come to. My parents, my teachers, my peers, my boss, my children, my bank loan, my spouse, my friends—all operate to limit my freedom, to dominate my time, to control me and to limit or to destroy my will.

The Shabbat is a weekly reminder that they may not succeed. Not only is it not inevitable that they should succeed; it is also wrong that I should let them succeed. Twenty-four hours each week, I have the right and the obligation to transcend all external powers and pressures, to be responsible only for me and to me—and to God. My pattern of Sabbath observances refreshes me within myself. It renews and refreshes those most intimate and precious of relationships which enhance and fulfill me. The technique of observance is less important to me than the fact of observance. Whether or not I drive my car is not important; whether or not I use the Shabbat for unique, non-routine, externally uncontrolled actions—that is important. For on Shabbat, I say to myself, I have rights, I am a self, I have a will. And from the Shabbat I derive the strength to be more of myself, to use more of the rest of the week to maximalize my existence.

Part of my self, intrinsic to me, is my Jewishness. Therefore, I use Shabbat on the day Jews have used it. I symbolize the enterprise by beginning the day, as Jews have done, with candlelighting, kiddush, family togetherness in light-hearted singing, joking freedom. I remind myself that generations of Jews found Shabbat so precious that they equated it with the messianic era, dubbed it a foretaste thereof. I breathe deeply within myself, I do the things which bring out the most in me to me—I use Shabbat to recapture me for me.

(Eugene J. Lipman, *Yamim Nora'im, Sinai Sermons.* Washington, D.C.: Temple Sinai, 1987)

EUGENE J. LIPMAN (1919-1994). *Rabbi, social activist, spiritual leader of Temple Sinai, Washington, D.C., and former president of the Central Conference of American Rabbis.*

A WOMAN'S PERSPECTIVE ON FREE WILL

Jewish women certainly have been affected by the women's liberation movement and consciousness raising, and that is one of the moving factors in reassessing our position and role in Jewish life. For me, and I can speak only for myself, it has to be done with understanding. In our past the Jewish family has been very important. In the past the Jewish home was where the father was king and the mother queen on Shabbat, regardless of the oppression of the outside world. The family has been the place where humane values were salvaged and nurtured, where peculiarities and uniqueness could thrive. What does family mean to us today? Is it important for us to maintain family strengths, or does liberation mean freedom from all the old traditional roles? Personally, I think not; to be truly liberated we must have freedom of choice, and in freedom of choice we can take those obligations and commitments that give meaning to our lives. So we have to find in our heritage those values— the force of a covenantal relationship that was accepted at Sinai–to make a positive Jewish way of life. Choices are never easy because with them comes the yoke of commitment. When we accept this commitment we should know that we must study. We must learn Torah for the sake of Torah. If we are to have aliyot, it should be because we are in the pursuit of knowledge, and on this there should be no regard for sex. This will not come easily, but we can begin. If women become talmudic scholars like Judy Hauptman, if women become rabbis, then they can begin to write books about great Jewish women, help to make *Halakhic* interpretations and have a voice in the changes necessary to give us equality in Jewish life. Being on congregational boards or becoming congregational presidents will not make these changes; these are administrative positions to which we bring a lot of expertise from our other organizational activities, but input in the learning and study programs–becoming scholars in our own right–will give us representation where we have not had it before. I would hope in the years to come that women will be astute enough not to jump in and take over but will be very conscious of the fact that for so long we did not have a voice, and now that we do, we will present our position and work for each and everyone, male and female, to have acceptance in the sight of God, man, and woman, and that women will maintain the strengths that they have had throughout the centuries of making their home their Temple and working for equality in their synagogues with the help of the men.

Then it can truly be said that the wonderful and mysterious preservation of the Jewish people is due to the Jewish woman. This is her glory, not alone in the history of her own people, but in the history of the world, and for all tomorrows.

(Suzanne Basinger, "Preserving the Covenant–The Challenge for Jewish Women,"
in *The Life of Covenant: The Challenge of Contemporary Judaism: Essays in Honor of Herman E. Schaalman*.
Chicago: Spertus College on Judaica Press, 1986)

SUZANNE BASINGER (1914-). *Past president of Emanuel Congregation in Chicago, the first woman to serve in that position. She has been either president or served on the board of directors of several major Jewish organizations and in 1971 was a delegate to the White House Conference on Aging.*

Moses Maimonides: A Brief Biography

Moses Maimonides was born on March 30, 1135, in Cordova, Spain. In rabbinical literature, he is also called **RaMBaM**–an acronym constructed by the name **R**abbi **M**oses **b**en **M**aimon. In some contexts, he is also referred to as *Hanesher Hagadol* (the Mighty Eagle).

Maimonides' father, Maimon ben Joseph–the *dayyan* of Cordova–was a man of outstanding piety and scholarship who traced his ancestry to Rabbi Yehudah Ha-Nasi, the compiler of the *Mishnah*. While little is known about Moses Maimonides' mother, legend suggests that Moses' father had a dream in which he was instructed to marry the daughter of a butcher who lived not far from Cordova. He took the dream seriously and married the woman. She died in childbirth, and Moses' father later remarried.

As is the case with many great scholars in our history–perhaps a way of maintaining hope for those children in our own midst who seem disinterested in study–a story is told that Moses was indifferent toward his education while he was still a child. The elder Maimonides was distressed about this attitude and called Moses to his side, chiding him about where a life of ignorance might lead, the shame it would bring to his family and to him. Following this upbraiding, Moses ran into the local synagogue, found a place to cower, and cried himself to sleep. When he awoke, he felt like a new person and committed himself to the arduous task of study. The boy then took himself to the house of the celebrated Rabbi Joseph ibn Migash, who had previously served as a teacher to the elder Maimonides, and diligently applied himself to study. Similar legends hold that Maimonides later returned to his native city of Cordova–while still a boy–and went straight to that same synagogue to deliver a scholarly discourse to surprise his father.

Cordova fell to the Almohads in 1148, and thirteen-year-old Moses and his family fled the religious persecution that followed. Little is known about him during the ten-year period that followed, as his family wandered throughout Spain. However, it was during this period that Maimonides probably began his commentary to the *Mishnah* and laid the foundation for much of the literary activity that occupied most of his adult life. During this period of turmoil in his life, he also wrote a short piece on the Jewish calendar (*Ma'amar Ha-Ibbur*), an essay on logic (*Millot Higgayon*), and collected notes for his commentary to several tractates of the Talmud.

In 1159/1160, the family settled in Fez, North Africa, where Maimonides studied under Rabbi Judah Ha-Kohen ibn Susan. In Fez, Maimonides encountered many Jews who had converted to Islam. This troubled him, so he wrote a letter to them, called *Iggeret Ha-Nechamah* (Letter of Consolation), suggesting that their prayers and good works would still make them considered as Jews. This concern over the large number of converts also prompted him to write *Iggeret Ha-Shemad* (Letter on Forced Conversion) and *Iggeret Kiddush Ha-Shem* (Letter of the Sanctification of the Divine Name). These subsequent letters are not as conciliatory as had been his previous efforts. Instead, he encourages people to emigrate rather than "transgress the Divine law." He wrote,

> In former times, Israelites were called upon to transgress the law by acts. Now, however, we are not asked to render active homage to idolatry but only to recite an empty formula that the Moslems themselves know we are uttering insincerely only to avoid the bigot. If ever under these circumstances, a Jew surrenders one's life for the sanctification of the Name of God before humans, he has done nobly well, and his reward is great before God. But if a person asks me, "Shall I be slain or utter the formula of Islam?" I answer, "Utter the formula and live."

Many took Maimonides' advice seriously. His own teacher Judah ibn Susan took his own life; Moses and his family fled Fez in 1165. They traveled to Israel and eventually arrived in Acre (Akko). As was customary, the family of Maimonides celebrated these stops along their family journey, marking them as family festivals, which were celebrated by many subsequent generations.

Following a short residence in the Land of Israel, where he visited many of its religious sites, Moses and his family moved to Egypt. Following a brief stay in Alexandria, they settled in Fostat (Old Cairo) in 1167. Moses' father died at about the same time. At that time, the majority of Jews in Cairo were Karaites, Jews who did not accept the post-biblical tradition of rabbinic interpretation found in sources like the *Mishnah* and Talmud. Instead, they drew upon only the Bible as their source of guidance for Jewish living. This caused great friction with the others in the community, the rabbinite Jews. Both groups accused each other of not being true Jews. Perhaps it was this implicit challenge to rabbinic authority that influenced Maimonides' decision to relocate to Cairo.

Moses' brother David supported the family so that Moses could devote himself to study and writing. Thus, one year after settling in Fostat, Maimonides completed his commentary to the *Mishnah* (1168). Then his brother David died, the result of drowning in the Indian Ocean while on a business trip. Stricken with grief, Maimonides was unable to function for an entire year. He refused to use his knowledge of the Jewish tradition in order to earn a livelihood. It was not until he was invited to become one of the physicians to al-Fadil (in 1185), the vizier (appointed by Saladin, whom he succeeded as ruler of Egypt after Saladin departed in 1174). That due to his fame in that position, Maimonides was named head of the Jewish community of Fostat in 1177.

During these years in Fostat, Maimonides achieved an amazing level of literary output. He finished his *Sefer Mitzvot* (1170). He composed his well-known epistle to Yemenite Jewry (1172), a response to a letter addressed to him by Rabbi Jacob al-Fayumi, which refers to the critical condition of the Jews in Yemen. In his reply, Maimonides attempts to prove that the sufferings of the Jews, together with the numerous instances of apostasy, were foretold by the prophets–especially by Daniel–and must not perplex the faithful. Attempts had been made in the past to do away with Judaism; they had invariably failed. The same would hold true for present attempts, for "religious persecutions are but a short duration."

In Egypt, he remarried, his first wife having died young. A son, Abraham, was born to the new couple, whom Moses personally educated. In addition, he devoted himself to his disciple Joseph ibn Sham'un (some suggest it was Ibn Akhnin), for whom he prepared his *Guide for the Perplexed*.

By 1180, Moses Maimonides finished his *Mishneh Torah* (A Summary of the Torah), a work that took him ten years to complete for "his own benefit, to save him in his advanced age the trouble and necessity of consulting the Talmud on every occasion." This work was designed to be a religious guide based on revelation and tradition. The *Mishneh Torah* was also called *Yad Ha-chazakah*, the Strong Hand. It was meant to be a definitive law code for all time that would eliminate other previous codes. While *Mishneh Torah* is still widely studied today, it never achieved the level of acceptance Maimonides had planned for.

Maimonides completed his *Guide for the Perplexed* in 1190/1191. In this very difficult philosophical work, composed in Arabic and written in Hebrew characters, he sought to provide a religious guide (like the *Mishneh Torah*) based on philosophy rather than on revelation and tradition. The work was translated into Hebrew by Rabbi Samuel ibn Tibbon during Rambam's own lifetime (who was consulted about the difficulty of certain Hebrew passages). Maimonides dedicated the work to his disciple Joseph, who was disappointed, for he felt it lacked the reconciliation between faith and science. A second translation was made by Yehudah Alharizi. The same year that the *Guide* was finished, Maimonides wrote to his student:

> I inform you that I have acquired a very great reputation in medicine among the great, such as the Chief Qadi, the Princes, the House of Al-Fadil (his protector), and other grandees, from whom I do not obtain a large fee. As for the ordinary people, I am placed too high for them to reach me. This obliges me continually to waste my day in Cairo visiting the (noble) sick. When I return to Fostat, I am too tired for the rest of the day and night to pursue my study of medical books, which I need. For, you know, how long and difficult this art is for a conscientious and exact man who does not want to state anything that he cannot support by argument and without knowing where it has been said and how it can be demonstrated.

Only four years after completing the *Guide*, Maimonides prepared a treatise on resurrection (1195). In a letter to his friend Rabbi Samuel ibn Tibbon in France, he wrote (1198):

> You will expose yourself in vain to the dangers of the journey, as you will not find a moment during the day or night to discuss with me. The Sultan resides in Cairo, and I dwell in Fostat. The distance between the two places is a double Sabbath day's journey (about a mile and a half). My duties to the Sultan are heavy. I must visit him early in the morning. If he feels weak, or any of his children or the inmates of his harem are ill, I cannot leave Cairo but must spend the greater part of my day in the palace. Also, if any of the officials falls ill, I have to attend to him, and I thus spend the whole day there. In brief, I repair to Cairo every day in the morning; and even if nothing unusual happens, I do not return to Fostat until the noon hour. Then I am fatigued and hungry, and I find the courts of my house full of people, prominent and common, gentlemen, theologians, and judges, waiting for my return. I dismount from my animal, wash

my hands, go forth to them, and entreat them to wait for me while I take a slight refreshment, my only meal in twenty-four hours. After that, I attend to the patients and prescribe for them. Patients go in and out until nightfall; or, I assure you, until two hours in the night. I talk to them lying on my back because of weakness. When the night falls, I feel so weak, I cannot speak any more. Thus no Jew can have a private discussion with me, except on the Sabbath. . . .

Moses Maimonides died on December 13, 1204 at the age of seventy; he was buried in Tiberias, Israel. In Fostat, the Jewish community mourned for three days; in Jerusalem, they fasted.

According to legend, as the funeral procession was going through the desert, it was attacked by a band of Bedouins. As soon as the robbers realized that they were about to desecrate the body of Maimonides, they refrained from their assault and hung their heads in shame. Forming a protective circle around the funeral cortege, they followed it all the way to the burial place in Palestine. For Maimuni, as they called him, was a man they all revered. Many times he had treated them for their illnesses without asking for pay for his services. In Cairo, there still stands an old prayer-house called the Synagogue of Maimonides. On the southern side there is a small shrine in which an "eternal light" is kept burning in memory of Rambam. It is said that in this shrine his body remained an entire week before it was taken to its burial place. The folks in Jerusalem lamented, "The glory has departed from Israel; the ark of *Adonai* has been taken away."

I. *Citations of Ancient and Medieval Works*

HEBREW BIBLE

NEW TESTAMENT

RABBINIC WORKS

MAIMONIDES

ARISTOTLE

II. Gleanings Authors

III. Names and Subjects